PRAISE FOR DEVOTIONS
ON F.I.R.E. YEAR TWO

Devotions on F.I.R.E. Year Two is not a traditional devotional book, which can lack biblical substance. It consists of intensive study, prayer, and hard work by the writer. Dr. Ken Burge's passion to know God's Word and to make Him known leaps off each page to the reader's eyes, mind, and heart! I highly recommend you to embark upon the daily journey, which will take you through the Bible in one year using the author's F.I.R.E. method. (I've personally benefited immensely by *Devotions on F.I.R.E.* and know you will share my experience through *Devotions on F.I.R.E. Year Two*.) Your unforgettable daily excursion takes you to the depth of God's holy Word and leaves you with relevant application. This excellent work will greatly bless each participant who commits to walk with the Lord.

— Shally Sagadal
Elementary school teacher and
missionary to the Philippines

Ever wanted to read through your Bible in one year, but you were not sure how to go about it? Well, you're in for a treat. Pastor Ken Burge, Sr. has created an easy to read and biblically sound devotional that is sure to light your F.I.R.E. and stoke your passion for the Word of God—365 days a year. Allow the Holy Spirit to illuminate your understanding and be a lamp unto your feet as you dive into each of Dr. Burge's power-packed devotions that seamlessly bring to life each daily Bible reading. You will not only walk away blessed by the Word of God, but will also leave with practical purpose from the employment point that follows each daily devotional. This labor of love from Pastor Burge will enable you to be a hearer and doer of the Word of God all year round.

— Bryan R. L. Buchanan
Licensed clinical professional counselor

I love this devotional! It is perfect for all ages as it provides Scripture passages and thought-provoking questions that help the reader to get their day on track. Dr. Burge has done a great job to remind us how applicable Scripture is in our daily lives, and how we can have an authentic personal relationship with God!

— Reagan Van Rees
Junior, Anchor Christian Collaborative

DEVOTIONS

ON

YEAR TWO

**A Daily Devotional
and 365 Day Plan
to Read through
The Bible**

Dr. Ken J. Burge, Sr.

Devotions on F.I.R.E. Year Two
Copyright @ 2019 by Ken J. Burge, Sr.
Published by Deep River Books
Sisters, Oregon
www.deepriverbooks.com

ISBN – 13: 9781632695130
Library of Congress: 2019915967

Printed in the USA
2019—First Edition
27 26 25 24 23 22 21 20 19   10 9 8 7 6 5 4 3 2 1

Cover design by Joe Bailen, Contajus Designs

Dedication

Serving the Lord has many advantages. One of the perks of ministry consists of meeting choice ministers of God. To personally know an individual who lives each and every day for Jesus is like finding a rare gem; however, to be intimately acquainted with an entire family that glorifies Jesus through all their actions is tantamount to discovering a necklace of fine pearls. I had this eureka moment when the Almighty brought the Sagadal family, who are our missionaries in the Philippines, into my life.

Felicisimo Sagadal is a pastor, church planter, and missionary. His zeal for the Lord exemplifies the heart of a man of God. Truly Fel (his nickname is much easier to pronounce) brings to the dear Filipino people the love of Jesus. By his side is my little sis (as I call her) in the Lord. Shally lives daily the traits of the virtuous woman in Proverbs 31. She has been an amazing advocate of my books, YouTube messages, and the Colmar Manor Bible Church. My dear little sis applies herself to the work of the Lord with vim and vigor.

There are three more pearls to be admired. Eunice is the oldest of the Sagadal children. Her passion is leading worship, feeding the poor children in the region, and representing her Lord. Next comes Kim; she likewise applies herself to minister in music and uses her technology skills for God's glory. She actively mentors younger saints to be like Jesus. Judah, whose name means "praise," brings glory to God like his father, mother, and two sisters. Clearly the Sagadal family, like a glorious string of pearls, is a unit for Jesus.

It is with great pleasure that I dedicate *Devotions on F.I.R.E. Year Two* to this precious Filipino family. I'm so thankful for your friendship, fellowship, and testimony for the King!

FOREWORD

BY KIMBERLY ANN BURGE

———◈———

I remember the first time I met Ken Burge. He had invited me to attend a Bible study. I was so excited. Ken lived down the street from me and I had often observed him as he drove by my home or picked up my brother to go to the gym. I was quietly hoping that the day would come when he would ask me to do something with him. This was the day—and a Bible study at that!

To my surprise, as I sat next to him at the Bible study, he called the meeting to order and began to teach. I was a bit intimidated. I hadn't realized until that moment that the *teacher* had invited me!

As I sat and listened to him open the Word of God and explain it so clearly, I was truly amazed that a young man of twenty knew so much about God. He was actively serving at Colmar Manor Bible Church—leading the youth ministry, the college and career group, and also teaching the Junior High Sunday School class. The more I got to know him, the more I realized that his love for the Bible guided everything he did.

As young as he was, he was dedicated to learning everything he could about this precious Book, reading it front to back at least once a year. His discipline and devotion to study was a challenge to me. What impressed me the most—having grown up in a Christian church— was how he applied what he read in his Bible. He took the truths from the Scripture and used the principles to guide his decisions. Ken walked with God daily and knew how to apply those truths into his workplace and home, using what he had gleaned to guide his day. I wanted that too—his love for the Bible was contagious! It definitely lit a spark that started me on a personal journey treasuring the Word of God!

I've been privileged and honored to share thirty-eight years with Ken. Through his ordination, becoming pastor of Colmar Manor Bible Church, many years of Bible College and seminary, training up our three precious sons, and now writing books, a day hasn't gone by that he didn't get up early to spend time with his Savior—reading His precious Book and gleaning its truths. His dedication convicted me, challenging me to be more consistent and purposeful in my daily devotions. This work is the tool that will ignite your Bible reading.

Devotions on F.I.R.E. Year Two guides you through the entire Bible in a year. Ken shares the wisdom and understanding that he has gleaned from years of study. He applies his unique F.I.R.E. method on every page. Each day there is a portion of Scripture to read from the Old and New Testaments. He asks a thought-provoking question that will pique your curiosity and help you get *familiar* with the text. Of course, he encourages us to rely on the Holy Spirit to help us *interpret* what we read. The interesting feature in this volume is that Ken often ties in truths revealing a *relationship* from both readings— that's not easy to do on your own! Each page ends with a task to accomplish encouraging us to *employ* the truths of Scripture in our daily lives!

INTRODUCTION TO DEVOTIONS ON F.I.R.E. YEAR TWO

The Lord has privileged me to disciple individuals for forty years. Several years ago, I started writing daily devotions for twelve men whom I train for ministry. After having them read through the Bible along with my daily devotion for one year, *Devotions on F.I.R.E.* emerged. My faithful apprentices matured over the course of one year from reading through the Bible and employing what they learned. Yet how could I build upon the foundation established?

God guided me to write *Devotions on F.I.R.E. Year Two* based upon my accumulated knowledge of the Scripture that is richly enhanced by reading through the Bible more than sixty times in forty years. This second volume often connects the *relationship* of both the Old and New Testament assigned portions of Scripture along with other relevant texts, which magnifies the glory of the living Word.

Now, let me explain the structure of this work and the meaning of F.I.R.E.

Devotions on F.I.R.E. Year Two is designed to have you read through the assigned portion of the Old and New Testament daily to complete the Bible in one year. Each day you will also read my devotion based upon the F.I.R.E. method of Bible study.

F.I.R.E. is the acronym used for our study. This mnemonic (memory) device stands for familiarity, interpretation, relationship, and employment.

F represents familiarity. Although I've been privileged to study the Bible at both the undergraduate and graduate levels, the emphasis was always upon observation as the first step of Bible study. The origin of the word "familiarity" derives from the Latin *familiaritas* and means "familiar" or "intimate." Bible study should originate from a deep-seated personal relationship with God. "Familiarity" roars out intimacy and relationship with the living God, while "observation" whimpers a frigid laboratory analysis of data.

Interpretation is the second stage of Bible study, represented here by the symbol **I**. Jesus has sent us a messenger to help us to understand the Scriptures—the eternal third member of the Godhead known as the Holy Spirit. Dependence upon Him is vital to enlighten our minds concerning God's truth. Jesus described the Holy Spirit as "the Spirit of truth" in John 16:13. He personally escorts us through the Bible, as the remainder of the verse says: "He will guide you into all truth."

Relationship becomes the third phase of our quest to understand the sacred text. The symbol **R** will stand for "relationship" throughout our travels. The Bible's value requires it to be treated with the utmost respect, "For the word of God is living and powerful, and sharper than any two-edged sword, piercing even to the division of soul and spirit, and of joints and marrow, and is a discerner of the thoughts and intents of the heart" (Hebrews 4:12). We will see how the life-giving parts ally with the whole.

The fourth and final part of this most excellent adventure is employment, represented by the symbol **E**. Employment, or application, began when those who originally received the living Word were given their authoritative marching orders. We too will transition together, in order to determine not only how those to whom the Bible first came responded, but also how we are called to respond today. God designed His Word to transform us into the image of Christ, and that cannot occur without us first personally employing the Bible to our lives.

January 1

Genesis 1–2, with Matthew 1

You are good, and do good (Psalm 119:68).

How should you respond to the goodness of God?

There are times when I use the call-and-response method during a sermon. For instance, if I call to the congregation, "God is good," they respond, "all the time." Genesis 1 and 2 testify that God is good all the time. On six occasions the Lord God stops and reflects upon His creation, and says, "it was good" (Genesis 1:4, 10, 12, 18, 21, 25). Then after the sixth day, which includes Adam's creation, He shares that "it was very good" (Genesis 1:31). Yet there is one time that God interjects, "It is not good that man should be alone" (Genesis 2:18). For this reason, He creates the first woman (Eve) from the man (Adam).

Likewise, God demonstrates His goodness by choosing another woman, Mary, who fulfills Scripture by giving birth to the Messiah (Matthew 1:22–23). Turning away from sin and to Him brings salvation for "the goodness of God leads you to repentance" (Romans 2:4).

Employment Point: *Celebrate the God who is good all the time.*

JANUARY 2

GENESIS 3–5, WITH MATTHEW 2

———

Now the birth of Jesus Christ was as follows (Matthew 1:18).

WHY DO PEOPLE DIE?

God previously warned Adam not to partake of the tree of the knowledge of good and evil "for in the day that you eat of it you shall surely die" (Genesis 2:17). Adam disobeys God and dies (Genesis 5:5). Since Adam was our representative, Paul writes, "For as in Adam all die" (1 Corinthians 15:22). The first man's disobedience establishes the principle of death for the living; therefore, our representative in Eden failed mankind, which has left no one unscathed.

On the other hand, Jesus existed before He was born on earth, and then lived to die so that all could live. The Greek text word order of Matthew 1:18 places the words "Jesus Christ" before "the birth" because Jesus, being God, lived before He was born. It took the sacrifice of the eternal Son of God to secure the salvation of those who come to Him through faith. Truly wise men still seek Him (Matthew 2:1–11).

EMPLOYMENT POINT: *Sincerely seek to worship King Jesus.*

———

January 3

Genesis 6–8, with Matthew 3

Repent, for the kingdom of heaven is at hand! (Matthew 3:2).

What does God expect from you in the midst of a wicked and violent world?

The Lord assesses not only the wickedness (Genesis 6:5) and violence (Genesis 6:11, 13) of the world, but Noah. "Noah was a just man, perfect in his generations. Noah walked with God" (Genesis 6:9). Noah focuses upon his daily walk with God and preaches to the unsaved world to repent for 120 years. Peter calls him "a preacher of righteousness" (2 Peter 2:5). He leads an exemplary life and receives the high honor of being placed beside Job and Daniel (Ezekiel 14:14, 20).

Like Noah, John the Baptist lived a balanced life by walking with his God and confronting the sinful world in which he lived. He says to the religious leaders, "Therefore bear fruits worthy of repentance" (Matthew 3:8). John the Baptist confronts the Pharisees and Sadducees boldly and calls Israel to renounce self-righteousness and turn to Jesus. The lives of these two pillars of the faith are worthy of imitation.

Employment Point: *Walk with God, and proclaim His Word.*

JANUARY 4

GENESIS 9–11, WITH MATTHEW 4

And do not be drunk with wine, in which is dissipation; but be filled with the Spirit (Ephesians 5:18).

HOW CAN YOU OVERCOME BEING TRIPPED UP BY THE ALLUREMENTS OF SATAN?

The first mention of wine in the Bible is found in Genesis 9:21: "Then he [Noah] drank of the wine and was drunk, and became uncovered in his tent." Noah literally and metaphorically stumbled over the fruit of his own vineyard. Even godly men falter. The following admonition from Paul applies to all saints: "Therefore let him who thinks he stands take heed lest he fall" (1 Corinthians 10:12).

Jesus, the Spirit-filled Son of God, is not duped by the Devil's enticement. He chooses the sword of the Spirit to fend off Satan. Jesus replies to the Wicked One's temptation, "Man shall not live by bread alone, but by every word that proceeds from the mouth of God" (Matthew 4:4). Jesus does not allow anything that this world has to offer control Him. We similarly will know victory over temptation if we heed Paul's command to repeatedly be filled (controlled) by God's Spirit.

EMPLOYMENT POINT: *Overcome temptation by allowing God's Word and Spirit to control you.*

JANUARY 5

GENESIS 12–14, WITH
MATTHEW 5:1–26

———◦———

You are the light of the world (Matthew 5:14).

WHAT SHOULD YOU DO WHEN GOD SAYS, "TAG, YOU'RE IT"?

God tagged Abraham and told him to separate from his family and follow Him (Genesis 12:1). What did Abraham do? He took his nephew Lot with him. Although Abraham's obedience to God is extraordinary because he left everything familiar to him, he didn't comply completely and brought Lot. Nephew Lot produces multiple headaches for the father of faith. It wasn't until "after Lot had separated from him" (Genesis 13:14) that God made a promise to Abraham about the land he would be given and the innumerable descendants who would derive from him (Genesis 13:15–17).

The Lord tagged Abraham to be the father of the Jewish nation who was to continue shining His light. Your heavenly Father has likewise tagged you. "You are the light of the world" (Matthew 5:14). As a result of being tagged, "Let your light so shine before men, that they may see your good works and glorify your Father in heaven" (Matthew 5:16).

EMPLOYMENT POINT: *Reflect God's light because He says, "Tag you're it."*

———◦———

JANUARY 6

GENESIS 15–17, WITH MATTHEW 5:27–48

———

He is a shield to those who put their trust in Him (Proverbs 30:5).

WHAT IS THE MOST REPEATED COMMAND IN THE BIBLE?

Abraham rescues Lot and perhaps fears retaliation (Genesis 14:1–16). God perceives this and says, "Do not be afraid, Abram" (Genesis 15:1). The most repeated command in the Bible is spoken to Abraham: "Do not be afraid." Like Abraham we live in a dangerous world and need reminding that we are invincible until the Lord calls us home. Only God knows the day of our death. Hebrews 9:27 reveals, "it is appointed for men to die once." Our security should derive from the Eternal One who continually hovers over His own children caring for us.

God is with us. The writer of Hebrews reminds us, "For He Himself has said, 'I will never leave you nor forsake you.' So we may boldly say: 'The LORD is my helper; I will not fear. What can man do to me?'" (Hebrews 13:5–6). Let's heed Agur's words: "He is a shield to those who put their trust in Him" (Proverbs 30:5).

EMPLOYMENT POINT: *Trust in God, as your protector.*

———

JANUARY 7

GENESIS 18–19, WITH MATTHEW 6

———◦———

Be anxious for nothing (Philippians 4:6).

ARE YOU A WORRYWART?

Abraham is concerned because he has relatives residing in Sodom and God is about to destroy that wicked city. He can choose to worry about the situation or he can pray; Abraham chooses the latter (Genesis 18:16–33). The father of faith opts to seek the Lord through prayer concerning this vital matter.

Similarly, Jesus understands the importance of prayer over worry. He instructs His disciples to stop worrying and have faith in God. He makes this point by giving an argument from the lesser to the greater: If God cares for the birds and the lilies of the field, then He will care more for His followers (Matthew 6:25–30). Our Lord further instructs His apprentices to stop worrying and seek God first, because He will subsequently care for their necessities (Matthew 6:31–33). Finally, Jesus tells His disciples to stop worrying because their futures are secure (Matthew 6:34). God's grace is sufficient every day; therefore, stop worrying.

EMPLOYMENT POINT: *Stop worrying, and commit everything to God through prayer.*

———◦———

JANUARY 8

GENESIS 20–22, WITH MATTHEW 7

Not everyone who says to Me, "Lord, Lord," shall enter the kingdom of heaven, but he who does the will of My Father in heaven (Matthew 7:21).

HOW SHOULD YOU RESPOND TO AN ABSURD REQUEST FROM GOD?

God has informed Abraham that he would be a great nation, and his seed would be as numerous as the sand by the sea. Now the Lord wants to know the following by commanding him to sacrifice his son: Does Abraham love Me more than anyone or anything? Loving the Lord above even family displays that He receives first place in our lives just as He requires (Matthew 10:37). Anything less shows that we are unfit to be in His service (Matthew 10:38–39).

The father of faith doesn't hesitate, but gets an early start the next morning for his three-day journey. Reaching his destination Abraham tells those with him, "Stay here with the donkey; the lad and I will go yonder and worship, and we will come back to you" (Genesis 22:5). God acknowledges Abraham's faith and praises him for loving the Lord above everyone else, which is demonstrated by his obedience (Genesis 22:12).

EMPLOYMENT POINT: *Demonstrate supreme love for God through your obedience.*

JANUARY 9

GENESIS 23–24, WITH MATTHEW 8

My soul, wait silently for God alone, for my expectation is from Him (Psalm 62:5).

ARE YOU WAITING UPON GOD TO PROVIDE THE RIGHT SPOUSE?

Abraham is a good father to Isaac. He seeks to arrange a marriage for Isaac that would please his Father. The Lord's plan for parents to guide their children hasn't changed. God honors Abraham who dispatches his servant to retrieve a wife for Isaac. We are told that when the servant returns home, with mission accomplished, we find Isaac meditating in the field (Genesis 24:63). Isaac keeps his focus upon the Lord, and God honors him with a spouse to be his complement.

Sadly, I've witnessed that when single Christians do not wait upon God, who faithfully works through parents, and *take the bull by the horns*, that they often experience deep and lasting wounds during the marriage. The ways of the Lord are always best. As the Lord brought Eve to Adam, wisdom cries out to look for the Lord's provision of a spouse, which the Creator has designed just for you!

EMPLOYMENT POINT: *Wait upon the Lord, for the spouse of His choosing.*

January 10

Genesis 25–26, with Matthew 9:1–17

———— ❦ ————

Whoever desires to come after Me, let him deny himself, and take up his cross, and follow Me (Mark 8:34).

Are you leading a life of self-denial?

Isaac has two sons: Esau and Jacob. God predicts, "the older shall serve the younger" (Genesis 25:23). Carnal Esau sells his birthright to Jacob (Genesis 25:30–34). The writer of Hebrews uses Esau as an example to warn us about fleshly lusts. He first tells us, "Pursue peace with all people, and holiness, without which no one will see the Lord" (Hebrews 12:14). Again the writer of Hebrews warns against fulfilling the lust of the flesh, "Lest there be any fornicator or profane person like Esau, who for one morsel of food sold his birthright" (Hebrews 12:16).

Don't choose instant gratification like Esau, which can cost you God's blessing (Hebrews 12:17). Remember, "the blessing of the LORD makes one rich, and He adds no sorrow with it" (Proverbs 10:22). Allow God's Spirit to lead. "Walk in the Spirit," writes Paul, "and you shall not fulfill the lust of the flesh" (Galatians 5:16).

Employment Point: *Choose God's path of self-denial, and experience His blessing.*

———— ❦ ————

January 11

Genesis 27–28, with Matthew 9:18–38

Let each one of you in particular so love his own wife as himself, and let the wife see that she respects her husband (Ephesians 5:33).

Do you have a Spirit-filled marriage?

God desires to bless His people through godly marriages, which produce spiritual children. Jacob is commanded not to take a heathen spouse (Genesis 28:2). Why? Genesis 28:3–4 shows marrying a believer as the path of blessing, "May God Almighty bless you, and make you fruitful and multiply you, that you may be an assembly of peoples; and give you the blessing of Abraham, to you and your descendants with you." The Lord delights to grace His children who honor Him in their marriages and families; this is the pathway of blessing.

In the Book of Malachi, God rebukes the Jewish males for divorcing their wives, and therefore wrecking the chance for godly descendants. One purpose for marriage is given in Malachi 2:15, "But did He not make them one, having a remnant of the Spirit? And why one? He seeks godly offspring." God simply blesses the godly!

Employment Point: *Strive to have a Spirit-filled marriage, leading to godly children.*

January 12

Genesis 29–30, with Matthew 10:1–23

Be sure your sin will find you out (Numbers 32:23).

What should you look for in a spouse, while guarding your heart from deceit?

God is simultaneously going to provide a bride for Jacob and teach the rascal about sowing and reaping. Jacob reaches his destination and observes not only a beautiful woman, but also one who works hard. Single Jacob is attracted to Rachel's beauty while observing her work ethic. Single Christians should not just note the attractiveness in a potential spouse, but also one who works hard for the Lord.

Moreover, recall that Jacob cunningly got both the birthright and blessing from his brother (Genesis 25, 27). Now he will reap the fruits of trickery at the hands of Laban, a master manipulator. Paul warns believers on this topic, "Do not be deceived, God is not mocked; for whatever a man sows, that he will also reap" (Galatians 6:7). Walking with the Lord and displaying integrity will keep you in the right path. "Be wise as serpents and harmless as doves" (Matthew 10:16).

Employment Point: *Seek a spouse who labors for Jesus, and guard your heart from deceit.*

January 13

Genesis 31–32, with Matthew 10:24–42

He who finds his life will lose it, and he who loses his life for My sake will find it (Matthew 10:39).

How has your prayer time changed you?

Jacob, the rascal, now becomes Jacob the deathly fearful man. Esau is reported to be in the vicinity, "So Jacob was greatly afraid" (Genesis 32:7) and said, "for I fear him" (Genesis 32:11). The supplanter finally displays honesty before God.

There are three lessons to be gleaned from Jacob's prayer. First, prayer should be costly (Genesis 32:24–25). Jacob left the prayer meeting with a limp! Two, pray persistently and expectantly (Genesis 32:26). "But he [Jacob] said, 'I will not let You go unless You bless me!'" The third lesson is as follows: Persistent and expectant prayers are honored (Genesis 32:27–30). Jacob's opponent blessed him, "Your name shall no longer be called Jacob, but Israel; for you have struggled with God and with men, and have prevailed" (Genesis 32:28). Hosea elaborates upon the life-changing event showing that Jacob wrestled with God (Hosea 12:2–6)!

Employment Point: *Pray hard, expecting God's blessing.*

JANUARY 14

GENESIS 33–35, WITH MATTHEW 11

———◦———

Honor your father and mother . . . that it may be well with you (Ephesians 6:2–3).

HAVE YOU CHOSEN TO REMAIN IN A SAFE PLACE?

Moses pens, "Now Dinah the daughter of Leah . . . went out to see the daughters of the land" (Genesis 34:1). Jacob's daughter gets into trouble because she wanders from her secure dwelling. Her curiosity led to rape, and then murder. Dinah's excursion from home to socialize with unbelievers had grave repercussions!

Let's spring forward two thousand years, when Joseph and Mary lost the Son of God. Joseph and Mary, thinking that Jesus was in the other's company, had left for home after being with Him in Jerusalem. They found Jesus in the temple. Although He is doing His Father's business, He understands the home in which He was placed. Luke records, "Then He went down with them and came to Nazareth, and was subject to them" (Luke 2:51). The end result is "Jesus increased in wisdom and stature, and in favor with God and men" (Luke 2:52). Blessings abound for being in the right place!

EMPLOYMENT POINT: *Remain under your God given authorities, for His blessing.*

———◦———

January 15

Genesis 36–37, with Matthew 12:1–21

———◆———

The fear of the LORD is the instruction of wisdom, and before honor is humility (Proverbs 15:33).

Are you teachable like Joseph and Jesus?

Meet Joseph, handsome, his father's favorite child, and about to experience severe testing from age seventeen until thirty. Being exalted by his father leads to his brothers' envy, and many trials. Great leaders submit to the training from the Father's school of preparation. Joseph honors God throughout life and subsequently receives recognition by the writer of Hebrews as a man of faith (Hebrews 11:22).

Isaiah predicts the following about Jesus seven hundred years before His birth: "He awakens Me morning by morning, He awakens my ear to hear as the learned. The Lord GOD has opened My ear; and I was not rebellious, nor did I turn away. I gave My back to those who struck Me, and My cheeks to those who plucked out the beard; I did not hide My face from shame and spitting" (Isaiah 50:4–6). Joseph and Jesus experience humiliation before exaltation, in God's school for great leaders.

EMPLOYMENT POINT: *Willingly submit to God's ways of training, like Joseph and Jesus.*

———◆———

JANUARY 16

GENESIS 38–40, WITH MATTHEW 12:22–50

———◈———

Flee sexual immorality (1 Corinthians 6:18).

WHY IS GENESIS 38 AND THE ACCOUNT ABOUT JUDAH INSERTED IN THE NARRATIVE ABOUT JOSEPH (GENESIS 37–50)?

I'm glad that you asked that question! Judah pays a prostitute to have relations with him, while Joseph flees from his temptation. The two stories are juxtaposed (placed side by side) to show the contrast between Judah and his perverted sons (Er and Onan) versus Joseph. As a slave, Joseph is placed in a dangerous setting where compromise could easily occur. We shouldn't put ourselves in an environment where we might yield to sin, but if we find ourselves being tempted, run (Romans 13:14)! Your exit strategy should consist of just one word: Run!

Those being tempted need to rush from temptation and zoom toward individuals who will keep them secure and accountable. Paul's advice is timeless; he writes, "Flee also youthful lusts; but pursue righteousness, faith, love, peace with those who call on the Lord out of a pure heart" (2 Timothy 2:22).

EMPLOYMENT POINT: *Sprint from temptation, and pursue holiness with godly saints.*

———◈———

JANUARY 17

GENESIS 41, WITH
MATTHEW 13:1–32

———— ◦ ————

Those who sow in tears shall reap in joy (Psalm 126:5).

WHY DID JESUS BEGIN SPEAKING PARABLES TO THE PEOPLE?

Jesus began speaking in parables "on the same day" (Matthew 13:1) that the religious leaders accuse Him of casting out demons by the power of the Devil (Matthew 12:22–32). It signifies Israel's rejection of King Jesus. He begins then speaking in parables for three reasons. First, it signifies that Israel has rejected Jesus. Next, the Lord teaches parables to reveal truth to His followers and conceal the truth from those who rejected Him (Matthew 13:11–13). Reason number three is to fulfill prophecy (see Isaiah 6:9–10 with Matthew 13:14–17).

Our mission is to spread the seed of God's Word just as our Lord proclaimed the message of the gospel prolifically. The psalmist writes about the blessing of heralding God's truth, "He who continually goes forth weeping, bearing seed for sowing, shall doubtless come again with rejoicing, bringing his sheaves with him" (Psalm 126:6). We need to go and do likewise!

EMPLOYMENT POINT: *Spread the seed of God's Word, trusting Him with the results.*

———— ◦ ————

January 18

Genesis 42–43, with Matthew 13:33–58

———◆———

The kingdom of heaven is like treasure hidden in a field, which a man found and hid; and for joy over it he goes and sells all that he has and buys that field (Matthew 13:44).

What is God's kingdom worth to you?

God's kingdom refers to His universal rule over those belonging to Him. You must be born again to enter the kingdom of God. Jesus informs Nicodemus, "Most assuredly, I say to you, unless one is born again, he cannot see the kingdom of God" (John 3:3). He stresses the point, "Do not marvel that I said to you ["you" is singular and directed toward Nicodemus], You ["you" is plural referring to all people] must be born again" (John 3:7).

Our Lord likens the kingdom to a hidden treasure located in a field. His kingdom is extremely valuable but not perceived by the human eye. One day a man exclaims "eureka," which means *I found it*. That is the meaning of the Greek term translated "found." He then hides the treasure in the field and sells everything he owns to purchase the field. God's kingdom surpasses any earthly treasure.

Employment Point: *Obtaining God's kingdom is worth tremendous sacrifice.*

———◆———

JANUARY 19

GENESIS 44–45, WITH
MATTHEW 14:1–21

———— ◈ ————

Even as Christ forgave you, so you also must do (Colossians 3:13).

HOW WELL DO YOU FORGIVE OTHERS?

Joseph is sold into slavery and knows firsthand the deep suffering from the hands of his brothers. Joseph's response, however, is "But now, do not therefore be grieved or angry with yourselves because you sold me here; for God sent me before you to preserve life" (Genesis 45:5). He understands, "it was not you who sent me here, but God" (Genesis 45:8). The betrayed brother understands God's sovereignty.

Are you quick to condemn others, but never judge yourself? When a woman is brought to Jesus in adultery, He tells those who want her stoned, "He who is without sin among you, let him throw a stone at her first" (John 8:7). How gracious has Jesus been to forgive your sin like the adulteress? Let's act upon His forgiveness. Paul says, "And be kind to one another, tenderhearted, forgiving one another, even as God in Christ forgave you" (Ephesians 4:32). Live as one who has been liberated!

EMPLOYMENT POINT: *Forgive as you've been forgiven.*

———— ◈ ————

January 20

Genesis 46–48, with Matthew 14:22–36

———◦———

Therefore He is also able to save to the uttermost those who come to God through Him, since He always lives to make intercession for them (Hebrews 7:25).

What should you do during life's storms?

After the feeding of the five thousand, "immediately Jesus made His disciples get into the boat and go before Him to the other side" (Matthew 14:22). Israel wants to make Jesus a king who will always feed them, so He protects His disciples from their selfish ambition (John 6:15). Jesus knows their desire for self-glorification and whisks them away from the multitude—to keep them from a spiritual implosion!

He prays for the disciples as a storm overtakes them (Matthew 14:23–24). Next, He reveals Himself to them (Matthew 14:25–27). We need to look to Him during the storms of life. Our Lord demonstrates His deity by walking upon the water. Often we get distracted during the storms of life rather than focusing upon the One who controls them. The disciples should not have feared the storm because Jesus dispatched them to the other side; He will bring you safely to shore!

Employment Point: *Believe Jesus' Word during a storm.*

———◦———

JANUARY 21

GENESIS 49–50, WITH
MATTHEW 15:1–20

Do not think that I came to destroy the Law or the Prophets. I did not come to destroy but to fulfill (Matthew 5:17).

DO YOU REGULARLY WORSHIP JESUS WHO ALONE FULFILLS THE LAW?

The Book of Genesis imparts three spectacular prophecies about Jesus. Moses gives us the earliest prediction about Jesus' virgin birth (Genesis 3:15). He refers to "her Seed," which points to His miraculous conception (Matthew 1:18–25; Galatians 4:4). Next, we have the connection between Genesis 12:3 and Galatians 3:8, which shows the Messiah coming from the line of Abraham and will bring salvation to the Gentiles ("all the families of the earth" in Genesis 12:3).

Finally, Moses foresees Jesus coming from the tribe of Judah (Genesis 49:8–10). John testifies to Jesus' triumph over death and unique character in Revelation 5. An angel tells him, "Behold, the Lion of the tribe of Judah, the Root of David, has prevailed to open the scroll" (Revelation 5:5). No wonder not only God the Father (Revelation 4:11), but also God the Son (Revelation 5:12) is noted as "worthy" to be worshiped in the book of Revelation!

EMPLOYMENT POINT: *Worship and adore Jesus, who alone fulfills the Law.*

JANUARY 22

EXODUS 1–3, WITH
MATTHEW 15:21–39

———◈———

I will praise You, for I am fearfully and wonderfully made (Psalm 139:14).

DO YOU VALUE LIFE?

The Pharaoh orders the execution of all Jewish male babies (Exodus 1:16). Shiphrah and Puah, who apparently oversee other midwives, do not heed the command of the king. They have another King. Moses writes, "But the midwives feared God, and did not do as the king of Egypt commanded them, but saved the male children alive" (Exodus 1:17). These two courageous women understood that babies are made in the image of God and should be protected.

Later in the book of Exodus, Moses teaches that anyone who harms a child within the mother's womb should be punished (Exodus 21:22–25). Like the two Hebrew midwives, the Law also values human life. Moreover, David writes, "For You formed my inward parts; You covered me in my mother's womb" (Psalm 139:13). "Covered" literally means *to weave together*. Human life is to be cherished because it is formed by the Creator's hand, and displays the handiwork of God!

EMPLOYMENT POINT: *Honor those who value life, to imitate God.*

———◈———

JANUARY 23

EXODUS 4–6, WITH MATTHEW 16

———◦◦◦———

I will build My church, and the gates of Hades shall not prevail against it (Matthew 16:18).

ARE YOU PARTNERING WITH JESUS TO BUILD HIS CHURCH?

Jesus laid down His life for the church to be born. Even His death wouldn't stop the process of reaching the masses. Countless Christians have also sacrificed their lives by spreading the gospel more than two thousand years. Tertullian, an early church father and martyr, said, "The blood of the martyrs is the seed of the church." God watered the seed of the Word through the ultimate sacrifice of dedicated saints.

My pastoral observation, after forty years of commitment to one local church, is that God greatly blesses the lives of those who sacrifice their time, money, service, location where they live, in order to align themselves with Jesus' church. Our future judgment occurs in the context of the church (1 Corinthians 3:11–15). Let's remember Jesus' words, "If anyone desires to come after Me, let him deny himself, and take up his cross, and follow Me" (Matthew 16:24). He rewards those who surrender themselves to the work of ministry!

EMPLOYMENT POINT: *Sacrificially partner with Jesus, to build His church.*

———◦◦◦———

January 24

Exodus 7–8, with
Matthew 17

———※———

This is My beloved Son, in whom I am well pleased. Hear Him!
(Matthew 17:5).

Have you exalted Jesus above all?

Jesus selects Peter, James, and John to have a mountaintop experience.
The Lord reveals His glory to them. Moses and Elijah also appear
and have a conversation with Jesus. (I wonder if Moses said to Jesus,
"Finally, after 1,400 years, I've made it to the Promised Land.") In
Peter's excitement he exclaims, "Lord, it is good for us to be here;
if You wish, let us make here three tabernacles: one for You, one
for Moses, and one for Elijah" (Matthew 17:4). Perhaps Peter thinks
about Zechariah 14:16–17, which connects the Feast of Tabernacles
with the kingdom.

Later the apostle to the Jews testifies about Jesus' glory being
revealed in 2 Peter 1:16–18. Peter might have made the right
connection with the Feast of Tabernacles and the kingdom of God;
however, he wrongly equates Moses and Elijah with Jesus. Jesus is the
eternal Son of God and should be exalted above everyone.

Employment Point: *Honor God's glorious Son above all men.*

———※———

January 25

Exodus 9–10, with Matthew 18:1–20

———

Bear one another's burdens, and so fulfill the law of Christ (Galatians 6:2).

Do you love the brethren by confronting those in sin?

We are privately to face those in sin. "Moreover if your brother sins against you, go and tell him his fault between you and him alone" (Matthew 18:15). Jesus wants the matter to stay private, so that the sinner can be restored to fellowship behind closed doors. He teaches that if the person doesn't repent, then you need to take one or two more witnesses with you (Matthew 18:16), based upon Deuteronomy 19:15. If that individual will not confess his sin, then the entire church is informed, and that person is put out of the church into Satan's domain (Matthew 18:17; 1 Corinthians 5:1–8).

The goal is reconciliation. Paul confronts a man who openly sins among the believers at Corinth (1 Corinthians 5:1–8). It seems that the man whom Paul excommunicated from the church later repents (2 Corinthians 2:5–11). Our goal should never be mere punishment, but to restore the saint by the above steps.

Employment Point: *Follow Jesus' directions about church discipline, to restore fallen saints.*

———

JANUARY 26

EXODUS 11–12, WITH MATTHEW 18:21–35

———※———

But if you do not forgive men their trespasses, neither will your Father forgive your trespasses (Matthew 6:15).

HAVE YOU CONSIDERED THE EXTENT OF GOD'S FORGIVENESS TO YOU?

Yesterday we learned from Jesus about the steps to confront those in sin. Today we'll focus upon the need to grant wholehearted forgiveness to individuals who have offended us. Rabbis taught in Jesus' day that you should forgive someone up to three times when they've sinned against you. Peter, being aware of this, thought he'd look spiritual to Jesus and asks, "How often shall my brother sin against me, and I forgive him? Up to seven times?" (Matthew 18:21). Jesus' response must have knocked the sandals right off Peter's feet: "I do not say to you, up to seven times, but up to seventy times seven" (Matthew 18:22). His response must have sent the fisherman reeling!

Jesus' parable then probes the debt of forgiveness we've received—which should be granted to others. Having the right focus is the key to forgiving others.

EMPLOYMENT POINT: *Forgive others for their trespasses, by contemplating the debt of Jesus' forgiveness to you.*

———※———

JANUARY 27

EXODUS 13–15, WITH MATTHEW 19:1–15

———————

Let the little children come to Me, and do not forbid them; for of such is the kingdom of heaven (Matthew 19:14).

ARE LITTLE CHILDREN IMPORTANT TO YOU?

Jesus has just given His view on marriage; it only naturally follows that He would address the topic of children. Parents bring both infants (Luke 18:15) and little children to Jesus that He might bless them. Sadly, the disciples don't value the little ones as they ought and try to hinder them from being brought to Jesus. The Lord expresses their value by stating: "Let the little children come to Me, and do not forbid them; for of such is the kingdom of heaven" (Matthew 19:14). Jesus says that infants and little children are in heaven.

God's special grace extends to infants and very little children, which enables them to enter heaven upon death. King David understands this and says after the death of his infant son, "I shall go to him, but he shall not return to me" (2 Samuel 12:23). Indeed, our Lord's grace reaches even into the womb to the unborn!

EMPLOYMENT POINT: *Don't hinder ministry to the little children, but pray for and bless them.*

———————

JANUARY 28

EXODUS 16–18, WITH MATTHEW 19:16–30

———◦———

See, we have left all and followed You (Matthew 19:27).

ARE YOU SACRIFICING THE TEMPORAL FOR THE ETERNAL?

The ruler loves his money more than his soul (Matthew 19:16–26). As Peter observes the rich man's departure, he asks Jesus, "See, we have left all and followed You. Therefore what shall we have?" (Matthew 19:27). Great question. Why should we put Jesus first in our lives and miss all the fun? Although sin has its pleasure for a season, sacrificing selfish gratification for God's future and lasting rewards shows foresight. Children of God need a retirement plan that is out of this world!

Jesus points out that our future blessing will far outweigh any momentary satisfaction. "And everyone who has left houses or brothers or sisters or father or mother or wife or children or lands, for My name's sake, shall receive a hundredfold, and inherit eternal life. But many who are first will be last, and the last first" (Matthew 19:29–30). Let's practice "present planned neglect" for future greatness!

EMPLOYMENT POINT: *Become the servant of all for future greatness.*

———◦———

January 29

Exodus 19–21, with Matthew 20:1–16

—————◆—————

I am the LORD your God, who brought you out of the land of Egypt, out of the house of bondage (Exodus 20:2).

ARE YOU HONORING THE PERSON AND WORK OF GOD?

We learn about our majestic God by studying both His person (who He is) and His work (what He does). The Ten Commandments reflect the nature of God. They instruct us about His character, which can be called His attributes or perfections. When the Father says "I am the LORD your God," He is declaring His eternality. God's name "LORD" derives from the verb *to be*. We can fully trust our God because He is the great "I am." Jesus makes the connection to the Father using these same words (John 8:58), which show His eternality.

Moreover, the eternal God displays His vast power by the ten plagues on Egypt, parting the Red Sea, and delivering the Israelites from four hundred years of captivity. His works are perfect; they are in complete harmony with His character and testify to His eternality. We should daily reflect upon the person and work of the Lord!

EMPLOYMENT POINT: *Revere the person and work of God.*

—————◆—————

January 30

Exodus 22–24, with Matthew 20:17–34

And whoever desires to be first among you, let him be your slave (Matthew 20:27).

How is your spiritual eyesight?

James and John come to Jesus unwittingly wearing blinders. They are self-centered and aspire to greatness. You sense their arrogance as they ask to sit on the right and left hand of Jesus in the kingdom. Remember, God resists the proud, but gives grace to the humble! Jesus exhibits humility unlike the self-centered brothers. He said earlier, "Take My yoke upon you and learn from Me, for I am gentle and lowly in heart, and you will find rest for your souls" (Matthew 11:29). Sadly, the Boanerges ("Sons of Thunder," Mark 3:17) hadn't grasped Jesus' teaching and ways.

Now reread the story of the blind men that become an object lesson displaying the pride and spiritual blindness of James and John (Matthew 20:29–34). The best way to remove blinders consists of serving others and spending time with godly Christians, who are not self-centered but God-centered, and imitate them (Matthew 20:26–28).

Employment Point: *Remain God-centered, by being the slave of all.*

JANUARY 31

EXODUS 25–26, WITH
MATTHEW 21:1–22

So the multitudes said, "This is Jesus, the prophet from Nazareth of Galilee" (Matthew 21:11).

ARE YOU BORN AGAIN?

There is a seeming tension in the Scripture about discerning who is saved. First Samuel 16:7 declares, "for man looks at the outward appearance, but the LORD looks at the heart." Yet Jesus says about false prophets, "You will know them by their fruits" (Matthew 7:16). Daniel predicts the exact day that Jesus would ride into Jerusalem (Daniel 9:24–27), which is called the Triumphal Entry. The prophecy began its 173,880-day countdown with the commencement to rebuild the walls in Jerusalem (Nehemiah 2:1–8). The Jewish people praise the Messiah but exalt a conquering king, not a suffering Savior (Matthew 21:1–11). John reveals their unbelief, "He came to His own, and His own did not receive Him" (John 1:11).

We need to make sure that we have turned from our sin and believed in Jesus; He took our sin upon Himself and conquered death. Let your unseen faith be displayed by a fruitful life!

EMPLOYMENT POINT: *Believe in Jesus' finished work on your behalf to be saved.*

FEBRUARY 1

EXODUS 27–28, WITH MATTHEW 21:23–46

By what authority are You doing these things? And who gave You this authority? (Matthew 21:23).

WHY DOES JESUS ANSWER TWO QUESTIONS WITH TWO QUESTIONS?

The two questions from Matthew 21:23 derive from Jesus cleansing the temple and healing the blind and the lame who were there (Matthew 21:12–14). Envious of Jesus' actions, the chief priests and elders question His authority. Yet He chooses not to answer them, but asks the following: "The baptism of John—where was it from? From heaven or from men?" (Matthew 21:25). With wisdom our Lord confronts the religious leaders with these two questions, to force them to contemplate where John received his authority.

Jesus knows that there is no reason to answer their questions unless they repent and acknowledge that John derived his authority from the Father. Similarly, Jesus' authority comes from above, but He will not give them additional revelation because they didn't honor God's earlier ambassador (John). Refusing to humble yourself under the mighty hand of God and disregard His messengers leads to hardening of the heart!

EMPLOYMENT POINT: *Honor God's authorities, to progress in your walk with Him.*

FEBRUARY 2

EXODUS 29–30, WITH MATTHEW 22:1–22

You also, as living stones, are being built up a spiritual house, a holy priesthood (1 Peter 2:5).

ARE YOU PURIFYING YOUR LIFE AS GOD'S PRIEST?

We are a royal priesthood (1 Peter 2:9). Yet we get contaminated in this morally filthy world and need God's cleansing through His forgiveness. God had a laver of bronze erected so that priests could wash before ministering. Moses admonishes, "So they shall wash their hands and their feet, lest they die" (Exodus 30:21). This symbolic act shows the need for a cleansed priesthood. The Lord servants shall "be holy, for I am holy" (Leviticus 11:44; 1 Peter 1:16).

A popular bumper sticker states: "Christians aren't perfect, just forgiven." This is true of even the apostle Paul, who in his old age calls himself the foremost of sinners (1 Timothy 1:15). John's words are needful for God's priests. He writes, "If we confess our sins, He is faithful and just to forgive us our sins and to cleanse us from all unrighteousness" (1 John 1:9). Let's strive to be a holy priesthood!

EMPLOYMENT POINT: *Confess your sins regularly, to be an effective priest.*

FEBRUARY 3

EXODUS 31–33, WITH MATTHEW 22:23–46

———◦———

The people sat down to eat and drink, and rose up to play (Exodus 32:6).

HOW ARE YOU SPIRITUALLY PROTECTING YOUR CHILDREN?

In the 1950s five percent of high school girls and ten percent of high school boys were sexually active. Spring forward to the year 2000, and those numbers jump to seventy percent for young ladies and eighty percent for young men. There are three m's that parents need to observe to protect their children. The first *m* is to guard your children's *music*. Satan loves to seduce the mind through carnal music. *Modesty* gives us the second *m*. When young men start to put improper pictures on their phones and young ladies dress provocatively, then further decline occurs.

The third *m* pertains to *morality*. What leads children down the path of destruction? It is the same thing that has always allured God's children to Satan's ways; they leave the realm of the godly for the immoral. Let's teach them to "flee youthful lusts," as Paul writes in 2 Timothy 2:22, and to "pursue righteousness, faith, love, peace with those who call on the Lord out of a pure heart."

EMPLOYMENT POINT: *Seek to guard your children's music, modesty, and morality.*

———◦———

FEBRUARY 4

EXODUS 34–36, WITH MATTHEW 23:1–22

———◦———

For the LORD your God is a consuming fire, a jealous God (Deuteronomy 4:24).

DID YOU KNOW THAT ONE OF GOD'S NAMES IS JEALOUS?

Moses writes, "For you shall worship no other god, for the LORD, whose name is Jealous, is a jealous God" (Exodus 34:14). Every instance of the adjective "jealous" appearing in the Old Testament is used of God (Exodus 20:5; Deuteronomy 4:24; 5:9; 6:15). Consider Deuteronomy 6:15, "For the LORD your God is a jealous God among you, lest the anger of the LORD your God be aroused against you and destroy you from the face of the earth." Clearly our Father calls us to Himself and will not permit His children to embrace pseudo gods.

All Christians have been guilty of idolatry at one time or another; however, the LORD is abundantly merciful. "For as the heavens are high above the earth," writes the psalmist, "so great is His mercy toward those who fear Him" (Psalm 103:11). Since the Lord is jealous for us, let's be zealous for Him!

EMPLOYMENT POINT: *Pursue your walk with the Lord, knowing that His name is Jealous.*

———◦———

FEBRUARY 5

EXODUS 37–38, WITH MATTHEW 23:23–39

O Jerusalem, Jerusalem, the one who kills the prophets and stones those who are sent to her! How often I wanted to gather your children together, as a hen gathers her chicks under her wings, but you were not willing! (Matthew 23:37).

DO YOUR DESIRES MATCH THE LORD'S?

Jesus lives up to His name, which means *Jehovah Savior*. The angel informs Mary, "for He will save His people from their sins" (Matthew 1:21). The Father dispatches the Son to be the Savior of the world. Luke offers the purpose for Jesus' first coming: "the Son of Man has come to seek and to save that which was lost" (Luke 19:10). Our Lord passionately pursued the unsaved and becomes the model evangelist for all those who identify with the deliverer of our soul!

Paul encourages Timothy to intercede for those who are in authority because God "desires all men to be saved and to come to the knowledge of the truth" (1 Timothy 2:4). We should align our motives to match God's; then we will track down unbelievers to share the good news of the gospel with them.

EMPLOYMENT POINT: *Seek to have the heart of God by desiring all people to be saved.*

FEBRUARY 6

EXODUS 39–40, WITH
MATTHEW 24:1–22

———◦———

Then the cloud covered the tabernacle of meeting, and the glory of the LORD filled the tabernacle (Exodus 40:34).

DOES GOD FILL YOUR TEMPLE WITH HIS GLORY?

The Lord's presence in our lives and homes should cause people to stand in awe. "And Moses was not able to enter the tabernacle of meeting, because the cloud rested above it, and the glory of the LORD filled the tabernacle" (Exodus 40:35). Today, Jesus' presence lives within each believer, which ultimately leads to our glorification. Paul states it as follows: "Which is Christ in you, the hope of glory" (Colossians 1:27). His presence should fill our lives as it did in the tabernacle.

The residents at Corinth also had a temple. Aphrodite (the Greek goddess of love) was worshiped through immoral practices in this structure that housed one thousand priestess-prostitutes. Paul reminds the saints at Corinth that their bodies are temples of the Holy Spirit and to "glorify God in your body and in your spirit, which are God's" (1 Corinthians 6:20). Let's have a suitable residence for the King of Kings!

EMPLOYMENT POINT: *Glorify God through your temple, and let His presence reign.*

———◦———

FEBRUARY 7

LEVITICUS 1–3, WITH MATTHEW 24:23–51

See then that you walk circumspectly, not as fools but as wise (Ephesians 5:15).

ARE YOU WISE OR FOOLISH?

Many people live as if judgment isn't coming. Consider the normal activities that were going on in Noah's day just before the global flood. "For as in the days before the flood, they were eating and drinking, marrying and giving in marriage, until the day that Noah entered the ark" (Matthew 24:38). Observe that "Noah" is singular here and the following verse speaks about "them all," which refers to all the people on the earth. "And did not know until the flood came and took them all away" (Matthew 24:39). God delivered Noah and destroyed the inhabitants of the earth.

David describes the fool as saying to himself, "There is no God" (Psalm 14:1). In other words, fools ignore the God who made them. Conversely, we are to be "redeeming the time, because the days are evil" (Ephesians 5:16). Your biological clock is ticking, so use every moment to bring glory to the Time Keeper!

EMPLOYMENT POINT: *Live wisely by using your time on earth for God's glory.*

FEBRUARY 8

LEVITICUS 4–6, WITH MATTHEW 25:1–30

The fool has said in his heart, "there is no God" (Psalm 53:1).

WHICH SET OF VIRGINS ARE YOU IMITATING?

At times Jesus introduces an important truth by repeating the word "amen." (Several examples are John 5:24, 25; 8:58, translated "most assuredly.") Similarly for emphasis, the important statement is repeated, "The fool has said in his heart, 'there is no God'" (Psalms 14:1; 53:1). Jesus tells the story of the ten virgins. He says, "Now five of them were wise, and five were foolish" (Matthew 25:2). Those who are foolish take their lamps but no oil with them (Matthew 25:3). In other words, they didn't prepare for the coming of the bridegroom, who they knew was returning but not when.

Jesus is coming again, but when? We need to be prepared for His return by daily walking with Him. Let's heed Paul's warning, "Awake, you who sleep, arise from the dead, and Christ will give you light. See then that you walk circumspectly, not as fools but as wise" (Ephesians 5:14–15).

EMPLOYMENT POINT: *Be wise and daily expect His return.*

FEBRUARY 9

LEVITICUS 7–9, WITH MATTHEW 25:31–46

———❖———

When the Son of Man comes in His glory, and all the holy angels with Him, then He will sit on the throne of His glory (Matthew 25:31).

DO YOUR WORDS AND WORKS TESTIFY TO YOUR SALVATION?

Jesus will come for the church in the Rapture and then will return with us after the Tribulation. Observe Jesus using the word "when" and not "if" He returns. Our Lord will fulfill the role as judge in His Second Coming. He will discern those who are saved (sheep) and separate them from the unsaved (goats). The saved enter the kingdom, but the unsaved go "into the everlasting fire" (Matthew 25:41).

As our words reveal our hearts ("For by your words you will be justified, and by your words you will be condemned"; Matthew 12:37), so do our deeds. Saints demonstrate their inner saving faith by caring for the needs of the brethren (Matthew 25:35–40). After all, we are saved to serve. "For we are His workmanship created in Christ Jesus unto good works" (Ephesians 2:10). Our words and works should display that the Lord has saved our soul and given us a new nature!

EMPLOYMENT POINT: *Let your words and works showcase your salvation.*

———❖———

FEBRUARY 10

LEVITICUS 10–12, WITH
MATTHEW 26:1–19

By those who come near Me I must be regarded as holy; and before all the people I must be glorified (Leviticus 10:3).

ARE YOU A PRESUMPTUOUS CHRISTIAN?

My dictionary defines "presumptuous" as follows: "A person failing to observe the limits of what is permitted or appropriate." Nadab and Abihu, the priestly sons of Aaron, were presumptuous. These two men went beyond the limits of God's tolerance, and He struck them dead. "So fire went out from the LORD and devoured them, and they died before the LORD" (Leviticus 10:2). Apparently they had been drinking and entered their sacred calling while drunk (Leviticus 10:8–10).

As a former youth pastor, and now pastor, I've witnessed too many Christians presume upon God's grace. Let Proverbs 29:1 be a warning to all of us. "He who is often rebuked, and hardens his neck," writes the wise man, "will suddenly be destroyed, and that without remedy." The Lord should be revered and approached with the utmost of respect and served with the same disposition.

EMPLOYMENT POINT: *Don't presume upon God's grace, and serve the Lord with a pure heart.*

FEBRUARY 11

LEVITICUS 13, WITH MATTHEW 26:20–54

Nevertheless, not as I will, but as You will (Matthew 26:39).

ARE YOU YIELDING TO GOD'S WILL?

Let's consider three key concepts gleaned from Jesus' three prayers (Matthew 26:36–46). One, prayerfully surrender to God's will (Matthew 26:36–40). Jesus courageously prays, "O My Father, if it is possible, let this cup pass from Me; nevertheless, not as I will, but as You will" (Matthew 26:39). Jesus came to implement the Father's will, not His own. Two, pray lest you yield to temptation (Matthew 26:41). The surest way to fall prey to Satan's trap is not submitting to God. Our Lord says, "Watch and pray, lest you enter into temptation. The spirit indeed is willing, but the flesh is weak" (Matthew 26:41). A prayer-driven life protects you!

Observe the third point is the same as the first: Prayerfully surrender to God's will (Matthew 26:42–46). Our hero prays in the face of death, "O My Father, if this cup cannot pass away from Me unless I drink it, Your will be done" (Matthew 26:42).

EMPLOYMENT POINT: *Pray while submitting to God's will, to overcome temptation.*

FEBRUARY 12

LEVITICUS 14, WITH
MATTHEW 26:55-75

———※———

For there is one God and one Mediator between God and men, the Man Christ Jesus (1 Timothy 2:5).

ARE YOU A MEMBER OF CLUB FAILURE?

Jesus patiently works with failures. If you have flunked a major spiritual test, then welcome to Club Failure. You are not alone! Our Lord predicts Peter's three denials, which the arrogant apostle didn't believe could happen to him. Matthew closes the incident as follows: "And Peter remembered the word of Jesus who had said to him, 'before the rooster crows, you will deny Me three times.' So he went out and wept bitterly" (Matthew 26:75).

Thankfully, Jesus intercedes for Club Failure members. Luke quotes Jesus in a parallel account, "Simon, Simon! Indeed, Satan has asked for you, that he may sift you as wheat. But I have prayed for you, that your faith should not fail; and when you have returned to Me, strengthen your brethren" (Luke 22:31-32). Be encouraged; Jesus, our eternal High Priest, prays for us continually (Hebrews 7:25).

EMPLOYMENT POINT: *Return to ministry knowing that Jesus prays for Club Failure members.*

———※———

FEBRUARY 13

LEVITICUS 15–17, WITH MATTHEW 27:1–31

<hr />

For the life of the flesh is in the blood, and I have given it to you upon the altar to make atonement for your souls (Leviticus 17:11).

DID YOU KNOW THAT JESUS WAS CURSED FOR YOU?

Leviticus 16 describes the Day of Atonement; it was a national day of fasting when the Jewish high priest offered a sacrifice for his own sin and then for the people. Jesus, our great High Priest, didn't need to offer a sacrifice for His sin, because He had none. Yet Jesus uniquely offered Himself as the sacrifice.

Our Lord suffers much; He receives a crown of thorns (Matthew 27:29). Indeed, Adam and Eve's sin originally impacted the earth with thorns (Genesis 3:18). Consider Galatians 3:13 to connect the dots. Paul writes, "Cursed is everyone who hangs on a tree" (Galatians 3:13). Jesus, the High Priest, took upon Himself our sin on the tree (cross). "For such a High Priest was fitting for us, who is holy, harmless, undefiled, separate from sinners, and has become higher than the heavens," pens the author of Hebrews (Hebrews 7:26).

EMPLOYMENT POINT: *Believe on the sinless High Priest who took the sin of the world upon Himself.*

<hr />

FEBRUARY 14

LEVITICUS 18–19, WITH MATTHEW 27:32–66

You shall love your neighbor as yourself (Leviticus 19:18).

WHAT OLD TESTAMENT VERSE IS QUOTED MORE THAN ANY OTHER IN THE NEW TESTAMENT?

Leviticus 19:18 surfaces more than any other passage in the New Testament (Matthew 5:43; 19:19; 22:39; Mark 12:31, 33; Luke 10:27; Romans 13:9; Galatians 5:14; James 2:8). Today is Valentine's Day in the United States; however, Jesus revealed His heart to the world not on Valentine's Day, but when He died on the cross. He displayed both a love for the individual for whom He died, and the world because Jesus' sacrifice is sufficient for all mankind.

Darkness covers the land for three hours as Jesus hangs upon the cross (Matthew 27:45). The darkness depicts the sin of the world being placed upon the Lamb of God. In Jesus' agony He cries out, "My God, My God, why have You forsaken Me?" (Matthew 27:46). Since the sin of the world is placed upon the Savior, the Father had to turn away. Nonetheless, Jesus exemplifies His love for mankind through His sacrifice.

EMPLOYMENT POINT: *Jesus loved His neighbor as Himself, and now we need to do likewise.*

February 15

Leviticus 20–21, with Matthew 28

Whoever desires to come after Me, let him deny himself, and take up his cross, and follow Me (Mark 8:34).

What two words should define your life?

Two words should describe your life; they are "make disciples." (This is one word in the Greek!) Jesus' directive derives from Matthew 28:18–20. Three participles ("go," "baptizing," and "teaching") are modifying one command ("make disciples"). Essentially, we are to train learners to follow Jesus according to His Word, which means the process continues by them training others.

Paul describes the regiment masterfully in 2 Timothy 2:2: "And the things that you have heard from me among many witnesses, commit these to faithful men who will be able to teach others also." Moreover, we should evaluate our impact locally and globally since we are to preach the gospel to every creature. Jesus gave a master plan to His apostles to reach nearby people and those far away (Acts 1:8). As Jesus trained His followers and then dispatched them to disciple others, we should do likewise. Pass the baton, so that the work of discipleship continues.

Employment Point: *Obey the Great Commission to fulfill your life mission.*

FEBRUARY 16

LEVITICUS 22–23, WITH MARK 1:1–22

So then faith comes by hearing, and hearing by the word of God (Romans 10:17).

DO YOU PRIZE THE PREACHED WORD?

Mark portrays the start of Jesus' ministry with the following words: "Jesus came to Galilee, preaching the gospel of the kingdom of God" (Mark 1:14). The gospel is action-oriented, and so is Jesus. Likewise, Matthew captures the urgency of Jesus' message: "Repent for the kingdom of heaven is at hand" (Matthew 4:17). Preaching is also a priority for Jesus' forerunner, John the Baptist (Mark 1:4–8). Paul, known for preaching the gospel wherever he goes, commands Timothy, "Preach the word! Be ready in season and out of season" (2 Timothy 4:2). Clearly the ministry of preaching has a firm foundation that must be built upon by each succeeding generation.

Are you ready to hear and obey the preached Word? Jesus gives a similar statement to each church in Revelation 2–3. Seven times He commands: "He who has an ear, let him hear what the Spirit says to the churches" (Revelation 2:7, 11, 17, 29; 3:6, 13, 22).

EMPLOYMENT POINT: *Be faithful to hear, and obey the preached Word.*

FEBRUARY 17

LEVITICUS 24–25, WITH MARK 1:23–45

For we walk by faith, not by sight (2 Corinthians 5:7).

DO YOUR CHOICES MIRROR FAITH IN THE ABILITY OF GOD'S WORD?

The Lord instructs His people to work their fields for six years, "but in the seventh year there shall be a Sabbath of solemn rest for the land" (Leviticus 25:4). He knows the following logical question is coming from the Israelites: "What shall we eat in the seventh year, since we shall not sow nor gather in our produce?" (Leviticus 25:20). Subsequently God answers the question calling His people to faith, "Then I will command my blessing on you in the sixth year, and it will bring forth produce enough for three years" (Leviticus 25:21). They were to believe His Word!

Likewise, today we are to trust God with our finances. Paul pens in the context of church giving, "He who sows sparingly will also reap sparingly, and he who sows bountifully will also reap bountifully" (2 Corinthians 9:6). The Lord cannot lie and always honors His promises; therefore, let's walk by faith.

EMPLOYMENT POINT: *Do what God requires of you, and watch Him supply your needs.*

FEBRUARY 18

LEVITICUS 26–27, WITH MARK 2

Draw near to God and He will draw near to you (James 4:8).

ARE YOU ARDENTLY STRIVING TO BE NEAR JESUS?

Our Lord would not be sidetracked from His calling to preach the gospel of the kingdom (Mark 1:38), so He continues heralding God's Word from a jam-packed house (Mark 2:2). Four friends of a paralyzed man will not be deterred from reaching Jesus, to the extent that they peel back the roof of the owner's home and lower the man down to Him. Jesus then forgives the man's transgressions while supernaturally and extemporaneously healing him.

Wonderfully these four men exemplify Hebrews 11:6. "But without faith it is impossible to please Him, for he who comes to God must believe that He is, and that He is a rewarder of those who diligently seek Him." The verb "diligently" comes from the root meaning *to seek* and also has an intensifier. With an intense resolve these men approach Jesus by faith. Let us by faith exemplify this same passion!

EMPLOYMENT POINT: *Diligently pursue Jesus by faith, and you will be rewarded for your effort.*

FEBRUARY 19

NUMBERS 1–2, WITH MARK 3:1–21

———◈———

Some [seed] fell on stony ground (Mark 4:5).

DO YOU HAVE A HARD HEART?

Jesus enters a synagogue "and a man was there who had a withered hand" (Mark 3:1). The verb "was" emerges from the imperfect tense and shows the man having continually been in that place. Perhaps he is a plant by the religious hypocrites in order to entrap Jesus on the Sabbath. Since Jesus doesn't operate based on the fear of man, "He had looked around at them with anger, being grieved by the hardness of their hearts, He said to the man, 'Stretch out your hand.' And he stretched it out, and his hand was restored as whole as the other" (Mark 3:5).

God's revelation through creation (general revelation) and the Word (special revelation) reveal His mighty power. These individuals reject His revelation, and as a result harden their own hearts. Spurning God's revelation leads to irreparable brokenness (Proverbs 29:1). Don't reject the Lord's general and special revelation!

EMPLOYMENT POINT: *Submit to the One who reveals His vast power through creation and the Word, in order not to have a hard heart.*

———◈———

FEBRUARY 20

NUMBERS 3–4, WITH
MARK 3:22–35

The soul who sins shall die (Ezekiel 18:20).

ARE YOU FLIRTING WITH DEATH?

The Lord distinguishes between right from wrong. Moses pens, "And the LORD God commanded the man, saying, 'of every tree of the garden you may freely eat; but of the tree of the knowledge of good and evil you shall not eat, for in the day that you eat of it you shall surely die'" (Genesis 2:16–17). Adam's transgression brings sin, suffering, and death to mankind; no one escapes its clutch.

Moving forward, Uzzah is a Kohathite, a priest. Numbers 4 informs us that the priests were strictly trained never to touch the ark of God, lest they die. Nonetheless, as we learn from 2 Samuel 6:7, "the anger of the LORD was aroused against Uzzah, and God struck him there for his error; and he died there by the ark of God" (2 Samuel 6:7). The Kohathite's disobedience by touching the ark brings about his swift destruction. Whether Adam or Uzzah, let's learn from their transgressions!

EMPLOYMENT POINT: *Stay away from death's door by honoring God's Word.*

FEBRUARY 21

NUMBERS 5–6, WITH MARK 4:1–20

———◦———

Go into all the world and preach the gospel to every creature (Mark 16:15).

ARE YOU FAITHFULLY SOWING THE SEED OF GOD'S WORD?

Our Lord gives the parable of the sower. "Parable" literally means *to cast alongside of.* A parable is designed to give a story derived from life that communicates a simple truth. Parables can be used to make a comparison or give a contrast. Jesus begins, "Listen! Behold, a sower went out to sow" (Mark 4:3). The apostles need to understand the meaning of this parable because they are the ones called upon to fulfill the Great Commission (Matthew 28:18–20).

You and I also have a heavenly calling to bring the gospel to the lost. Jesus informs us where the enablement comes from to accomplish the divine task. Luke writes, "But you shall receive power when the Holy Spirit has come upon you; and you shall be witnesses to Me" (Acts 1:8). The Lord Jesus dispatched His Spirit at Pentecost and now indwells all God's children, which empowers us to witness.

EMPLOYMENT POINT: *Scatter the seed of God's Word wherever you go.*

———◦———

FEBRUARY 22

NUMBERS 7, WITH
MARK 4:21–41

———— ◈ ————

By which have been given to us exceedingly great and precious promises (2 Peter 1:4).

ARE YOU STANDING UPON THE PROMISES OF GOD?

The writer of the second gospel introduces the account of Jesus' disciples going through a storm, "on the same day" (Mark 4:35). Our Lord had instructed His followers all day and then chooses to test their knowledge. Just the words, "Let us cross over to the other side" (Mark 4:35) should have assured the twelve that they were destined to reach the shore. These eight words from the Lord's lips are enough to guarantee His disciples that they will reach the other side!

A great windstorm arises on the Sea of Galilee, which is approximately 690 feet below sea level and surrounded by mountains. The twelve panic as their boat rapidly fills with water. And where is Jesus? "But He was in the stern, asleep on a pillow" (Mark 4:38). After He awakened, Jesus rebukes the storm and corrects His disciples for lacking faith. Furthermore, Jesus is going to the other side to free a demon-possessed man.

EMPLOYMENT POINT: *Cling to the promises of God.*

———— ◈ ————

FEBRUARY 23

NUMBERS 8–10, WITH
MARK 5:1–20

For You are my rock and my fortress; therefore, for Your name's sake, lead me and guide me (Psalm 31:3).

ARE YOU FOLLOWING THE LEADER?

God delights to guide His children. He even leads His disobedient children in the wilderness. "At the command of the LORD the children of Israel would journey," writes Moses, "and at the command of the LORD they would camp; as long as the cloud stayed above the tabernacle they remained encamped" (Numbers 9:18). The Almighty displays His longing to be out in front of His children as a light unto their path. Clearly He wants us to follow the leader.

Likewise, Jesus follows the Father's direction. "And when He had come out of the boat, immediately there met Him out of the tombs, a man with an unclean spirit" (Mark 5:2). As the Spirit of God led Jesus into the wilderness to be tempted by the Devil (Mark 1:12; Luke 4:1), He followed His Father's guidance to deliver a man who was demon-possessed (Mark 5:1–13). His guidance is purposeful!

EMPLOYMENT POINT: *Follow God's lead, because He directs us to set the captives free and to do His will.*

February 24

Numbers 11–13, with Mark 5:21–43

———

But I say to you that for every idle word men may speak, they will give account of it in the day of judgment (Matthew 12:36).

What is the Lord hearing from your lips?

Israel isn't pleased with God's provision. Moses reports, "Now when the people complained, it displeased the LORD; for the LORD heard it" (Numbers 11:1). A cursory review of their recent past would have reminded them that the Lord delivered them from 430 years of bondage, provided manna daily for their breakfast, and cared for all their needs. How could they complain so freely after the Lord had extended repeatedly His goodness to them?

We would do well to daily ponder and thank God for His spiritual (Ephesians 1:3; 2:6) and physical provision (Philippians 4:19). Let's focus upon Philippians 2:14–15 to establish this habit. "Do all things without complaining and disputing, that you may become blameless and harmless, children of God without fault in the midst of a crooked and perverse generation, among whom you shine as lights in the world." Let's continually offer thanksgiving to our spiritual and physical provider!

EMPLOYMENT POINT: *Please God's ears by daily praising Him with your lips.*

———

FEBRUARY 25

NUMBERS 14–15, WITH
MARK 6:1–32

Now faith is the substance of things hoped for, the evidence of things not seen (Hebrews 11:1).

IS YOUR FAITH STIFLED BY SIGHT?

Faith is our title deed to claim God's promises. The Lord opens the door for the Israelites to enter Canaan. All they need to do is believe and act upon the promise. Sadly, ten of the twelve spies return with a bad report to Moses because they live by sight and not faith. Moses pens, "There we saw the giants (the descendants of Anak came from the giants); and we were like grasshoppers in our own sight, and so we were in their sight" (Numbers 13:33). God's children should have been focusing upon the greatness of their God, which would have made the inhabitants of Canaan look like midgets!

Subsequently "the LORD said to Moses: 'How long will these people reject Me? And how long will they not believe Me, with all the signs which I have performed among them?'" (Numbers 14:11). Consequently because of their unbelief they could not enter the land (Hebrews 3:19).

EMPLOYMENT POINT: *Use your title deed of faith to inherit God's promises.*

February 26

Numbers 16–17, with Mark 6:33–56

Be of good cheer! It is I; do not be afraid (Mark 6:50).

Are you looking for God's glory during a storm?

The disciples participate in their first miracle with Jesus' feeding of the five thousand. He quickly puts the disciples on a boat because the crowd desires a king who will provide for them, so He protects them from their own pride (Mark 6:45; John 6:15; Luke 22:24). Jesus knows that His followers are prone to self-centeredness, and that He must protect them from selfish ambition, which would eventually ruin them.

As Jesus goes to pray the disciples are caught up in a great storm. He "would have passed them by" (Mark 6:48). The term "passed by" is used in the Greek translation of the Old Testament (Exodus 33:22; 1 Kings 19:11) referring to a theophany. A theophany is a visible manifestation of God. Jesus reveals His deity by walking on the water. We need to look for God to intervene during the storms of life by displaying His divine nature and attributes.

EMPLOYMENT POINT: *Anticipate the God-Man to reveal Himself to you during a storm of life.*

FEBRUARY 27

NUMBERS 18–20, WITH MARK 7:1–13

To whom much is given, from him much will be required (Luke 12:48).

DO YOU GRASP YOUR ACCOUNTABILITY TO GOD?

Moses has a unique relationship with God. Faithfully this choice servant does the Lord's bidding, and the Lord communes with Moses face to face (Numbers 12:7–8). Yet, "to whom much has been committed, of him they will ask the more" (Luke 12:48). After Miriam, Moses' sister, was buried, God tells the prophet, "Take the rod; you and your brother Aaron gather the congregation together. Speak to the rock before their eyes, and it will yield its water" (Numbers 20:8). All that Moses needs to do is take God at His Word and act upon it by speaking to the rock.

Regretfully, Moses disobeys God by striking the rock and then steals the glory that alone belongs to Him (Numbers 20:12). "Therefore let him who thinks he stands take heed lest he fall," writes Paul (1 Corinthians 10:12). Moses' disobedience keeps him from entering Canaan. We should be quick to give the glory that solely belongs to the Almighty!

EMPLOYMENT POINT: *Obey God completely, lest you forfeit blessings.*

FEBRUARY 28

NUMBERS 21–23, WITH
MARK 7:14–37

And I, if I am lifted up from the earth, will draw all peoples to Myself (John 12:32).

ARE YOU DIRECTING THE UNSAVED TO THE CROSS?

The Lord sent fiery serpents to bite the Israelites because of their grumbling (Numbers 21:4–9). God structures an unconventional way for those bitten to be healed. "The Lord said to Moses, 'Make a fiery serpent, and set it on a pole; and it shall be that everyone who is bitten, when he looks at it, shall live'" (Numbers 21:8). Faith takes God at His Word and acts upon His prescribed method of healing.

God has an unusual means to save the world. Jesus tell Nicodemus, "And as Moses lifted up the serpent in the wilderness, even so must the Son of Man be lifted up, that whoever believes in Him should not perish but have eternal life" (John 3:14–15). Let's point people to the cross. "For God so loved the world that He gave His only begotten Son, that whoever believes in Him should not perish but have everlasting life" (John 3:16). Let's walk by faith and not sight!

EMPLOYMENT POINT: *Direct the lost to look upon the cross by faith.*

March 1

Numbers 24–27, with Mark 8

———◦◉◦———

Whoever desires to come after Me, let him deny himself, and take up his cross, and follow Me (Mark 8:34).

Are you a dedicated disciple?

Jesus' followers are often called disciples. A disciple is a lifelong learner. There are three commands that Jesus imparts to His apprentices in Mark 8:34. First He says, "Let him deny himself." The aorist verb, which refers to past time, speaks about a once-and-for-all commitment. You are purchased by Jesus' shed blood; your life belongs to Him. Self-denial means that you daily live by the motto: Not my will be done, but Your will! You exist to serve Him, not yourself.

Jesus then uses a second past tense verb (aorist) and gives the imperative, "and take up his cross." Our Lord is crucified for us; we now are positionally co-crucified with Him (Galatians 2:20). We are to die to self and imitate Jesus to do the Father's will. The third command is given with a present tense verb. When Jesus says, "follow Me," the idea is to continually be His disciple.

Employment Point: *Deny self, take up your cross, and continually follow Jesus.*

———◦◉◦———

MARCH 2

NUMBERS 28–29, WITH MARK 9:1–29

He also predestined to be conformed to the image of His Son (Romans 8:29).

ARE YOU DAILY BECOMING MORE LIKE JESUS?

Moses makes an interesting request of God in Exodus 33:18, "Please, show me Your glory." The gracious Father gives Moses a partial look at His glory. In Mark 9, Jesus takes three of His followers, Peter, James, and John, and displays His glory to them. Excitingly, there are two Old Testament guests invited to this exclusive showing: Moses and Elijah. Mark describes the transfiguration as follows: "His clothes becoming shining, exceedingly white, like snow, such as no launderer on earth can whiten them" (Mark 9:3). Jesus, the Son of Man, reveals that He is also the Son of God.

We are now to display Jesus' glory. Paul describes the process of progressive sanctification, "But we all, with unveiled face, beholding as in a mirror the glory of the Lord, are being transformed into the same image from glory to glory, just as by the Spirit of the Lord" (2 Corinthians 3:18).

EMPLOYMENT POINT: *Daily walk with Jesus to display His glory.*

MARCH 3

NUMBERS 30–31, WITH MARK 9:30–50

⎯⎯⎯◦◦◦⎯⎯⎯

The last will be first, and the first last (Matthew 20:16).

DO YOU DESIRE TO BE GREAT FOR GOD?

Those desiring to be great for God should apply the following. First, *future greatness comes from present service* (Mark 9:33–35). As the disciples debate which of them will be the greatest in the kingdom, Jesus says, "If anyone desires to be first, he shall be last of all and servant of all" (Mark 9:35). Jesus then gives a living object lesson to His apprentices; He places a child before them. With that said, here is the second application: *Serve those least esteemed by society to please God* (Mark 9:36–37). Children had no social status in Jesus' day; therefore, to ascend to greatness, you need to first embrace a lowly mindset.

The third application, from Mark 9:38–41, follows: *Service to Jesus brings future rewards.* Even a cup of cold water in Jesus' name brings a lasting reward (Mark 9:41). Jesus will return and reward His faithful servants. Let's live for the benefit package that is out of this world!

EMPLOYMENT POINT: *Employ the above three points for future greatness.*

⎯⎯⎯◦◦◦⎯⎯⎯

MARCH 4

NUMBERS 32–33, WITH MARK 10:1–31

———

Train up a child in the way he should go, and when he is old he will not depart from it (Proverbs 22:6).

WHY INVEST IN CHILDREN'S SPIRITUAL NEEDS?

Apparently the disciples of Jesus didn't highly value children. "Then they [parents] brought little children to Him, that He might touch them; but the disciples rebuked those who brought them" (Mark 10:13). But what did the Maker of the children think? "But when Jesus saw it, He was greatly displeased and said to them, 'Let the little children come to Me, and do not forbid them; for of such is the kingdom of God'" (Mark 10:14).

Not only does Jesus receive children into His kingdom, yet unless adults become like little children by humbling themselves, they cannot enter His kingdom. Jesus adds, "Assuredly, I say to you, whoever does not receive the kingdom of God as a little child will by no means enter it" (Mark 10:15). As little children are dependent upon adults for all their needs, sinners need to rely solely upon Jesus for salvation.

EMPLOYMENT POINT: *Serve the little children, while imitating their humility.*

———

MARCH 5

NUMBERS 34–36, WITH MARK 10:32–52

———◦———

For I have given you an example, that you should do as I have done to you (John 13:15).

WHAT HAPPENS WHEN YOU IGNORE THE CROSS?

Three lessons are to be gleaned from the disciples ignoring the cross (Mark 10:35–45). One, *ignoring the cross leads to selfish ambition* (Mark 10:35–37). James and John heard Jesus vividly describe His betrayal, suffering, scourging, and death, and still ask to sit on His right and left hand in the kingdom. Two, *ignoring the cross leads to spiritual ignorance* (Mark 10:38–41). The Sons of Thunder (James and John) do not comprehend that Jesus is referring to suffering and death by the object lessons of "the cup" and "baptism." We miss the basic teachings of Jesus when we shy away from the cross.

Our third point is as follows: *Sacrificially serve Jesus for future greatness* (Mark 10:42–45). Our Lord shares, "whoever desires to become great among you shall be your servant" (Mark 10:43). Greatness begins with a descent to serving one another for the glory of God.

EMPLOYMENT POINT: *Employ the above lessons to be great for Jesus.*

———◦———

MARCH 6

DEUTERONOMY 1–2, WITH MARK 11:1–19

For we walk by faith, not by sight (2 Corinthians 5:7).

ARE YOU A RARE PERSON OF FAITH?

Only two adult males (Joshua and Caleb) who are delivered from Egypt receive the privilege to enter the Promised Land. Moses writes about Caleb, "he shall see it, and to him and his children I am giving the land on which he walked, because he wholly followed the LORD" (Deuteronomy 1:36). Two out of more than 603,550 men (see Numbers 1:46–47, which excludes the Levites) shows how few adults exhibited faith in God after seeing the ten plagues on Egypt and the Red Sea parting.

Moreover, although Jesus seems broadly supported during the Triumphal Entry (Mark 11:1–11), it was superficial. This is expressed by the object lesson of the cursing of the fig tree by Jesus immediately after the Triumphal Entry (Mark 11:12–14). The tree has an appearance of fruit but is barren, just like the nation. As John records, "He came to His own, and His own did not receive Him" (John 1:11).

EMPLOYMENT POINT: *Believe God's Word and obey it to please Him.*

MARCH 7

DEUTERONOMY 3–4, WITH MARK 11:20–33

There we saw the giants . . . and we were like grasshoppers in our own sight (Numbers 13:33).

IS YOUR FAITH GREATER THAN THE BIGGEST OBSTACLE YOU FACE?

Og's name makes me think of a big ugly goon. Of course, I wouldn't have said that to Og's face because he's a giant (Deuteronomy 3)! God instructs Moses about the oversized hater of Israel, "Do not fear him, for I have delivered him and all his people and his land into your hand" (Deuteronomy 3:2). Now that's a God-sized promise. Yet the Lord takes down the *big oaf* demonstrating that nothing is impossible with Him.

As Israel looked to the Lord, by faith turn to Jesus. Our Savior's disciples saw Him curse the fig tree (Mark 11:12–14), which withered and died. Jesus then says, "Have faith in God. For assuredly, I say to you, whoever says to this mountain, 'Be removed and be cast into the sea,' and does not doubt in his heart, but believes that those things he says will be done, he will have whatever he says" (Mark 11:22–23).

EMPLOYMENT POINT: *Trust God for the impossible.*

MARCH 8

DEUTERONOMY 5–7, WITH MARK 12:1–27

Let Us make man in Our image (Genesis 1:26).

WHAT RESPONSIBILITY COMES FROM BEING MADE IN GOD'S IMAGE?

Some deny that God exists in three persons: Father, Son, and Holy Spirit. They point to Deuteronomy 6:4, "Hear, O Israel: The LORD our God, the LORD is one!" Yet the Hebrew term "one" refers to a *one of unity* as it is used of Adam and Eve becoming "one flesh" (Genesis 2:24). Moses shows our responsibility to the Trinity in Deuteronomy 6:5, "You shall love the LORD your God with all your heart." After all, we are made in His image. Truly the image is marred because of the Fall (Genesis 1:26; 5:3), but mankind still reflects God's image (James 3:9).

In Mark 12:13–17, the Pharisees and Herodians seek to entrap Jesus. He asks for a denarius, which bears Caesar's image. He famously says, "Render to Caesar the things that are Caesar's, and to God the things that are God's" (Mark 12:17). As taxes are paid to Caesar whose image is on the coin, we are to love God whose image we bear.

EMPLOYMENT POINT: *Give government their due, and to God who created you.*

MARCH 9

DEUTERONOMY 8–10, WITH MARK 12:28–44

And you shall remember that the LORD your God led you all the way these forty years in the wilderness, to humble you and test you, to know what was in your heart, whether you would keep His commandments or not (Deuteronomy 8:2).

WHAT IS THE GREATEST COMMANDMENT?

Jesus answers that question, "And you shall love the LORD your God with all your heart, with all your soul, with all your mind, and with all your strength. This is the first commandment" (Mark 12:30). In essence, we are commanded to love the Lord completely. Our visibly hidden Creator deserves that His children love Him with their entire being. The One who implanted and designed each of us in the womb commands nothing less than complete and wholehearted loyalty to Him.

Yet our God is invisible. What concrete or visible way can we display that we fully love Him? Jesus continues, "And the second, like it, is this: 'You shall love your neighbor as yourself'" (Mark 12:31). The word "like" conveys *equal to*. We display our love for the God unable to be seen by loving our able to be seen neighbor.

EMPLOYMENT POINT: *Demonstrate your love for the invisible God by loving your visible neighbor.*

MARCH 10

DEUTERONOMY 11–13, WITH MARK 13:1–13

Beloved, do not believe every spirit, but test the spirits, whether they are of God; because many false prophets have gone out into the world (1 John 4:1).

DO YOU BIBLICALLY EVALUATE PROCLAIMED MESSAGES?

Deuteronomy 13 gives a warning to the saints for them not to be duped by those who claim to be prophets, dreamers of dreams, and workers of wonders, when in actuality they point people away from the true God. Moses commands, "You shall walk after the Lord your God and fear Him, and keep His commandments and obey His voice; you shall serve Him and hold fast to Him" (Deuteronomy 13:4). The man of God understands the necessity to walk with God and reject idolatry.

Jesus gives a similar warning in Mark 13. He says, "Take heed that no one deceives you. For many will come in My name, saying, 'I am He,' and will deceive many" (Mark 13:5–6). We are to test the spirits by evaluating the content of a message. Satan desires children of God to wander from the truth of the Bible and veer off course to the path of destruction.

EMPLOYMENT POINT: *Discern the truth from the lie by evaluating every message by the Bible.*

MARCH 11

DEUTERONOMY 14–16, WITH MARK 13:14–37

But you are a chosen generation, a royal priesthood, a holy nation, His own special people (1 Peter 2:9).

ARE YOU DEDICATED TO GOD AND SEPARATED FROM WORLDLINESS?

Israel is not to mingle with the heathen nations around them lest they adopt their immoral practices. God's prescribed diet for the nation helps to accomplish this end (Deuteronomy 14:1–21). Moses explains, "For you are a holy people to the LORD your God, and the LORD has chosen you to be a people for Himself, a special treasure above all the peoples who are on the face of the earth" (Deuteronomy 14:2). The Lord God is holy and calls His children to imitate their spiritual Father.

In Mark 13, Jesus predicts the activities of the Antichrist. Once he sets up the abomination of desolation, which is an idol that comes to life (Revelation 13:11–18), Jesus warns, "then let those who are in Judea flee to the mountains" (Mark 13:14). The Lord desires His children to withdraw from wickedness because we are His chosen people. He calls us to flee from ungodliness and run to Him!

EMPLOYMENT POINT: *Separate from ungodliness as God's precious possession.*

MARCH 12

DEUTERONOMY 17–19, WITH MARK 14:1–25

You shall not sacrifice to the LORD your God a bull or sheep which has any blemish or defect, for that is an abomination to the LORD your God (Deuteronomy 17:1).

ARE YOU OFFERING GOD YOUR BEST?

Mark 14:1–11 gives us a contrast between two sacrifices; one is self-serving while the other is God-serving. Point one is as follows: *Religious hypocrites slither to silence the righteous* (Mark 14:1–2). "The chief priest and the scribes," writes Mark, "sought how they might take Him [Jesus] by trickery and put Him to death" (Mark 14:1). Those who should have received Jesus with open arms seek His demise!

Mark strategically inserts another contrasting story. *Render sacrifices to Jesus worthy of remembrance* imparts the second point (Mark 14:3–9). Mary's sacrifice costs three hundred days' pay for the average day laborer (John 12:5). What a sacrifice! Our third point returns to the former account: *Religious hypocrites sell out the righteous* (Mark 14:10–11). Mary's sacrifice shows her adoration for Jesus, whereas Judas' words reveal a selfish heart. We should choose to regularly display our affection for Jesus.

EMPLOYMENT POINT: *Render sacrifices to Jesus worthy of remembrance.*

MARCH 13

DEUTERONOMY 20–22, WITH MARK 14:26–50

There is no fear in love; but perfect love casts out fear, because fear involves torment (1 John 4:18).

ARE YOU A FEARFUL PERSON?

Fear can be paralyzing. Moses writes concerning the principles of warfare, "The officers shall speak further to the people, and say, 'What man is there who is fearful and fainthearted? Let him go and return to his house, lest the heart of his brethren faint like his heart'" (Deuteronomy 20:8). Fear is contagious and spreads rapidly; it must be contained, or else it can impact an entire army.

Moreover, an independent spirit can produce fear. Jesus predicts Peter's three denials. Arrogantly, the apostle responds, "If I have to die with You, I will not deny you!" (Mark 14:31). Heartbreakingly, while Jesus prays in Gethsemane, Peter sleeps. No wonder Jesus would say, "Watch and pray, lest you enter into temptation" (Mark 14:38). If Peter had been prayerful, which would have demonstrated a dependence upon God, then his level of courage would have been elevated. Let's expel fear through prayer!

EMPLOYMENT POINT: *Prayerfully depend upon Jesus to keep you courageous for Him.*

MARCH 14

DEUTERONOMY 23–25, WITH MARK 14:51–72

Ascribe greatness to our God. He is the Rock, His work is perfect; for all His ways are justice (Deuteronomy 32:3–4).

HAVE YOU PERSONALLY EXPERIENCED GOD'S RIGHTEOUSNESS?

The Old Testament Law reveals God's just nature. Moses pens, "If there is a dispute between men, and they come to court, that the judges may judge them, and they justify the righteous and condemn the wicked" (Deuteronomy 25:1). Human judges were to be chosen that would represent the character of God, and render decisions that the Almighty Judge would give His judicial nod of approval.

Yet Mark records about the religious leaders, "Now the chief priests and all the council sought testimony against Jesus to put Him to death, but found none" (Mark 14:55). Likewise, Pilate declares thrice that he finds no fault in Jesus (John 18:38; 19:4, 6). This is why John says of Jesus, "Behold! The Lamb of God who takes away the sin of the world" (John 1:29). Also, Paul testifies, "For He [God] made Him [Jesus] who knew no sin to be sin for us, that we might become the righteousness of God in Him" (2 Corinthians 5:21).

EMPLOYMENT POINT: *Receive God's righteousness through Jesus' perfect sacrifice.*

MARCH 15

DEUTERONOMY 26–27, WITH
MARK 15:1–26

And if children, then heirs—heirs of God and joint heirs with Christ (Romans 8:17).

WHAT DID JESUS DO TO MAKE US HIS PRIZED POSSESSION?

Moses is preparing the Israelites to enter Canaan. He writes, "Also today the LORD has proclaimed you to be His special people" (Deuteronomy 26:18). God set His exceptional love upon Israel and elevated their status among the nations. They were called to be the Father's cherished treasure, and to represent Him to the nations. His light is to be reflected through their lives.

Today church age saints have an exalted status (Ephesians 1:3; 2:6). We enjoy these blessings because of the following reason: *Jesus died among sinners to save sinners* (Mark 15:24–32). Our Savior identified with sinful humanity; He was crucified between two sinners while Roman soldiers were at His feet gambling for His clothing. Mark reports, "And when they crucified Him, they divided His garments, casting lots for them to determine what every man should take. Now it was the third hour [9 am], and they crucified Him" (Mark 15:24–25).

EMPLOYMENT POINT: *Relish your prized standing before God, remembering what it cost.*

MARCH 16

DEUTERONOMY 28, WITH MARK 15:27–47

Then the veil of the temple was torn in two from top to bottom (Mark 15:38).

DO YOU DAILY ENTER GOD'S PRESENCE?

Only one designated man enters the Holy of Holies annually. Jesus' death changes this forever. Mark writes, "And Jesus cried out with a loud voice, and breathed His last. Then the veil of the temple was torn in two from top to bottom" (Mark 15:37–38). That which separates the Holy of Holies from all men and women—but one Jewish priest annually—is rent from top to bottom signifying that all people are invited through Jesus' death.

We are encouraged to draw near to God "by a new and living way which He consecrated for us, through the veil, that is, His flesh" (Hebrews 10:20). Paul assures us concerning salvation, "There is neither Jew nor Greek, there is neither slave nor free, there is nether male nor female; for you are all one in Christ Jesus" (Galatians 3:28). The new covenant has provided all people equal access to the Father through the Son.

EMPLOYMENT POINT: *Enter God's holy presence through Jesus' sacrifice.*

MARCH 17

DEUTERONOMY 29–30, WITH MARK 16

———◆———

That I may know Him and the power of His resurrection (Philippians 3:10).

DO YOU KNOW GOD INTIMATELY AND PROCLAIM THE GOSPEL REGULARLY?

God has unveiled Himself to us through the Bible that we might know Him personally and obey Him completely. Moses writes, "The secret things belong to the LORD our God, but those things which are revealed belong to us and to our children forever, that we may do all the words of the law" (Deuteronomy 29:29). The term "revelation" literally means *to unveil*. Our Father uncovers for us His nature and ways through the Scriptures. Study them thoroughly; enjoy the sacred privilege to know Him and make Him known.

Moreover, Jesus' loyal ladies go early Sunday morning to anoint His body for burial (Mark 16:1). Shortly thereafter they discover He's raised from the dead. Jesus later commands His disciples, "Go into all the world and preach the gospel to every creature" (Mark 16:15). God was manifested in the flesh to redeem us to the Father. We have now been commissioned to know Him intimately and to herald the gospel.

EMPLOYMENT POINT: *Know Him through the revealed Word, and proclaim Him broadly.*

———◆———

MARCH 18

DEUTERONOMY 31–32, WITH
LUKE 1:1–23

One generation shall praise Your works to another, and shall declare Your mighty acts (Psalm 145:4).

ARE YOU PASSING ON YOUR FAITH TO THE NEXT GENERATION?

Christianity is one generation away from extinction. Moses, who was about to die, writes, "Gather the people together, men and women and little ones, and the stranger who is within your gates, that they may hear and that they may learn to fear the Lord your God" (Deuteronomy 31:12). He desires to pass the baton of faith to those who are about to enter Canaan; they are entrusted with this sacred mission.

Spring forward about 1,500 years, to when a godly couple learns that they will be the parents to John the Baptist. Zacharias and Elizabeth are described as follows: "And they were both righteous before God, walking in all the commandments and ordinances of the Lord blameless" (Luke 1:6). This godly couple reared a Spirit-filled son who "will turn many of the children of Israel to the Lord their God" (Luke 1:16). Imagine what God can do through Spirit-filled Christians to reach and train future generations.

EMPLOYMENT POINT: *Instruct and model godliness for the next generation.*

MARCH 19

DEUTERONOMY 33–34, WITH LUKE 1:24–56

But since then there has not arisen in Israel a prophet like Moses (Deuteronomy 34:10).

WHERE DOES THE LIFE OF MOSES DIRECT US?

Moses dies and God buries him. He is the only person recorded in the Scripture that God buries. The prophet Moses would point people to a future Prophet. He writes, "The LORD your God will raise up for you a Prophet like me from your midst" (Deuteronomy 18:15). Peter connects Moses' prediction to Jesus (Acts 3:22–26).

Jesus is more than a prophet. Marvel at the angel's words to Mary: "Do not be afraid, Mary, for you have found favor with God. And behold, you will conceive in your womb and bring forth a Son, and shall call His name Jesus. He will be great, and will be called the Son of the Highest; and the Lord God will give Him the throne of His father David. And He will reign over the house of Jacob forever, and of His kingdom there will be no end" (Luke 1:30–33). Jesus will fulfill the prediction given to David (2 Samuel 7:12–16) and will have an eternal house, throne, and kingdom.

EMPLOYMENT POINT: *Worship Jesus who is Prophet, Priest, and King!*

MARCH 20

JOSHUA 1–3, WITH
LUKE 1:57–80

Be strong in the LORD and in the power of His might (Ephesians 6:10).

FROM WHENCE COMES YOUR STRENGTH?

God repeatedly commands Joshua to "be strong" (Joshua 1:6, 7, 9, 18). Where would he derive the strength for the daunting task ahead? Joshua 1:8 gives us the answer: "This Book of the Law shall not depart from your mouth, but you shall meditate in it day and night, that you may observe to do according to all that is written in it. For then you will make your way prosperous, and then you will have good success." Moreover, thankfully Joshua experienced great training at Moses' feet. Wisely he learned the importance and benefits of obeying the Lord.

Also, Elizabeth and Zacharias have a son who needs strength; he is none other than John the Baptist. As his parents walk with God, so John would follow in their godly path. Luke summarizes John's physical and spiritual progress, "So the child grew and became strong in spirit" (Luke 1:80). He walked wisdom's path!

EMPLOYMENT POINT: *Stay strong by feeding on God's Word and walking by faith.*

MARCH 21

JOSHUA 4–6, WITH
LUKE 2:1–24

———◦———

As Commander of the army of the LORD I have now come (Joshua 5:14).

ARE YOU FOLLOWING THE LEADER?

All of God's great leaders are great followers. Joshua is perhaps contemplating the impossible task of conquering Jericho. "And it came to pass, when Joshua was by Jericho, that he lifted his eyes and looked, and behold, a Man stood opposite him with His sword drawn in His hand. And Joshua went to Him and said to Him, 'Are You for us or for our adversaries?'" (Joshua 5:13). (I believe the Commander is the preincarnate Jesus.) The unexpected visitor says, "No, but as Commander of the army of the LORD I have now come" (Joshua 5:14). The human leader of God's people wisely yields to His Commander and is told that he stands upon holy ground.

Likewise, the Lord guides shepherds 1,400 years later to Bethlehem where they also will stand upon holy ground (Luke 2:8–16). Following the guidance of the Leader will take you into His holy presence; the journey is worth the effort.

EMPLOYMENT POINT: *Bow before your Commander, and yield always to His direction.*

———◦———

March 22

Joshua 7–8, with Luke 2:25–52

And the men of Ai struck down about thirty-six men (Joshua 7:5).

Are you daily getting your marching orders from God?

After Jericho is defeated Joshua assesses Ai and believes it can easily be conquered. Sadly, thirty-six lives are lost. Wisdom demands that we consult God in every situation and not live by past performance. This unlearned lesson becomes even more glaring in light of Joshua 9 and the Gibeonites. Logic does not compare to the mind and wisdom of the Lord; therefore, pray for wisdom in all matters.

Furthermore, the Hebrew name "Joshua" is translated by the Greek term "Jesus." Both names convey salvation by God. As Jesus develops in His manhood, we find Him asking questions and interacting with the rabbis (Luke 2). Imagine being His poor parents who lost the Son of God! (This isn't one of their finer moments!) After tracking Him down and questioning Jesus' activity, He says, "Why did you seek Me? Did you not know that I must be about My Father's business?" (Luke 2:49).

Employment Point: *Wisely consult the Father daily, to care skillfully for His business.*

MARCH 23

JOSHUA 9–10, WITH
LUKE 3

———※———

They did not ask counsel of the LORD (Joshua 9:14).

DO YOU SEEK GOD'S COUNSEL IN ALL MATTERS?

The Gibeonites don't want to be decimated like the other inhabitants of Canaan. "But when the inhabitants of Gibeon heard what Joshua had done to Jericho and Ai, they worked craftily, and went and pretended to be ambassadors" (Joshua 9:3–4). Instead of the Israelites consulting God about the situation, they acted hastily. This agreement would cost Israel dearly, because other nations came and attacked Gibeon and Israel was obligated to protect them (Joshua 10:4–6).

Yet God uses these things to defeat the Canaanites who assemble against the Israelites and Gibeonites. Daylight was quickly waning and God honors Joshua's request. He said, "Sun, stand still over Gibeon; and Moon, in the Valley of Aijalon" (Joshua 10:12). "So the sun stood still," records Joshua, "and the moon stopped, till the people had revenge upon their enemies" (Joshua 10:13). God extends mercy to His people despite their lack of wisdom to consult Him in all affairs.

EMPLOYMENT POINT: *Consult God always before making rash decisions.*

———※———

MARCH 24

JOSHUA 11–13, WITH
LUKE 4:1–32

———◆———

Then Jesus, being filled with the Holy Spirit, returned from the Jordan (Luke 4:1).

WHAT'S YOUR POWER SOURCE?

Luke 4 testifies to the importance of Spirit-filled living. Jesus identifies with mankind by being baptized by John the Baptist. "Then Jesus, being filled with the Holy Spirit, returned from the Jordan and was led by the Spirit into the wilderness" (Luke 4:1). Jesus yields to both the Spirit and Word of God and experiences victory over Satan. The confluence (two things coming together) of the Spirit and Word are given in Luke 4:4. "But Jesus answered him [Satan], saying, 'It is written, *Man shall not live by bread alone, but by every word of God.*'"

Before Jesus teaches, Luke 4:14 informs us, "Then Jesus returned in the power of the Spirit to Galilee." Once again the empowering Spirit is evident. Jesus quotes from Isaiah 61 in Luke 4:18, showing the twin virtues of the Word and Spirit. Our Lord displays two things that every child of God needs for empowerment: a dependence upon the eternal Word of God and the eternal Spirit!

EMPLOYMENT POINT: *Be controlled by God's Spirit, and the Word for victorious living.*

———◆———

MARCH 25

JOSHUA 14–15, WITH LUKE 4:33–44

———

I am as strong this day as on the day that Moses sent me (Joshua 14:11).

WHERE DO YOU DERIVE YOUR POWER AND PURPOSE?

Caleb, at age eighty-five, speaks to Joshua about conquering a particular mountain (Joshua 14:12). Our aged strong man derives robustness from the Lord. Decades earlier Moses promises Caleb an inheritance "because you have wholly followed the LORD my God" (Joshua 14:9). Caleb and Joshua outlive their peer group because of their obedience and faith in God's Word. "And Joshua blessed him, and gave Hebron to Caleb the son of Jephunneh as an inheritance . . . because he wholly followed the LORD God of Israel" (Joshua 14:13–14).

Jesus also completely follows the Lord. His Father guided Him to the extent that when people pressed Jesus to stay in a certain town, "He said to them, 'I must preach the kingdom of God to the other cities also, because for this purpose I have been sent'" (Luke 4:43). Our Lord had regular conference calls with the Father, which clearly kept Him understanding His heart and direction.

EMPLOYMENT POINT: *Wholly follow the Lord to receive strength and guidance.*

———

MARCH 26

JOSHUA 16–18, WITH
LUKE 5:1–16

Follow Me, and I will make you fishers of men (Matthew 4:19).

ARE YOU SUCCESSFULLY CATCHING SOULS?

Jesus' presence forever changes life. He stands by the Sea of Galilee when the multitude crowd Him to hear God's Word (Luke 5:1). Since two boats are close at hand, He gets into one of them and begins to teach. Luke continues, "When He had stopped speaking, He said to Simon, 'Launch out into the deep and let down your nets for a catch'" (Luke 5:4). Peter hesitates because they fished all night and caught nothing, but says, "nevertheless at Your word I will let down the net" (Luke 5:5). "And when they had done this, they caught a great number of fish" (Luke 5:6). Jesus then reassures him, "Do not be afraid. From now on you will catch men" (Luke 5:10).

"From now on" is a favorite expression of Luke (Luke 1:48; 12:52; 22:69; Acts 18:6) showing that God's intervention changes things permanently. This is true of Mary (Luke 1:48, translated "henceforth"), Peter (Luke 5:10), and Paul (Acts 18:6). The Lord's intervention into our lives has also forever changed us!

EMPLOYMENT POINT: *Follow Jesus for life-changing ministry.*

MARCH 27

JOSHUA 19–20, WITH LUKE 5:17–39

So he left all, rose up, and followed Him (Luke 5:28).

DO YOU BELIEVE THAT JESUS CAN SAVE THE WEALTHY?

After the rich young ruler walks away from Jesus, He says, "For it is easier for a camel to go through the eye of a needle than for a rich man to enter the kingdom of God" (Luke 18:25). Yet when Jesus comes upon the affluent Levi (Matthew), the tax collector, "He said to him, 'Follow Me.' So he left all, rose up, and followed Him" (Luke 5:27–28). The Greek term for "all," in "left all" (Luke 5:28) means *the whole* or *universally*. Matthew forsakes everything to follow Jesus, which shows that he passes "through the eye of a needle." All things are truly possible with God!

Moreover, "Then Levi gave Him a great feast in his own house. And there were a great number of tax collectors and others who sat down with them" (Luke 5:29). Matthew universally leaves all to follow Jesus and sacrifices to reach others. This recent convert demonstrates his new nature by generously feeding others after he lost his livelihood in order for them to meet the King.

EMPLOYMENT POINT: *Trust Jesus to reach the rich.*

MARCH 28

JOSHUA 21–22, WITH
LUKE 6:1–26

Be anxious for nothing, but in everything by prayer (Philippians 4:6).

DO YOU HAVE EXTENDED TIMES IN PRAYER BEFORE A MAJOR DECISION?

There is only one instance in the New Testament where there is an all-night prayer meeting. It is recorded in Luke 6:12: "Now it came to pass in those days that He [Jesus] went out to the mountain to pray, and continued all night in prayer to God." Jesus then calls twelve disciples to Himself, whom He names apostles.

The greater the decision, the more time you should take to pray. Our Lord needs to choose His successors who would subsequently reach the world with the gospel. Such an important decision should never be hastily made.

Furthermore, the parallel passage in Mark states, "And He went up on the mountain and called to Him those He Himself wanted. And they came to Him. Then He appointed twelve, that they might be with Him and that He might send them out to preach" (Mark 3:13–14). Jesus depended upon the Father's guidance so that these individuals would be the right men to fulfill the Great Commission.

EMPLOYMENT POINT: *Set aside enough time to pray on important matters.*

MARCH 29

JOSHUA 23–24, WITH
LUKE 6:27–49

But as for me and my house, we will serve the LORD (Joshua 24:15).

HAVE YOU CHOSEN TO SERVE THE LORD?

Joshua understands his responsibility to guide the nation Israel, but also his own family. He points to the crossroads and says to the Israelites, "Choose for yourselves this day whom you will serve, whether the gods which your fathers served that were on the other side of the River, or the gods of the Amorites, in whose land you dwell. But as for me and my house, we will serve the LORD" (Joshua 24:15). The home presents the most natural surrounding to make disciples.

Disciple-makers realize that those they train will resemble the trainer. Jesus says, "A disciple is not above his teacher, but everyone who is perfectly trained will be like his teacher" (Luke 6:40). Moreover, great leaders correct flaws that they don't want to pass down to the next generation. First they remove the planks in their own eyes, and then they instruct others (Luke 6:41). Let's desire to be like the Master Disciple-Maker and commence the training at home.

EMPLOYMENT POINT: *Disciple your family and others with personal integrity.*

MARCH 30

JUDGES 1–2, WITH
LUKE 7:1–30

———◆———

Therefore I urge you, imitate me (1 Corinthians 4:16).

WHAT ARE YOU IMPARTING TO THE NEXT GENERATION?

Joshua's life positively impacts the next generation. "So the people served the LORD all the days of Joshua, and all the days of the elders who outlived Joshua" (Judges 2:7). Sadly, subsequent generations didn't do as well. The theme of Judges is that "everyone did what was right in his own eyes" (Judges 21:25). In essence, they followed their own hearts!

John the Baptist also left an imprint on the following generation; he humbly prepared the people to receive Jesus. Our Lord highly praises him. "For I say to you, among those born of women there is not a greater prophet than John the Baptist. . . . And when all the people heard him, even the tax collectors justified God, having been baptized with the baptism of John" (Luke 7:28–29). Spurgeon said the righteous carves his name upon the rock, but the wicked writes his remembrance in the sand. Which will be your legacy?

EMPLOYMENT POINT: *Leave a godly legacy for the next generation.*

———◆———

MARCH 31

JUDGES 3–5, WITH
LUKE 7:31–50

But a woman who fears the LORD, she shall be praised (Proverbs 31:30).

ARE YOU HUMBLY SERVING THE LORD?

Deborah willingly offers her service for the Lord. God uses her to deliver the nation from the hands of Sisera, a king in Canaan, who severely oppressed the Israelites. She musters Barak to lead an army and the Lord produces a miraculous victory by using a torrential downpour for their advantage (Judges 5:19–23). Her encouragement leads to Barak being named in the "Hall of Faith" in Hebrews 11:32.

Today's second lady in our devotion is nameless, but she humbles herself at the Savior's feet. Luke uses three imperfect tense verbs (wiped, kissed, and anointed) showing continuous action in past time describing her actions. He writes about the woman's sacrificial act with the costly oil, "and wiped them with the hair of her head; and she kissed His feet and anointed them with the fragrant oil" (Luke 7:38). The woman's hair, which the Bible calls her glory (1 Corinthians 11:15), is used to show her gratitude.

EMPLOYMENT POINT: *Humble yourself to boldly serve the Lord.*

APRIL 1

JUDGES 6–7, WITH LUKE 8:1–21

———◦———

For God has not given us a spirit of fear, but of power and of love and of a sound mind (2 Timothy 1:7).

ARE YOU BOLDLY SERVING THE LORD?

God calls timid Gideon to deliver His people from the Midianites. The reluctant hero is hiding in a cave threshing wheat. "And the Angel of the LORD appeared to him, and said to him, 'The LORD is with you, you mighty man of valor!'" (Judges 6:12). With God's help Gideon becomes courageous. All glory belongs to God; therefore, He scales back a huge army of men and reduces their number to three hundred. Almighty God structures the army so that only He could be credited with a victory over the enemy of Israel. He is the children of Israel's greatest asset.

Gideon creatively devises an unusual plan to defeat Midian. He distributes "a trumpet into every man's hand, with empty pitchers, and torches inside the pitchers" (Judges 7:16). God honors Gideon's faith. "For the time would fail me to tell of Gideon . . . who through faith subdued kingdoms . . . out of weakness were made strong, became valiant in battle" (Hebrews 11:32–34).

EMPLOYMENT POINT: *Trust God to give you inner strength.*

———◦———

APRIL 2

JUDGES 8–9, WITH LUKE 8:22–56

———◦———

Let us cross over to the other side of the lake (Luke 8:22).

DO YOU TRUST JESUS' PROMISES?

Jesus' words are true and should be honored. Our Lord has an appointment on the other side of the lake; He is going to endure stormy seas to free a captive. Luke writes, "But as they sailed He fell asleep. And a windstorm came down on the lake, and they were filling with water, and were in jeopardy" (Luke 8:23). The disciples panic and awake their sleeping Lord. He calms the storm and then asks, "Where is your faith?" (Luke 8:25). He has a divine appointment to set free a man who is held captive by demons (Luke 8:26–40).

Please remember that even in the storms of life that Jesus is with you and there are exciting opportunities on the other side of the storm. Relax; He is in the boat with you and will honor His promises. The waters might be choppy for a while, but be patient, because the Lord could have a divine appointment on the other side.

EMPLOYMENT POINT: *Rely upon Jesus in turbulent times, while anticipating future opportunities.*

———◦———

APRIL 3

JUDGES 10–11, WITH LUKE 9:1–36

Let every man be swift to hear, slow to speak, slow to wrath (James 1:19).

DO YOU CONSIDER YOUR WORDS BEFORE SPEAKING?

Although Jephthah exhibits great courage for the Lord, he utters a rash vow, which costs his daughter's life (Judges 11:29–40). Hurried speech generally is nonproductive. Solomon concurs, "Do not be rash with your mouth, and let not your heart utter anything hastily before God. For God is in heaven, and you on earth; therefore let your words be few" (Ecclesiastes 5:2). Prayerful and thoughtful utterances should be the norm for children of God; they could be lifesaving!

Peter also should have used discretion before speaking to Jesus at His transfiguration. The quick-to-speak apostle suggests to Jesus, "let us make three tabernacles: one for You, one for Moses, and one for Elijah" (Luke 9:33). He erroneously equates Moses and Elijah with Jesus. No wonder the Father speaks: "This is My beloved Son. Hear Him!" (Luke 9:35). Let's heed James' counsel to "be swift to hear, slow to speak" (James 1:19).

EMPLOYMENT POINT: *Prayerfully and thoughtfully choose your words, to honor God.*

APRIL 4

JUDGES 12–14, WITH LUKE 9:37–62

———◆———

I have made a covenant with my eyes (Job 31:1a).

WHY THEN SHOULD I LOOK UPON A YOUNG WOMAN (JOB 31:1B)?

Samson has a major problem; he lustfully uses his sight. Throughout the account on Samson (Judges 13:1–16:31), he keeps gazing upon the wrong objects. He reaps what he sows with the removal of his eyes (Judges 16:21). Consider Paul's inspired words, "Do not be deceived, God is not mocked; for whatever a man sows, that he will also reap" (Galatians 6:7).

Conversely, Jesus calls His followers to have godly ambitions. He models this in Luke 9:51. "Now it came to pass, when the time had come for Him to be received up, that He steadfastly set His face to go to Jerusalem." Jesus understands His mission and concentrates on the goal. Luke informs us about two men who didn't grasp the wholehearted dedication that Jesus demands of His followers (Luke 9:59–61). To the one man, Jesus says, "No one, having put his hand to the plow, and looking back, is fit for the kingdom of God" (Luke 9:62).

EMPLOYMENT POINT: *Avoid distractions by focusing upon the things of God.*

———◆———

APRIL 5

JUDGES 15–17, WITH
LUKE 10:1–24

———◈———

I press toward the goal for the prize of the upward call of God in Christ Jesus (Philippians 3:14).

HOW IS YOUR SPIRITUAL EYESIGHT?

Samson loses his eyes and then his life, and Israel continues in a downward spiral. Mighty Samson focused upon unsuitable objects; the nation of Israel also has a selfish gaze. Judges 17:6 sums up their spiritual dullness. "In those days there was no king in Israel; everyone did what was right in his own eyes." The strong man and the entire nation fasten their eyes upon ill-suited things for God's people.

Centuries later Jesus dispatches seventy witnesses to Israel. Their sights are set by Jesus to display God's mighty power to them. They express to Jesus upon returning, "Lord, even the demons are subject to us in your name" (Luke 10:17). Jesus, knowing that people generally don't handle power well, tells them, "Nevertheless do not rejoice in this, that the spirits are subject to you, but rather rejoice because your names are written in heaven" (Luke 10:20).

EMPLOYMENT POINT: *Focus upon the joy of your salvation while serving others.*

———◈———

APRIL 6

JUDGES 18–19, WITH LUKE 10:25–42

But one thing is needed, and Mary has chosen that good part (Luke 10:42).

HAVE YOU PUT OUT THE WELCOME MAT FOR JESUS?

Martha, Mary, and Lazarus make a wise decision by entertaining Jesus. Today's first point comes from their example: *Welcome Jesus in your home* (Luke 10:38–39). Permit Jesus to govern your house. Like Martha, we easily get distracted with daily chores. "But Martha was distracted with much serving" (Luke 10:40). Her mind is pulled in many directions and she misses time with Jesus. *Welcome Jesus into your head* gives us point number two (Luke 10:40). Keep Jesus and His Word central in your thinking and don't allow lesser things to distract you.

Finally, *welcome Jesus into your heart* (Luke 10:41–42). Listen to Jesus lovingly refocusing Martha. "Martha, Martha, you are worried and troubled about many things. But one thing is needed, and Mary has chosen that good part, which will not be taken away from her" (Luke 10:41–42). Let's choose to keep God's Word central to our lives as our number-one priority, because it is eternal!

EMPLOYMENT POINT: *Welcome Jesus into your head, home, and heart.*

APRIL 7

JUDGES 20–21, WITH LUKE 11:1–28

You are good, and do good (Psalm 119:68).

DO YOU FAITHFULLY ASK GOD TO MEET YOUR NEEDS?

You might want to underline the often-repeated word "ask" in Luke 11:9–13. Jesus commands, "Ask, and it will be given to you; seek, and you will find; knock, and it will be opened to you" (Luke 11:9). The three verbs "ask," "seek," and "knock" emerge as imperatives (commands) in the present tense, which means keep on asking, keep on seeking, and keep on knocking. James reminds us, "Yet you do not have because you do not ask" (James 4:2).

Jesus uses an *a fortiori* argument (an argument from the lesser to greater) in Luke 11:11–13. He begins with a loving father who is asked by his son for bread, fish, or an egg. The father, because he loves his son, will not give him anything harmful, but what is good. Jesus then says, 'If you then, being evil, know how to give good gifts to your children, how much more will your heavenly Father give the Holy Spirit to those who ask Him!" (Luke 11:13).

EMPLOYMENT POINT: *Ask God daily to meet your needs, because He is good.*

APRIL 8

RUTH 1–4, WITH
LUKE 11:29–54

———◆———

For all the people of my town know that you are a virtuous woman (Ruth 3:11).

DO PEOPLE KNOW YOU FOR BEING MORALLY EXCELLENT?

Ruth is a virtuous woman who exhibits moral excellence during the time of the judges when everyone followed their own corrupted hearts (Judges 21:25; Ruth 1:1). When she comes to the fork in the road, whether to follow her mother-in-law and the God of Israel, or to go back to her motherland and pagan belief system, she chooses God. "But Ruth said: 'Entreat me not to leave you, or to turn back from following after you; for wherever you go, I will go; and wherever you lodge, I will lodge; your people shall be my people, and your God, my God'" (Ruth 1:16).

A virtuous woman is not only precious in God's sight, but also to her husband. Proverbs 31:10 enlightens us, "Who can find a virtuous wife? For her worth is far above rubies." Moreover, "her children rise up and call her blessed; her husband also, and he praises her" (Proverbs 31:28). A virtuous woman should be honored for her strength of character!

EMPLOYMENT POINT: *Bless the virtuous woman in your life.*

———◆———

April 9

1 Samuel 1–3, with Luke 12:1–34

Talk no more so very proudly; let no arrogance come from your mouth, for the LORD is the God of knowledge (1 Samuel 2:3).

ARE YOU GOD-RELIANT OR SELF-RELIANT?

Hannah's childlessness leads her to pour out her soul to God. Eli believes she is drunk because of her fervent prayer. She responds, "No, my lord, I am a woman of sorrowful spirit. I have drunk neither wine nor intoxicating drink, but have poured out my soul before the LORD" (1 Samuel 1:15). God honors Hannah's petition and provides a son who would learn to say, "Speak, for Your servant hears" (1 Samuel 3:10). Observe the nexus between a praying mom and a son who serves God.

Conversely, the rich fool in Luke 12:13–21 didn't consider God's ways. He is preoccupied with materialism and dies not experiencing the joy of an obedient ear to God. The Lord says, "Fool! This night your soul will be required of you; then whose will those things be which you have provided?" (Luke 12:20). He personifies the meaning of the word "fool," because he lived as if there is no God.

EMPLOYMENT POINT: *Hear and heed the Word of God, to live wisely.*

April 10

1 Samuel 4–6, with
Luke 12:35–59

———◆———

And behold, I am coming quickly, and My reward is with Me, to give to every one according to His work (Revelation 22:12).

When does a master serve a slave?

Jesus begins our parable by saying, "Let your waist be girded and your lamps burning" (Luke 12:35). In other words, be ready always to serve your master. Then Jesus pronounces a blessing upon His vigilant servants. "Blessed are those servants whom the master, when he comes, will find watching. Assuredly, I say to you that he will gird himself and have them sit down to eat, and will come and serve them" (Luke 12:37). Can you imagine how amazing it will be to have the Son of Man serve you when He returns?

We don't know when Jesus will return, so the admonition to be watchful is emphasized. As we await the Rapture, which is the imminent return of Christ, let us not grow weary in our service for the Master. His reward to serve us when He comes back should inspire us greatly; let's stay focused upon the prize!

EMPLOYMENT POINT: *Faithfully serve the Master, and He will serve you upon returning.*

———◆———

April 11

1 Samuel 7–9, with Luke 13:1–21

O God, lift up Your hand! (Psalm 10:12).

Whose hand are you depending upon?

The word "hand" or "hands" occurs often in 1 Samuel 7 (1 Samuel 7:3, 8, 13, 14). Samuel says to the Israelites, "If you return to the LORD with all your hearts, then put away the foreign gods and the Ashtoreths from among you, and prepare your hearts for the LORD, and serve Him only; and He will deliver you from the hand of the Philistines" (1 Samuel 7:3). Later Samuel is asked, "Do not cease to cry out to the LORD our God for us, that He may save us from the hand of the Philistines" (1 Samuel 7:8). God honors their request, "And the hand of the LORD was against the Philistines" (1 Samuel 7:13).

In Luke 13, Jesus comes upon a needy woman. Luke records, "And He laid His hands on her, and immediately she was made straight, and glorified God" (Luke 13:13). Jesus, who is God in flesh, touches this woman and physically made her straight. Similarly, submitting to His mighty hand will impact us spiritually.

Employment Point: *Depend continually upon God's powerful hand.*

APRIL 12

1 SAMUEL 10–12, WITH LUKE 13:22–35

And He gave them their request, but sent leanness into their soul (Psalm 106:15).

ARE YOU WALKING THE NARROW PATH?

Height equals sight for the children of Israel. They want a visible king (1 Samuel 8:20), instead of trusting the invisible God. As some great kings were tall, so was Saul. "He was taller than any of the people from his shoulders upward" (1 Samuel 10:23). Interestingly, Samuel says, "Do you see him whom the Lord has chosen, that there is no one like him among all the people?" (1 Samuel 10:24). Israel got their request, but also experienced "leanness [skimpiness] into their soul" (Psalm 106:15). We should imitate the apostle Paul who writes, "For we walk by faith, not by sight" (2 Corinthians 5:7).

We get into trouble when we desire to be like the world. Jesus' disciples ask Him, "Lord, are there few who are saved?" (Luke 13:23). He responds, "Strive to enter through the narrow gate, for many, I say to you, will seek to enter and will not be able" (Luke 13:24).

EMPLOYMENT POINT: *Walk the narrow path through faith in the invisible God.*

APRIL 13

1 SAMUEL 13–14, WITH LUKE 14:1–24

The LORD has sought for Himself a man after His own heart (1 Samuel 13:14).

HOW DOES DAVID MIRROR GOD'S HEART?

Saul takes on a role that he is not qualified to perform; it is the role of a priest (1 Samuel 13:5–23). Samuel informs the disobedient king, "You have done foolishly. You have not kept the commandment of the LORD your God. . . . But now your kingdom shall not continue. The LORD has sought for Himself a man after His own heart" (1 Samuel 13:13–14). Rejecting God's Word spoken through the man of God moves the Lord to replace Saul with David.

Paul gives us insight to David being a man after God's own heart. "And when He had removed him [Saul], He raised up for them David as King, to whom also He gave testimony and said, 'I have found David the son of Jesse, a man after My own heart, who will do all My will'" (Acts 13:22). David reflects a heart for God by seeking to fully obey Him; we should seek to have the same heart!

EMPLOYMENT POINT: *Obey all of God's will, to mirror His heart.*

APRIL 14

1 SAMUEL 15–16, WITH LUKE 14:25–35

Behold, to obey is better than sacrifice (1 Samuel 15:22).

ARE YOU DOING THE RIGHT MATH?

Saul does the human math, which is selfish, and doesn't complete God's will. He is commanded, "Now go and attack Amalek, and utterly destroy all that they have" (1 Samuel 15:3). He partially complies because his math doesn't match God's. Samuel then asks Saul a revealing question. "Has the LORD as great delight in burnt offerings and sacrifices, as in obeying the voice of the LORD?" (1 Samuel 15:22). The self-centered king didn't grasp, "For My thoughts are not your thoughts" (Isaiah 55:8), proclaims the Lord.

More than one thousand years later, Jesus asks, "For which of you, intending to build a tower, does not sit down first and count the cost, whether he has enough to finish it?" (Luke 14:28). He encourages us to do the math with heaven's calculator. We are to count the cost and place Jesus first in our lives by doing the heavenly calculation—since God created us, Jesus died for us, and He promises us heaven.

EMPLOYMENT POINT: *Do the math with heavenly computations.*

APRIL 15

1 SAMUEL 17–18, WITH LUKE 15:1–10

For with God nothing will be impossible (Luke 1:37).

ARE YOU TRUSTING GOD TO ACCOMPLISH GREAT THINGS?

There is perhaps more detail about Goliath's physical stature than any other biblical character. At nine feet and nine inches tall, he is Israel's biggest visible nightmare. Our first point is as follows: *The enemy is enormous and intimidating* (1 Samuel 17:1–11). Israel wants a visible king to lead them; therefore, God gives them their request but humbles them by a greater physical king than their own. *Engage the enemy with the eyes of faith* imparts our second point (1 Samuel 17:12–38). David knows the invisible God intimately and that He is greater than any physical obstacle.

Finally, take heart by the third point. *Overcome the impossible for God's glory* (1 Samuel 17:39–58). This is exactly what David does when he uses the smooth stone to fell the giant and lop off his head. We should take heart, "for with God nothing will be impossible" (Luke 1:37).

EMPLOYMENT POINT: *Overcome the impossible with the eyes of faith, for the glory of God.*

APRIL 16

1 SAMUEL 19–21, WITH LUKE 15:11–32

———◦◦———

Before honor is humility (Proverbs 15:33).

HAVE YOU HUMBLED YOURSELF BEFORE GOD?

David has been anointed king, killed Goliath, and has a ladies' praise team. His victories over the Philistines lead to the following: "The women sang as they danced, and said: 'Saul has slain his thousands, and David his ten thousands'" (1 Samuel 18:7). As Saul contemplates these words, he becomes angry and subsequently jealous of David (1 Samuel 18:8). He then attempts to kill him. Why does God permit this? Proverbs 15:33 enlightens us, "The fear of the LORD is the instruction of wisdom, and before honor is humility."

Our loving Father prepares His children for greatness through humility. Even Jesus, the eternal Son of God, experiences great humiliation before being exalted to God's right hand and given the name above all names (Philippians 2:5–11). The Lord trains His great servants through this process so that they can continually receive His grace and accomplish great things. Let's follow the path of the Son of Man!

EMPLOYMENT POINT: *Submit to God's path to honor through humility.*

———◦◦———

APRIL 17

1 SAMUEL 22–24, WITH LUKE 16:1–18

Fear God. Honor the king (1 Peter 2:17).

DO YOU HONOR YOUR AUTHORITIES?

Saul, who is Israel's first king, seeks to kill God's designated successor: David. As David is on the lam, because the demon-driven king is pursuing him, he gets an opportunity to kill Saul. The sweet psalmist of Israel declines having his men eliminate Saul, speaking these words: "The LORD forbid that I should do this thing to my master, the LORD's anointed, to stretch out my hand against him, seeing he is the anointed of the LORD" (1 Samuel 24:6).

David practices what he preaches; he endures this trial keeping his eyes upon the Lord and waiting patiently upon His timing to remove Saul and establish his kingdom. He writes, "My soul, wait silently for God alone, for my expectation is from Him" (Psalm 62:5). Moreover, David's life can be contrasted with the unjust steward (Luke 16:1–13) because he honors his authorities (God and Saul), unlike the unscrupulous manager. Furthermore, the unjust steward only honors himself!

EMPLOYMENT POINT: *Honor God by respecting His authorities.*

APRIL 18

1 SAMUEL 25–26, WITH LUKE 16:19–31

———◦———

And being in torments in Hades (Luke 16:23).

DO YOU BELIEVE IN THE POWER OF THE GOSPEL?

David spares Saul's life for a second time (1 Samuel 26). The man after God's own heart may have granted him permission to live, but only God can save a soul. Jesus pulls back the covers of heaven and hades briefly. He tells about a rich man, who didn't care about the things of God, which is shown by his neglect of the beggar daily at his gate (Luke 16:20). Subsequently the beggar dies and has heavenly escorts to Abraham's bosom. By way of contrast, note the plural use of "torment" to describe the rich man's suffering. "And being in torments in Hades" is how Jesus depicts the wealthy man's agony (Luke 16:23). The rich man petitions Abraham to send Lazarus to his brothers as a witness. Abraham responds, "If they do not hear Moses and the prophets, neither will they be persuaded though one rise from the dead" (Luke 16:31). God's Word is to be honored above sight!

EMPLOYMENT POINT: *Trust in the gospel's power to reach the unsaved.*

———◦———

APRIL 19

1 SAMUEL 27–29, WITH LUKE 17:1–19

The heart is deceitful above all things, and desperately wicked (Jeremiah 17:9).

DOES SUCCESS IN LIFE COME FROM FOLLOWING YOUR HEART?

David has two opportunities to snuff out Saul's life and seize the promised throne. The king in waiting defers to God's perfect timing. However, afterward as recorded in 1 Samuel 27:1, "David said in his heart, 'now I shall perish someday by the hand of Saul. There is nothing better for me than that I should speedily escape to the land of the Philistines; and Saul will despair of me, to seek me anymore in any part of Israel. So I shall escape out of his hand.'" David discourages himself because he follows his heart instead of God's Word.

The Lord anointed David and told him that he would be Israel's next king (1 Samuel 16). Knowing that the Almighty made this promise should have sustained David even during grievous trials. "He who trusts in his own heart is a fool," writes the wise man, "but whoever walks wisely will be delivered" (Proverbs 28:26).

EMPLOYMENT POINT: *Trust in God's Word and not your heart.*

APRIL 20

1 SAMUEL 30–31, WITH LUKE 17:20–37

Be strong in the Lord and in the power of His might (Ephesians 6:10).

WHERE DO YOU TURN WHEN OVERWHELMED BY LIFE'S CIRCUMSTANCES?

David, a man on the run, is placed in an impossible situation. He and his band of outcasts travel fifty miles from Aphek to Ziklag to find that their wives and children have been taken captive by the Amalekites. The writer captures the emotion of the setting: "Now David was greatly distressed, for the people spoke of stoning him, because the soul of all the people was grieved, every man for his sons and his daughters" (1 Samuel 30:6a). David doesn't remain under the circumstances but "strengthened himself in the LORD his God" (1 Samuel 30:6b).

David learned a valuable lesson caring for his father's flock from predators in the wilderness: God is present even when you are alone. Again on this occasion he demonstrates his unique courage as against the giant (1 Samuel 17). Let's imitate David who writes, "when my heart is overwhelmed; lead me to the rock that is higher than I" (Psalm 61:2).

EMPLOYMENT POINT: *Encourage yourself in the Lord when your heart is overwhelmed.*

APRIL 21

2 SAMUEL 1–3, WITH
LUKE 18:1–17

———◦◦◦———

Beloved, do not avenge yourselves, but rather give place to wrath; for it is written, "Vengeance is Mine, I will repay," says the Lord (Romans 12:19).

HOW LONG UNTIL THE LORD RIGHTS THE WRONGS YOU'VE EXPERIENCED?

In Jesus' parable, a woman appears before an unjust judge who doesn't care for justice or the things of God. Nonetheless this lady returns daily with her grievance. The judge relents, "Yet because this widow troubles me I will avenge her, lest by her continual coming she weary me" (Luke 18:5). The Greek verb "weary" was used in secular language as a boxing metaphor meaning *to hit under the eye*. If you will, this woman is jabbing the judge daily under the eye by her persistent punches (petitions).

Jesus gives a comparison to make His point, "And shall God not avenge His own elect who cry out day and night to Him, though He bears long with them?" (Luke 18:7). Keep pleading for God's justice; the day will come when the Judge will personally right every wrong! Our faith in the Lord should not waver during times of oppression.

EMPLOYMENT POINT: *Petition God faithfully to enact justice when you've been wronged.*

———◦◦◦———

April 22

2 Samuel 4–6, with
Luke 18:18–43

———◦———

Counsel in the heart of man is like deep water, but a man of understanding will draw it out (Proverbs 20:5).

Do you adequately show the lost their need to be saved?

Wise counselors and faithful evangelists understand the following concept: A person needs to understand his own sin before coming to Jesus. Although the rich young ruler looks ripe for salvation, Jesus knows better. Our Lord shows the man his need to replace self-righteousness with God's righteousness. That is why Jesus confronts him with certain commandments and then follows up, "You still lack one thing. Sell all that you have and distribute to the poor, and you will have treasure in heaven; and come, follow Me" (Luke 18:22). Jesus exposes the man's heart—and reveals that he has another God (materialism) and is covetous.

Similarly, we need to share the message, "for all have sinned and fall short of the glory of God" (Romans 3:23). Indeed, "for the wages of sin is death, but the gift of God is eternal life in Christ Jesus our Lord" (Romans 6:23). Let's call sinners to repentance and point them to the Savior!

Employment Point: *Show the lost their sin through the Law, and then give the gospel.*

———◦———

April 23

2 Samuel 7–9, with
Luke 19:1–28

Every good gift and every perfect gift is from above (James 1:17).

Are you humbled by God's kindness to you?

David gives God first place in his life. He desires to build God a house; however, the Lord says no to David, and that He will build him an eternal house, throne, and kingdom (2 Samuel 7:12–16). Jesus, who is David's greatest descendant, will fulfill this promise (Luke 1:30–33). David's response to God's favor is as follows: "Then King David went in and sat before the Lord; and he said: 'Who am I, O Lord God? And what is my house, that You have brought me this far?'" (2 Samuel 7:18).

Furthermore, our Savior says to Zacchaeus who humbles himself to see Jesus, "Today salvation has come to this house, because he also is a son of Abraham; for the Son of Man has come to seek and to save that which was lost" (Luke 19:9–10). The wee little man demonstrates humility by climbing a tree to see the Savior!

Employment Point: *Humbly receive God's gifts to you and remain thankful.*

APRIL 24

2 SAMUEL 10–12, WITH LUKE 19:29–48

———◦———

Then the LORD sent Nathan to David (2 Samuel 12:1).

HOW WELL DO YOU REPRESENT THE ONE WHO SENT YOU AS HIS AMBASSADOR?

Observe the repeated word "sent" in 2 Samuel 11 (2 Samuel 11:1, 3, 4, 6, 14, 27). David is the all-powerful king who authoritatively dispatches people to do his bidding—even when it is wrong. He not only commits adultery but murder. God is intimately aware of the king's cover-up and conveys a message through His prophet. "Then the LORD sent Nathan to David" (2 Samuel 12:1). Nathan points out the errors of David's way, and exclaims, "You are the man!" (2 Samuel 12:7).

God also sent Jesus to us. "But when the fullness of the time had come, God sent forth His Son" (Galatians 4:4). King Jesus is rejected (John 1:11). He points out during His Triumphal Entry that the Jews didn't grasp that He is the Prince of Peace (Luke 19:42). As the Father sent the Son to save the world (John 3:17), we are dispatched on a search and rescue mission to the unsaved (Mark 16:15).

EMPLOYMENT POINT: *Represent Jesus well, who sends you to a lost world.*

———◦———

APRIL 25

2 SAMUEL 13–14, WITH LUKE 20:1–26

Be sure your sin will find you out (Numbers 32:23).

HAVE YOU CONSIDERED THE PRINCIPLE OF SOWING AND REAPING?

God's Word teaches the above timeless truth (Numbers 32:23). King David reaps the whirlwind because of his disobedience to the Father. Second Samuel 13 informs us about the gross immorality in David's family—that of incest. The apostle Paul instructs us, "Do not be deceived, God is not mocked; for whatever a man sows, that he will also reap" (Galatians 6:7). David would have saved himself a lot of heartache if he had heeded Moses' admonition, "be sure your sin will find you out" (Numbers 32:23).

It is true that the apple doesn't fall far from the tree in this account. David's son, Absalom, rebels against his father and incites an attempt to overthrow the kingdom. I wonder if David would have committed adultery with Bathsheba and had Uriah murdered had he thought about the consequences of his sin? Paul writes, "For he who sows to his flesh will of the flesh reap corruption" (Galatians 6:8). Let's count the cost and not do anything that dishonors God and brings His chastening hand upon us!

EMPLOYMENT POINT: *Avoid sin's path by considering sowing and reaping.*

April 26

2 Samuel 15–16, with Luke 20:27–47

———◆———

They profess to know God, but in works they deny Him (Titus 1:16).

Are you discerning?

Absalom is a hypocrite. He pretends to care for the people in order to have a following, but then splits the kingdom by rebelling against his father. Of course, all of this wouldn't have happened if David hadn't sinned; yet Absalom is responsible for his actions. David committed adultery with Bathsheba in private. Yet "Absalom went in to his father's concubines in the sight of all Israel" (2 Samuel 16:22). Absalom loves attention; however, his pride leads to his sudden and irreparable downfall!

Let's consider Jesus' warning to His generation. "Then, in the hearing of all the people, He said to His disciples, 'Beware of the scribes, who desire to go around in long robes, love greetings in the marketplaces, the best seats in the synagogues, and the best places at feasts'" (Luke 20:45–46). Wisdom cries out that we should characterize people by their actions, and not just their words!

EMPLOYMENT POINT: *Don't follow those who practice a double standard in life.*

———◆———

APRIL 27

2 SAMUEL 17–18, WITH LUKE 21:1–19

Now all these things happened to them as examples, and they were written for our admonition (1 Corinthians 10:11).

DO YOU LOVE DRAWING ATTENTION TO YOURSELF?

Absalom has long flowing hair and craves attention. It becomes a spectacle. "And when he cut the hair of his head—at the end of every year he cut it because it was heavy on him—when he cut it, he weighed the hair of his head at two hundred shekels [about five pounds] according to the king's standard" (2 Samuel 14:26). Who would have thought that a haircut could lead to a public showing?

Moreover, Paul writes, "Does not even nature itself teach you that if a man has long hair, it is a dishonor to him?" (1 Corinthians 11:14). The Bible teaches us that "pride goes before destruction, and a haughty spirit before a fall" (Proverbs 16:18). Absalom flees from Joab's soldiers and gets his head caught in a tree (2 Samuel 18:9) and is subsequently killed (2 Samuel 18:14–15). He longed for followers in life, but was surrounded by adversaries in death (2 Samuel 18:15).

EMPLOYMENT POINT: *Live humbly by drawing attention to the Lord, and not self.*

April 28

2 Samuel 19–20, with Luke 21:20–38

He came to His own, and His own did not receive Him (John 1:11).

What consequences did the Jews experience for rejecting Jesus?

There is a hefty price to pay for shunning Jesus. In Luke 21:20–24 Jesus predicts the decimation of Jerusalem in AD 70. Our Lord says, "And they will fall by the edge of the sword, and be led away captive into all nations. And Jerusalem will be trampled by Gentiles until the times of the Gentiles are fulfilled" (Luke 21:24). Josephus, a Jewish historian, estimated that 1.1 million people were killed in AD 70. Nothing presently good or beneficial in the future will come to those who turn away the Savior of the world!

The rejection of Jesus permits the Gentiles to continue having some form of rulership over Israel until the time of Jesus' Second Coming. That is what is meant by Jesus' expression "the times of the Gentiles." Let's trust in the One who promises, "Heaven and earth will pass away, but My words will by no means pass away" (Luke 21:33).

Employment Point: *Submit to Jesus, to have His future blessing.*

APRIL 29

2 SAMUEL 21–22, WITH LUKE 22:1–30

For I have given you an example, that you should do as I have done to you (John 13:15).

DO YOU WANT TO BE GREAT FOR JESUS?

Jesus' disciples long to be great, but not for Jesus. Luke writes, "Now there was also a dispute among them, as to which of them should be considered the greatest" (Luke 22:24). Our Lord doesn't correct them for desiring to be great; however, He does redirect them to change their worldly posture to a heavenly disposition. In essence, Jesus guides His followers from being self-serving to becoming the servants of all.

Our Lord exposes their mindset. He says, "The kings of the Gentiles exercise lordship over them, and those who exercise authority over them are called benefactors. But not so among you; on the contrary, he who is greatest among you, let him be as the younger, and he who governs as he who serves" (Luke 22:25–26). Greatness comes from making yourself last of all and the slave of all (Mark 10:43–44). This pattern Jesus establishes for all His apprentices!

EMPLOYMENT POINT: *Imitate Jesus for future greatness, by being the slave of all.*

April 30

2 Samuel 23–24, with Luke 22:31–53

———◦———

Be strong in the Lord and in the power of His might (Ephesians 6:10).

Are you loyal to God's leaders?

David is spiritually and physically strong. The Lord surrounds the king with loyal subjects who possess courage. The author of 2 Samuel gives us a list of David's mighty men and their accomplishments in 2 Samuel 23. Here is the first of three points: *Loyal servants are willing to stand alone* (2 Samuel 23:8–12). The author pens about Shammah, "But he stationed himself in the middle of the field, defended it, and killed the Philistines. So the LORD brought about a great victory" (2 Samuel 23:12). Shammah's invisible Partner honors the warrior of faith with an amazing conquest.

Loyal servants are willing to sacrificially serve their leader imparts point two (2 Samuel 23:13–17). David's faithful men risk their lives just to bring him a cool drink of water from Bethlehem. Let the third point resonate in your thinking: *Loyal servants will be honored* (2 Samuel 23:18–39). God's Word recognizes them!

Employment Point: *Practice the above three points, for God to honor you.*

———◦———

130

MAY 1

1 KINGS 1–2, WITH LUKE 22:54–71

———— ◦◦◦ ————

Now I tell you before it comes, that when it does comes to pass, you may believe that I am He (John 13:19).

HOW HAS BIBLE PROPHECY IMPACTED YOU?

David reminds Solomon that God predicted his reign and subsequent building of the temple. "Behold, a son shall be born to you, who shall be a man of rest; and I will give him rest from all his enemies all around. His name shall be Solomon...He shall build a house for My name, and he shall be My son, and I will be his Father; and I will establish the throne of his kingdom over Israel forever" (1 Chronicles 22:9–10). Jesus will fulfill this promise at His Second Coming (Luke 1:30–33).

Furthermore, Jesus told Peter that he would deny Him. Luke reports, "And the Lord turned and looked at Peter. Then Peter remembered the word of the Lord, how He had said to him, 'Before the rooster crows, you will deny Me three times.' So Peter went out and wept bitterly" (Luke 22:61–62). God's Word eternally remains faithful and true!

EMPLOYMENT POINT: *Live confidently for Jesus, because the Bible is trustworthy.*

———— ◦◦◦ ————

MAY 2

1 KINGS 3–5, WITH LUKE 23:1–26

Teacher, we want You to do for us whatever we ask (Mark 10:35).

WHAT DO YOU DESIRE FROM GOD?

James and John long to be personally great so they request to sit on Jesus' right and left hand in His future kingdom. Compare them to Solomon who is Israel's new king. God approaches the inexperienced ruler. "Ask! What shall I give you?" (1 Kings 3:5). Solomon humbly requests for wisdom to govern the nation. The Lord not only honors his request, but also adds riches to the king. God highly respects and elevates those who seek to glorify Him with their petitions.

In life, there is nothing wrong with the desire to accomplish great things, as long as God has placed that yearning upon your heart. The Lord had given Joseph dreams about being a future ruler, and brought these to pass by setting him up as the second leader in Egypt, which also meant that he could provide for his family. Whatever your calling, it is prudent to seek God's wisdom.

EMPLOYMENT POINT: *Seek God's wisdom to fulfill His dreams for your life.*

MAY 3

1 KINGS 6–7, WITH
LUKE 23:27–38

———◦———

Father, forgive them, for they do not know what they do (Luke 23:34).

DO YOU FORGIVE OTHERS AS JESUS DID?

Jesus suffered and "all who desire to live godly in Christ Jesus will suffer persecution" (2 Timothy 3:12). Not only will the godly be persecuted from those outside the faith, but also at times we will be attacked from those within our circle of faith. Earlier Jesus tells His followers, "And if he [a brother or sister in the Lord] sins against you seven times in a day, and seven times in a day returns to you, saying, 'I repent,' you shall forgive him" (Luke 17:4).

No wonder the apostles respond to this seemingly impossible calling from Jesus, "Increase our faith" (Luke 17:5). You have to look no further than the cross for the strength to do the impossible. Paul writes, "And be kind to one another, tenderhearted, forgiving one another, even as God in Christ forgave you" (Ephesians 4:32). Our Lord loves to operate in the realm of the impossible. Allow Him to enable you to forgive as you've been forgiven!

EMPLOYMENT POINT: *Imitate Jesus who freely forgave others.*

———◦———

MAY 4

1 KINGS 8–9, WITH
LUKE 23:39–56

———◦◦◦———

Having boldness to enter the Holiest by the blood of Jesus
(Hebrews 10:19).

DO YOU DAILY GO TO THE HOLIEST?

Luke writes, "Now it was about the sixth hour [12 pm], and there
was darkness over all the earth until the ninth hour [3 pm]. Then the
sun was darkened, and the veil of the temple was torn in two" (Luke
23:44–45). The literal darkness over the cross depicts the sin of the
world being placed upon the sinless One. Paul pens, "For He [God]
made Him [Jesus] who knew no sin to be sin for us, that we might
become the righteousness of God in Him" (2 Corinthians 5:21).
Only Jesus could satisfy the wrath of God being our substitute.

Moreover, the veil was torn from top to bottom showing that
all people may enter the Holy of Holies. Through Christ, let's take
advantage to "come boldly to the throne of grace, that we may obtain
mercy and find grace to help in time of need" (Hebrews 4:16). Let's
enter "by a new and living way which He consecrated for us, through
the veil, that is, His flesh" (Hebrews 10:20).

EMPLOYMENT POINT: *Enter the Holiest regularly, because of Jesus'*
sacrifice.

———◦◦◦———

MAY 5

1 KINGS 10–11, WITH LUKE 24:1–35

———◆———

Did not our heart burn within us while He talked with us on the road, and while He opened the Scriptures to us? (Luke 24:32).

DO YOU DAILY MARVEL AT GOD'S WISDOM CONTAINED IN THE BIBLE?

The Queen of Sheba traveled far to hear the wisdom of Solomon. As she is awed by his wisdom and knowledge, she says, "Happy are your men and happy are these your servants, who stand continually before you and hear your wisdom!" (1 Kings 10:8). She traversed land and sea to glean wisdom from the world's wisest man, and experienced no disappointment; the Queen of Sheba learned much!

A descendant of Solomon, Jesus, conquers death and walks and talks with two of His followers. He travels incognito; they didn't originally know that it was Jesus with them. After He explains the prophecies pertaining Himself, they say, "Did not our heart burn within us while He talked with us on the road, and while He opened the Scriptures to us?" (Luke 24:32). Jesus is wiser than the greatest wise man who ever walked the earth. Hear Him!

EMPLOYMENT POINT: *Allow God's Word daily to give you "biblical heartburn."*

———◆———

MAY 6

1 KINGS 12–13, WITH LUKE 24:36–53

———◆———

He who walks with wise men will be wise, but the companion of fools will be destroyed (Proverbs 13:20).

FROM WHOM DO YOU TAKE COUNSEL?

Solomon dies, and his son Rehoboam becomes king. He seeks counsel from two groups of people to determine how to rule his kingdom. The neophyte king "consulted the elders who stood before his father Solomon" (1 Kings 12:6). Unwisely he rebuffs their counsel and turns to his peers, which leads to a division of the land. God earlier predicted this division, but the selfish ruler is responsible for the poor counsel he heeds.

Rehoboam governs the southern kingdom and Jeroboam the northern kingdom. Jeroboam also seeks counsel. "Therefore the king asked advice, made two calves of gold, and said to the people, 'It is too much for you to go up to Jerusalem. Here are your gods, O Israel, which brought you up from the land of Egypt!'" (1 Kings 12:28). Unlike Rehoboam and Jeroboam, we need to seek godly counsel from mature believers, for "he who walks with wise men will be wise" (Proverbs 13:20).

EMPLOYMENT POINT: *Seek counsel from godly people, and heed their advice to walk in wisdom.*

———◆———

MAY 7

1 KINGS 14–15, WITH JOHN 1:1–28

In the beginning was the Word, and the Word was with God, and the Word was God (John 1:1).

ARE YOU WALKING WITH THE WORD?

Only in John's writings do we find Jesus described as "the Word." The apostle of love depicts Jesus as eternally God in John 1:1. "Was" appears three times in this verse in the imperfect tense, which shows continuous action in past time. The tense communicates that Jesus always existed in the past, dwelt continually with the Father, and is eternally God. Jesus existed before time, but chose to step into time (Galatians 4:4). Our author continues, "And the Word became flesh and dwelt among us" (John 1:14). In other words, the eternal Son of God became the God-Man.

Jesus, the eternal Son of God, became like us so that one day we could be fully conformed to His image through our glorification. Jesus will return again. John describes His Second Coming: "He was clothed with a robe dipped in blood, and His name is called the Word of God" (Revelation 19:13).

EMPLOYMENT POINT: *Worship the Word, who eternally existed with the Father and will come again.*

MAY 8

1 KINGS 16–18, WITH JOHN 1:29–51

He must increase, but I must decrease (John 3:30).

ARE YOU WILLING TO STAND ALONE FOR GOD?

Great men and women of God have a common trait: They are willing to stand alone. In 1 Kings 18, Elijah throws down the gauntlet to the 450 prophets of Baal, proclaiming that he serves the only living God. Observe the silence when the false prophets cry out to their god, "O Baal, hear us!" and 1 Kings 18:26 continues, "But there was no voice; no one answered." Yet when Elijah calls out to God "the fire of the LORD fell and consumed the burnt sacrifice" (1 Kings 18:38). The Lord honors Elijah for trusting in the power of the Almighty in the midst of the enemy's camp!

Similarly, John the Baptist is willing to stand alone and point people to Jesus. He declares, "Behold! The Lamb of God who takes away the sin of the world! This is He of whom I said, 'After me comes a Man who is preferred before me, for He was before me'" (John 1:29–30). Both Elijah and John rely upon the Lord.

EMPLOYMENT POINT: *Stand alone for God, awaiting His display of vast power.*

MAY 9

1 KINGS 19–20, WITH JOHN 2

He restores my soul (Psalm 23:3).

HOW SHOULD YOU OVERCOME DEPRESSION?

All of us suffer from depression occasionally. God's prescription for Elijah's depression is found in 1 Kings 19. *Allow God to care for you* is our first point (1 Kings 19:1–8). When Elijah desires death, God nourishes him physically. Permit yourself time for rest, refreshment, and healthy food. Our second point is as follows: *Seek God's presence during depression* (1 Kings 19:9–14). Get into the Word and let the Word get into you. First Kings 19:11 shares, "And behold, the LORD passed by," which refers to a theophany—that is, God manifests His presence to the depressed disciple. You need to enjoy God's company always, particularly when you are feeling down.

Serve God for His reorientation imparts our third point (1 Kings 19:15–21). The Lord dispatches Elijah to anoint a king and a prophet for ministry. God graciously helps the self-absorbed prophet to focus upon others. Directing your attention upon serving others guards the heart from selfishness.

EMPLOYMENT POINT: *Apply these employment points to overcome depression.*

MAY 10

1 KINGS 21–22, WITH JOHN 3:1–21

———◦◦◦———

I say to you, unless one is born again, he cannot see the kingdom of God (John 3:3).

DO YOU STAY ON THE RIGHT MESSAGE?

Jesus reveals to Nicodemus his greatest need. He says, "Do not marvel that I said to you, 'You must be born again'" (John 3:7). The first "you" in this verse is singular and points to Nicodemus, while the second "you" is plural and directs us to the need of all people. Since Nicodemus is familiar with the Old Testament, Jesus gives him an illustration from Numbers 21 about the fiery serpents biting the grumbling Israelites.

The Master of evangelism expresses the need for those bitten to look up to the brazen serpent upon the pole to be healed (John 3:14–15). He then connects the dots, and says, "For God so loved the world that He gave His only begotten Son, that whoever believes in Him should not perish but have everlasting life" (John 3:16). Like Jesus, we should direct people to look upon the cross by faith. After all, "It is finished!" (John 19:30).

EMPLOYMENT POINT: *Repeatedly tell people to be born again.*

———◦◦◦———

MAY 11

2 KINGS 1–3, WITH JOHN 3:22–36

Please let a double portion of your spirit be upon me (2 Kings 2:9).

WHERE IS THE LORD GOD OF ELIJAH? (2 KINGS 2:14).

Elisha asks the above question when he receives the mantle of Elijah to carry on his prophetic role. Elijah's disciple knows that his master is about to go to heaven, and that he lacks the power to succeed his powerful mentor. For this reason he clings to his leader, who tests him three times by attempting to shrug off the determined follower (2 Kings 2:2, 4, 6).

How committed are you to stay attached to the Vine, Jesus Christ, in order to accomplish His will through your life? As Elisha clings to Elijah seeking heavenly help, we need to abide in Jesus. Our Lord says, "Abide in Me, and I in you. As the branch cannot bear fruit of itself, unless it abides in the vine, neither can you, unless you abide in Me" (John 15:4). God's power flows through the life of individuals who stay connected to the Lord by walking closely with Him.

EMPLOYMENT POINT: *Walk with Jesus for divine enablement to minister.*

MAY 12

2 KINGS 4–5, WITH
JOHN 4:1–30

———◦◦◦———

God resists the proud, but gives grace to the humble (James 4:6).

DO YOU HUMBLY FOLLOW GOD?

Naaman the Syrian is a commander of his army and a man of character; however, he is a leper (2 Kings 5:1). He travels to Israel because a
servant girl informs him that Elisha, who lives there, could heal him.
Once this important man arrives Elisha doesn't go to greet him, but
sends his servant who tells the commander to dip seven times in the
Jordan River (2 Kings 5:10). At first he refuses, but then is persuaded
to take the prophet at his word, and is healed. Elisha treats the commander in this fashion to teach him humility because "God resists the
proud, but gives grace to the humble" (James 4:6).

Similarly, Jesus humbles the Samaritan woman informing her,
"for you have had five husbands, and the one whom you now have is
not your husband" (John 4:18). Subsequently she believes in Jesus.
God's favor reached an enemy combatant of Israel (Naaman the Syrian) and a person normally hated by Jews (a Samaritan).

EMPLOYMENT POINT: *Humble yourself before God to receive His*
grace.

———◦◦◦———

MAY 13

2 KINGS 6–8, WITH JOHN 4:31–54

The LORD opens the eyes of the blind (Psalm 146:8).

HOW DO YOU PRAY FOR GOD'S SERVANTS AND THE SPIRITUALLY BLIND?

Elisha informs the king of Israel about Syria's battle plans. So, the king believes there is a traitor in his midst. A servant reports to the king about Elisha who "tells the king of Israel the words that you speak in your bedroom" (2 Kings 6:12). Therefore the king dispatches an army to seize Elisha and the prophet's servant panics after seeing them. Elisha tells him, "Do not fear, for those who are with us are more than those who are with them" (2 Kings 6:16). Here's your first employment point: *Pray for God's servants' spiritual sight* (2 Kings 6:13–17).

After leading the blind army to the king of Israel, Elisha prays, "LORD, open the eyes of these men, that they may see" (2 Kings 6:20). *Pray for the blind to see* is our second employment point (2 Kings 6:20). Satan has rendered sightless the minds of the spiritually blind (2 Corinthians 4:3–4). They need "the God who commanded light to shine out of darkness" (2 Corinthians 4:6) to open their eyes.

EMPLOYMENT POINT: *Pray for God's servants' spiritual sight, and for the blind to see.*

143

MAY 14

2 KINGS 9–11, WITH
JOHN 5:1–24

The Father judges no one, but has committed all judgment to the Son (John 5:22).

HOW DO YOU PREPARE TO STAND BEFORE JESUS?

John pens his gospel demonstrating Jesus' deity, and that believing on His finished work saves you (John 20:30–31). The Jewish leaders understand Jesus' claim and respond, "Therefore the Jews sought all the more to kill Him, because He not only broke the Sabbath [John 5:1–16], but also said that God was His Father, making Himself equal with God" (John 5:18). They grasp Jesus' self-assertion that He is eternally God.

Jesus is God and our future judge. John writes, "For the Father judges no one, but has committed all judgment to the Son" (John 5:22). Knowing these things should motivate us to prepare to stand before Jesus. Paul's goal should be our goal. He pens, "Therefore we make it our aim, whether present or absent, to be well pleasing to Him. For we must all appear before the judgment seat of Christ" (2 Corinthians 5:9–10). Let's walk with Jesus now, to be ready to stand before Him in the future (1 John 2:28).

EMPLOYMENT POINT: *Please God daily, to prepare to meet Jesus.*

MAY 15

2 KINGS 12–14, WITH JOHN 5:25–47

———◈———

And the Scripture cannot be broken (John 10:35).

DO YOU TRUST BIBLE PROPHECY?

Jesus assesses the unbelieving Jews by making two "if" statements in John 5:46–47. The first "if" is a second-class condition, which means assuming the statement to be false. Our Lord says, "For if you believed Moses, you would believe Me; for he wrote about Me" (John 5:46). The idea from the Greek text is "if" you believed Moses and his writings, which you don't, you would have believed Me. Jesus exposes the unbelief of those whom He addresses.

Next Jesus gives a first-class condition, which means assuming the statement to be true. "But if you do not believe his writings, how will you believe My words?" (John 5:47). That is, "since" you haven't relied upon Moses' writing, this is why you won't believe My words either. Today's devotion shows that when you don't put your trust in the Scriptures that point to Jesus, then you don't model belief in Him. Faith in Jesus directly connects to believing the eternal Word!

EMPLOYMENT POINT: *Honor Jesus by believing the prophecies that point to Him.*

———◈———

MAY 16

2 KINGS 15–17, WITH
JOHN 6:1–21

———◦———

Jesus took the loaves, and when He had given thanks He distributed them to the disciples (John 6:11).

WHY SHOULD YOU PARTNER WITH JESUS?

Jesus has His disciples participate in the feeding of the 5,000. The large group is thoroughly fed. He gave them "as much as they wanted" (John 6:11). John reports, "Therefore when Jesus perceived that they were about to come and take Him by force to make Him king, He departed again to a mountain by Himself alone" (John 6:15). Jesus doesn't want to become a pseudo–king who provides food for the multitudes, but comes to be their Savior and King.

The Lord protects His disciples by sending them away by boat from the multitude. In the midst of a storm, "they saw Jesus walking on the sea and drawing near the boat; and they were afraid" (John 6:19). He says, "It is I; do not be afraid" (John 6:20). The disciples need to look upon God's glory and not their own; He shields them from a crowd who would promote their selfishness to focus upon Him!

EMPLOYMENT POINT: *Glorify God through your partnership with Jesus.*

———◦———

MAY 17

2 KINGS 18–19, WITH JOHN 6:22–44

I am the bread of life (John 6:35).

WHAT SATISFIES YOUR SOUL?

The things that God originally intends for good can become an idol to us. For instance, the bronze serpent the Lord used in Numbers 21. When the Israelites were bitten and then looked upon the object in faith, they were restored to health. God structured a means for those bitten by the serpents to be made well.

Centuries later, godly king Hezekiah destroys the object. "He removed the high places and broke the sacred pillars, cut down the wooden image and broke in pieces the bronze serpent that Moses had made; for until those days the children of Israel burned incense to it, and called it Nehushtan" (2 Kings 18:4). An idol is sort of like a proper noun; it can derive from a person, place, or thing. Only Jesus can truly satisfy the soul. He shares, "I am the bread of life. He who comes to Me shall never hunger, and he who believes in Me shall never thirst" (John 6:35).

EMPLOYMENT POINT: *Find your soul's satisfaction in Jesus.*

MAY 18

2 KINGS 20–22, WITH JOHN 6:45–71

I rejoice at Your word as one who finds great treasure (Psalm 119:162).

HOW MUCH TIME WOULD ELAPSE BEFORE YOU DISCOVERED THAT YOUR BIBLE IS MISPLACED?

The southern kingdom of Judah doesn't realize that the Old Testament is no longer a part of their national fabric. Josiah becomes king and the Lord confronts his heart through the discovery of God's Word. "Then Hilkiah the high priest said to Shaphan the scribe, 'I have found the Book of the Law in the house of the LORD.' And Hilkiah gave the book to Shaphan, and he read it" (2 Kings 22:8). Revival begins with the revealed Word of God!

The story continues, "Now it happened, when the king heard the words of the Book of the Law, that he tore his clothes" (2 Kings 22:11). Rent garments reveal a repentant heart. God blesses those who hear and heed the Bible. "Blessed is he who reads and those who hear the words of this prophecy, and keep those things which are written in it" (Revelation 1:3). Choose to read, hear, and then obey the sacred Scripture for the blessing of the Lord.

EMPLOYMENT POINT: *Discover God's Word anew, and let the revival begin.*

MAY 19

2 KINGS 23–25, WITH
JOHN 7:1–31

Because zeal for Your house has eaten me up (Psalm 69:9).

HOW ZEALOUS ARE YOU FOR THE LORD?

Josiah's zeal for the Lord is recorded in 2 Kings 23. He receives the highest of praise, "Now before him there was no king like him, who turned to the LORD with all his heart, with all his soul, and with all his might, according to all the Law of Moses; nor after him did any arise like him" (2 Kings 23:25). Why is he different? He diligently guards his heart. Centuries later John writes, "Little children, keep yourselves from idols" (1 John 5:21).

God honors those who wholeheartedly pursue Him. Jesus' invitation stands today for those who want to forsake the best that the world has to offer, and be contented with His Spirit. "If anyone thirsts," says Jesus, "let him come to Me and drink. He who believes in Me, as the Scripture has said, out of his heart will flow rivers of living water" (John 7:37–38). Only Jesus can satisfy your soul!

EMPLOYMENT POINT: *Let God's Spirit fill your life with contentedness and zeal.*

MAY 20

1 CHRONICLES 1–2, WITH JOHN 7:32–53

———◈———

As we have borne the image of the man of dust, we shall also bear the image of the heavenly Man (1 Corinthians 15:49).

HAVE YOU TRANSITIONED FROM ADAM TO JESUS?

First Chronicles 1–9 pertains to the royal line of David. It begins with Adam; Luke's genealogy begins with Jesus (Luke 3:23) and takes us back to Adam (Luke 3:38). There are two key personages in history: Adam and Jesus. Adam was our representative. Paul writes, "Just as through one man sin entered the world, and death through sin, and thus death spread to all men, because all sinned" (Romans 5:12).

Whereas Adam failed, Jesus succeeded. The apostle continues, "For if by the one man's offense death reigned through the one, much more those who receive abundance of grace and of the gift of righteousness will reign in life through the One, Jesus Christ" (Romans 5:17). Be encouraged, "As we have borne the image of the man of dust, we shall also bear the image of the heavenly Man" (1 Corinthians 15:49). Adam failed as our representative, but Jesus emerged victorious!

EMPLOYMENT POINT: *Believe on Jesus, who conquered sin and death in your behalf.*

———◈———

MAY 21

1 CHRONICLES 3–5, WITH JOHN 8:1–20

I am the light of the world (John 8:12).

ARE YOU WALKING IN GOD'S LIGHT?

Jesus enters the temple before morning light. The majority of Greek manuscripts say "very early in the morning" (John 8:2) He arrives at the temple to teach. Religious leaders who bring a woman caught in adultery rudely interrupt him. They seek to entrap Jesus by asking what should be done to her. Our Lord knows that answering not to stone her would violate the Law, but to have her put to death would cause tension between Jesus and the Roman government.

It isn't important what Jesus writes on the ground, since Scripture doesn't record His words. Rather, it is how He writes on the ground that should be our focus; He writes with the finger of God, like the Law was written (Exodus 31:18). God's conviction comes upon the people and they leave from the oldest to the youngest. The adulteress who came to Jesus in darkness then leaves exposed to God's light.

EMPLOYMENT POINT: *Walk in God's light by following the Light of the World.*

MAY 22

1 CHRONICLES 6–7, WITH JOHN 8:21–36

———◦———

I am the way, the truth, and the life. No one comes to the Father except through Me (John 14:6).

HAS THE TRUTH SET YOU FREE?

Pilate sarcastically asks Jesus, "What is truth?" (John 18:38). Previously to a different audience Jesus said, "And you shall know the truth, and the truth shall make you free" (John 8:32). Our Lord came to reveal truth to us. John writes, "For the law was given through Moses, but grace and truth came through Jesus Christ" (John 1:17). Have you placed your faith in Jesus? His grace is available to you. The term "grace" means *favor*. We do not deserve the gift of eternal life. Yet Jesus freely offered Himself on the cross to be our sin bearer.

Subsequently Jesus conquered death, which demonstrates that He is God. You are saved or born again by placing your faith in Jesus who "is the true God and eternal life" (1 John 5:20). Once you depend solely upon Him to be your Savior, then you experience John 8:36: "Therefore if the Son makes you free, you shall be free indeed."

EMPLOYMENT POINT: *Be spiritually free by placing your faith in Jesus.*

———◦———

MAY 23

1 CHRONICLES 8–10, WITH JOHN 8:37–59

Before Abraham was, I AM (John 8:58).

ARE YOU HONORING DAVID'S GREATEST DESCENDANT?

First Chronicles 10:1–29:30 pertains to the reign of David. The transition from ungodly Saul to righteous David emerges in 1 Chronicles 10:13–14. "So Saul died for his unfaithfulness which he had committed against the LORD, because he did not keep the word of the LORD, and also because he consulted a medium for guidance. But he did not inquire of the LORD; therefore He killed him, and turned the kingdom over to David the son of Jesse."

God promises David an eternal house, throne, and kingdom (2 Samuel 7:12–16), which Jesus will fulfill (Luke 1:30–33). He is the God-Man who conquers death. He boldly proclaims, "Most assuredly, I say to you, before Abraham was, I AM" (John 8:58). Jesus equates Himself with the Father (Exodus 3:13–14). Let's praise Him: "Worthy is the Lamb who was slain to receive power and riches and wisdom, and strength and honor and glory and blessing!" (Revelation 5:12).

EMPLOYMENT POINT: *Lavish David's greatest descendant with praise.*

MAY 24

1 CHRONICLES 11–13, WITH JOHN 9:1–23

Now as Jesus passed by, He saw a man who was blind from birth (John 9:1).

WHAT MIRACLE IS NEVER PERFORMED IN THE OLD TESTAMENT?

No account exists of sight being given to someone born blind in the Old Testament. John writes about Jesus, "He spat on the ground and made clay with the saliva; and He anointed the eyes of the blind man with the clay. And He said to him, 'Go, wash in the pool of Siloam' (which is translated, Sent). So he went and washed, and came back seeing" (John 9:6–7). Saliva was considered a curative in Jesus' day. Perhaps Jesus is allowing the blind man to hear what is about to transpire through spitting on the ground. The clay reminds us about Adam's creation from the ground.

Finally, Jesus tests the man's faith by giving him an assignment; he follows through and receives his sight. John records, "but these are written that you may believe that Jesus is the Christ, the Son of God, and that believing you may have life in His name" (John 20:31).

EMPLOYMENT POINT: *Rely fully upon the One who gives sight to the blind.*

MAY 25

1 CHRONICLES 14–16, WITH JOHN 9:24–41

———◦———

God is Spirit, and those who worship Him must worship in spirit and truth (John 4:24).

ARE YOU APPROPRIATELY WORSHIPING THE LORD?

David's attempt to return the ark of God to the tabernacle resulted in failure. Uzza, a Kohathite, was trained never to touch the ark of God lest he would die (see Numbers 4:15); he touched it, and God killed him (1 Chronicles 13:9–10). Later David is told why his effort to return the ark of God brought about Uzza's death, "For because you did not do it the first time [referring to the priests' sanctification described in 1 Chronicles 15:12], the LORD our God broke out against us, because we did not consult Him about the proper order" (1 Chronicles 15:13).

Whether it is worship under the old covenant for Israel or the new covenant for the church, God's Word should always be the source of our authority to please Him. Paul writes to a church whose worship is topsy-turvy, "Let all things be done decently and in order" (1 Corinthians 14:40). God's holy Word, which reveals truth, should govern worship.

EMPLOYMENT POINT: *Worship God according to His Word.*

———◦———

MAY 26

1 CHRONICLES 17–19, WITH JOHN 10:1–21

———◈———

I took you from the sheepfold, from following the sheep, to be ruler over My people Israel (1 Chronicles 17:7).

ARE YOU FOLLOWING THE GOOD SHEPHERD?

David is a good shepherd; he cares for his father's flock by protecting the sheep from lions and bears (1 Samuel 17:34). God promotes him to shepherd Israel. Although the Lord doesn't permit the man after His own heart to build the temple, yet He promises David an eternal house, throne, and kingdom (1 Chronicles 17:12–14).

A thousand years after David comes another good shepherd from his lineage. Jesus says, "I am the good shepherd. The good shepherd gives His life for the sheep" (John 10:11). Our Lord often repeats His pledge (John 10:15, 17, 18; 15:13). Jesus, the Good Shepherd, is worthy of our loyalty as the writer of Hebrews states, "Now may the God of peace who brought up our Lord Jesus from the dead, that great Shepherd of the sheep, through the blood of the everlasting covenant, make you complete in every good work to do His will" (Hebrews 13:20–21).

EMPLOYMENT POINT: *Follow the Good Shepherd who laid down His life for you.*

———◈———

MAY 27

1 CHRONICLES 20–22, WITH JOHN 10:22–42

For the children ought not to lay up for the parents, but the parents for the children (2 Corinthians 12:14).

ARE YOU MAKING SACRIFICES FOR THE NEXT GENERATION?

King David is a man after God's own heart and loves his son Solomon. The warrior David isn't permitted to build the temple, so he makes necessary provision for Solomon to accomplish the sacred task. "Now David said, 'Solomon my son is young and inexperienced, and the house that is to be built for the LORD must be exceedingly magnificent, famous and glorious throughout all countries. I will now make preparation for it.' So David made abundant preparations before his death" (1 Chronicles 22:5).

Similarly God the Father and Jesus His Son make an excellent pair, even surpassing David and Solomon. Together they make provision for the world's salvation. Jesus testifies that He gives the gift of eternal life, and that both He and His Father secure the souls of the saved (John 10:28–30). We should seek to have a heart like David and God the Father through our provisions for others.

EMPLOYMENT POINT: *Serve the next generation and others, through your sacrifices.*

MAY 28

1 CHRONICLES 23–25, WITH JOHN 11:1–17

———◦◉◦———

These are written that you may believe that Jesus is the Christ (John 20:31).

ARE YOU INCREASING IN FAITH?

If there is ever a man who needs to experience his name's meaning, it's Lazarus. His name means *God is my help*. Jesus has a warm relationship with Lazarus and his sisters Mary and Martha. Jesus allows Lazarus to die in order to teach a profound lesson to His followers. Although Mary and Martha summons the Lord because Lazarus is ill, Jesus permits him to die and to remain in that state for four days. Jesus gives the purpose of His delay, "I am glad for your sakes that I was not there, that you may believe" (John 11:15). He allows Lazarus to die to strengthen the faith of Martha, Mary, and His disciples.

Jesus prescribes trials so that our faith will not be an inch deep and a mile wide. James writes, "My brethren, count it all joy when you fall into various trials, knowing that the testing of your faith produces patience" (James 1:2–3).

EMPLOYMENT POINT: *Trust Jesus during a trial, which will build your faith.*

———◦◉◦———

MAY 29

1 CHRONICLES 26–27, WITH JOHN 11:18–46

———◦———

I am the resurrection and the life (John 11:25).

DO YOU BELIEVE THIS?

John's gospel conveys Jesus' seven great "I am" statements. The fifth such declaration appears in the account of Lazarus' resurrection. "I am" refers to Exodus 3:13–14. Moses asks God, "Indeed, when I come to the children of Israel and say to them, 'The God of your fathers has sent me to you,' and they say to me, 'What is His name?' what shall I say to them?" (Exodus 3:13). God's response, "I AM WHO I AM. And He said, Thus you shall say to the children of Israel, 'I AM has sent me to you'" (Exodus 3:14). Three times the verb "I AM" emerges in Exodus 3:14; it derives from the verb *to be*. In other words, it conveys that God is eternal—He has always existed.

Moreover, our Lord's "I am" statement to Martha in John 11:25 communicates that Jesus, the eternal One, raises the dead and imparts everlasting life. He then asks her, "Do you believe this?" (John 11:26).

EMPLOYMENT POINT: *Believe in Jesus, who is the resurrection and the life.*

———◦———

May 30

1 Chronicles 28–29, with John 11:47–57

For this is the love of God, that we keep His commandments. And His commandments are not burdensome (1 John 5:3).

What is your top priority?

David provides an abundance of provisions for the temple to be built by Solomon; however, the building of the temple isn't the aging father's top priority. He desires foremost to see his son walk with God. King David prays, "And give my son Solomon a loyal heart to keep Your commandments and Your testimonies and Your statutes, to do all these things, and to build the temple for which I have made provision" (1 Chronicles 29:19). Solomon himself would later write, "A wise son makes a glad father, but a foolish son is the grief of his mother" (Proverbs 10:1).

David's predecessor didn't obey his heavenly Father and lost his kingdom. Samuel says to Saul, "Has the LORD as great delight in burnt offerings and sacrifices, as in obeying the voice of the LORD? Behold, to obey is better than sacrifice, and to heed than the fat of rams" (1 Samuel 15:22).

EMPLOYMENT POINT: *Prioritize God's Word in your life, and instruct others to do the same.*

MAY 31

2 CHRONICLES 1–3, WITH JOHN 12:1–19

The fear of the LORD is the beginning of wisdom (Psalm 111:10).

ASK! WHAT SHALL I GIVE YOU? (2 CHRONICLES 1:7).

Solomon responds to the above question from God, "Now give me wisdom and knowledge, that I may go out and come in before this people" (2 Chronicles 1:10). The young king understands that the wisdom from above is more valuable than silver and gold.

In John 12, Mary the sister of Lazarus (who had just been raised from the dead) offers a sacrificial gift to the giver of life and wisdom. John writes, "Then Mary took a pound of very costly oil of spikenard, anointed the feet of Jesus, and wiped His feet with her hair. And the house was filled with the fragrance of the oil" (John 12:3). This perfume is valued at three hundred denarii, which is equivalent to three hundred days' pay for the average laborer. Solomon in his youth, and Mary, understand something of great importance: Nothing compares to knowing God personally and serving Him well.

EMPLOYMENT POINT: *Pursue God's wisdom through the Word and prayer, while humbly serving at Jesus' feet.*

JUNE 1

2 CHRONICLES 4–6, WITH JOHN 12:20–50

———◦———

Father, glorify Your name (John 12:28).

WHY SHOULD YOU GLORIFY GOD?

The Westminster shorter catechism asks: What is the chief end of man? The answer, Man's chief end is to glorify God, and to enjoy Him forever. At the dedication of the temple, Solomon "praised the Lord, saying: 'For He is good, for His mercy endures forever'" (2 Chronicles 5:13). God is so pleased with the dedication "that the priests could not continue ministering because of the cloud; for the glory of the Lord filled the house of God" (2 Chronicles 5:14).

Glorify God in everything; Jesus did! Our Lord pours out His heart, saying, "Now My soul is troubled, and what shall I say? 'Father, save Me from this hour?' But for this purpose I came to this hour. 'Father, glorify Your name'" (John 12:27–28). The Father honors Solomon's desire to bring Him glory; He does the same for Jesus. He replies, "Then a voice came from heaven, saying, 'I have both glorified it and will glorify it again'" (John 12:28).

EMPLOYMENT POINT: *Seek to glorify God through all you say and do.*

———◦———

JUNE 2

2 CHRONICLES 7–9, WITH JOHN 13:1–17

Greater love has no one than this, than to lay down one's life for his friends (John 15:13).

WHAT LESSON DOES JESUS TEACH HIS DISCIPLES ABOUT WASHING FEET?

"For I have given you an example, that you should do as I have done to you," says Jesus (John 13:15). Our Lord loves His followers. John writes, "having loved His own who were in the world, He loved them to the end" (John 13:1). Jesus loves the disciples with all of His holy essence.

In the same context of our passage today, Luke says about Jesus' apostles, "Now there was also a dispute among them, as to which of them should be considered the greatest" (Luke 22:24). The footwashing is more than a lowly act of service; Jesus shows His disciples through this deed that He willingly lays down His life for them, and they must choose to do the same for each other. His soon-coming death will model that greatness comes from a life of self-denial and sacrifice. Jesus culminates His lesson as follows: "blessed are you if you do them" (John 13:17).

EMPLOYMENT POINT: *Imitate Jesus by humbly serving the family of God.*

June 3

2 Chronicles 10–12, with John 13:18–38

Now I tell you before it comes, that when it does come to pass, you may believe that I am He (John 13:19).

What does Jesus' ability to predict the future tell us about Him?

God is not controlled by time, since He created it. Also, He knows the past, present, and future perfectly. Our all-knowing God predicts that Rehoboam, the son of Solomon, will have part of his kingdom taken away (2 Chronicles 10:15).

Moreover, Jesus informs His followers that there is a traitor in the band of disciples. He predicts this so that His apprentices at the fulfillment of this forecast might better grasp His deity. The words, "I am" in John 13:19 point to Jesus' deity and that He is equal in His nature to God the Father (Exodus 3:13–14). Our Lord also foretells Peter's denials with specifics (John 13:36–38), which later perfectly come to pass. We can fully rely upon the God who can predict Rehoboam's divided kingdom, Judas' betrayal, and Peter's three denials. The One who created time knows all periods of time!

Employment Point: *Trust Jesus wholly because He knows your past, present, and future.*

JUNE 4

2 CHRONICLES 13–16, WITH JOHN 14

—————

If you ask anything in My name, I will do it (John 14:14).

WHAT DOES GOD REQUIRE OF YOU TO ACCOMPLISH GREAT THINGS FOR HIM?

Asa is facing the Ethiopian "army of a million men and three hundred chariots" (2 Chronicles 14:9). Yet he cries out to God, which shows an utter dependence upon Him, and wins the battle. Sadly, later he relies upon the arm of strength (the Syrians) for victory over the northern kingdom of Israel. Although his actions are foolish, the one thing God looks for in His servants is revealed. "For the eyes of the LORD run to and fro throughout the whole earth, to show Himself strong on behalf of those whose heart is loyal to Him" (2 Chronicles 16:9). Our Lord scans the globe for men and women of faith whose hearts are fully surrendered to Him.

After Jesus says to His disciples, "If you ask anything in My name, I will do it," He adds, "If you love Me, keep My commandments" (John 14:14–15). Obedience is essential to unleash the Lord's power.

EMPLOYMENT POINT: *Be completely loyal to Jesus, to accomplish great things for God.*

—————

JUNE 5

2 CHRONICLES 17–19, WITH JOHN 15

———◦———

Abide in Me, and I in you (John 15:4).

WHAT IS KEY TO A FRUITFUL LIFE FOR GOD?

David, a man after God's own heart, becomes the standard for the southern kings of Judah. Jehoshaphat imitates him by walking with God, seeking Him, and delighting in His ways (2 Chronicles 17:3–6). "Therefore the LORD established the kingdom in his hand; and all Judah gave presents to Jehoshaphat, and he had riches and honor in abundance" (2 Chronicles 17:5).

Jesus, the greatest descendant of David, becomes the standard for His disciples. He says to them, "This is My commandment, that you love one another as I have loved you" (John 15:12). Jesus promises a productive life to those who stay close to Him. "I am the vine, you are the branches. He who abides in Me, and I in him, bears much fruit; for without Me you can do nothing" (John 15:5). Staying close to the heart of God by daily walking with Jesus produces a fruitful existence on earth and treasures in heaven!

EMPLOYMENT POINT: *Walk with Jesus and bear much fruit for God.*

———◦———

JUNE 6

2 CHRONICLES 20–22, WITH JOHN 16:1–15

Position yourselves, stand still and see the salvation of the LORD (2 Chronicles 20:17).

HOW SHOULD YOU POSITION YOURSELF WHEN THE ENEMY OF YOUR SOUL OVERWHELMS YOU?

Satan and his allies, the world and the flesh, stand united against you. Similarly, several nations aligned themselves to fight godly Jehoshaphat and the kingdom of Judah. The wise king knows he's outmatched; therefore, he turns to the great Equalizer in prayer (2 Chronicles 20:3–12). The divine response follows: "Do not be afraid nor dismayed because of this great multitude, for the battle is not yours, but God's" (2 Chronicles 20:15).

As Jehoshaphat prudently seeks God and is delivered from his adversaries, you must pursue the same course of action. Consider Paul's counsel, "Finally, my brethren, be strong in the Lord and in the power of His might. Put on the whole armor of God, that you may be able to stand against the wiles of the devil. For we do not wrestle against flesh and blood, but against principalities, against powers, against the rulers of the darkness of this age" (Ephesians 6:10–12).

EMPLOYMENT POINT: *Turn to God and rely upon Him to defend you.*

JUNE 7

2 CHRONICLES 23–25, WITH JOHN 16:16–33

Do not be deceived: Evil company corrupts good habits (1 Corinthians 15:33).

WHO ARE YOUR SPIRITUAL ADVISORS?

King Joash is blessed to receive guidance from godly Jehoiada. The writer of 2 Chronicles 24:2 reveals, "Joash did what was right in the sight of the LORD all the days of Jehoiada the priest." Once Jehoiada died, "the leaders of Judah came and bowed down to the king. And the king listened to them" (2 Chronicles 24:17). Consequently the king is led astray, and the nation served idols.

Unlike Joash, eleven of the twelve apostles carry on the work of Jesus after He died, rose from the dead, and ascended to heaven. He had prepared them for His departure and subsequent opposition (John 16:16–33). Our Lord says to them shortly before His death, "These things I have spoken to you, that in Me you may have peace. In the world you will have tribulation; but be of good cheer, I have overcome the world" (John 16:33).

EMPLOYMENT POINT: *Apply what your godly spiritual advisors teach you, so that you remain steadfast in the faith.*

JUNE 8

2 CHRONICLES 26–28, WITH JOHN 17

I have finished the work which You have given Me to do (John 17:4).

HOW CAN YOU REMAIN LOYAL TO GOD UNTIL YOUR EARTHLY WORK IS DONE?

Uzziah had a fifty-two-year reign as king over Judah. He starts strong; however, he fails miserably in the end. The king did what was right, "and as long as he sought the LORD, God made him prosper" (2 Chronicles 26:5). Yet he didn't handle his popularity well. "So his fame spread far and wide, for he was marvelously helped till he became strong" (2 Chronicles 26:15). Uzziah then oversteps his God-given boundaries, exuding pride, and seeks to offer incense in the temple (2 Chronicles 26:16). Being a king did not give him the authority to serve as a priest, and this led to God striking him with leprosy.

Unlike Uzziah, Jesus completes His God-given mission. He humbly continues praying to the Father until His death, which shows a pattern for leading a dependent life. He chooses spending His last minutes with the Father in prayer before being arrested.

EMPLOYMENT POINT: *Pray unceasingly to finish life's journey well.*

June 9

2 Chronicles 29–31, with John 18:1–23

And bowing His head, He gave up His spirit (John 19:30).

Who ultimately determined that Jesus would die?

Jesus is arrested by about six hundred troops while in Gethsemane. Perhaps they expected Him to flee, because they "came there with lanterns, torches, and weapons" (John 18:3). Our Lord willingly identifies Himself with the words "I am," which testify to His deity. Amazingly, "they drew back and fell to the ground" (John 18:6). Jesus had given them a glimpse of His glory, which knocked them over. Clearly Jesus is not apprehended against His will; God's will is being accomplished!

Earlier Jesus testifies about His life, "No one takes it from Me, but I lay it down of Myself" (John 10:18). He is in total control; Jesus' demeanor portrays the second part of the contrasting proverb: "The wicked flee when no one pursues, but the righteous are bold as a lion" (Proverbs 28:1). We should also remain calm when trials come, because our sovereign Lord governs the universe.

Employment Point: *Yield to the One who freely gave up His life for you.*

JUNE 10

2 CHRONICLES 32–33, WITH JOHN 18:24–40

—◆—

Pilate said to Him, "What is truth?" (John 18:38).

WHAT IS THE DIFFERENCE BETWEEN PERCEPTION AND REALITY?

The Assyrian army enters Judah and surround Jerusalem. The *perception* is that Hezekiah would be better off surrendering than to allow the city to be decimated. The Assyrian king taunts Hezekiah and disparages the LORD God (2 Chronicles 32:9–19). Yet Hezekiah understands *reality*. He says, "Be strong and courageous; do not be afraid nor dismayed before the king of Assyria, nor before all the multitude that is with him; for there are more with us than with him" (2 Chronicles 32:7). The God of truth, who places you in the majority when He is on your side, sends His angel to smite the Assyrian army, and Sennacherib is subsequently murdered (2 Chronicles 32:21).

Similarly Pilate, the Roman governor, seemingly has the upper hand with Jesus, which is the *perception*. In *reality* Jesus could easily defeat Pilate. Jesus says, "If My kingdom were of this world, My servants would fight, so that I should not be delivered to the Jews" (John 18:36).

EMPLOYMENT POINT: *Trust in the God of truth above perception.*

—◆—

JUNE 11

2 CHRONICLES 34–36, WITH JOHN 19:1–22

———◦———

I find no fault in Him (John 18:38; 19:4, 6).

WOULD THERE BE ENOUGH EVIDENCE TO CONVICT YOU OF BEING A CHRISTIAN?

The Jewish authorities couldn't make a case against Jesus. Paul says, "And though they found no cause ["cause" is translated "fault" in John 18:38; 19:4, 6] for death in Him, they asked Pilate that He should be put to death" (Acts 13:28). This explains why Jesus qualifies to be the unique spotless Lamb of God.

Although Josiah isn't perfect, yet he is a man of integrity. "And he did what was right in the sight of the LORD, and walked in the ways of his father David; he did not turn aside to the right hand or to the left" (2 Chronicles 34:2). Josiah lived in a corrupt world, but didn't submit to its values. We must walk with integrity like Josiah and follow Jesus' path. "For to this you were called, because Christ also suffered for us, leaving us an example, that you should follow His steps" (1 Peter 2:21).

EMPLOYMENT POINT: *Live for Jesus, so that others could convict you of being a Christian.*

———◦———

JUNE 12

EZRA 1–2, WITH
JOHN 19:23–42

It is finished! (John 19:30).

WHAT IS THE MEANING OF JESUS' SIXTH SAYING ON THE CROSS?

The Greek term *tetelestai* is a perfect tense verb, which conveys a completed action with the results continuing. This word has been found written across tax bills in Jesus' day signifying "paid in full." No wonder the crying out of "paid in full" precedes Jesus' seventh statement on the cross: "Father, into Your hands I commit My spirit" (Luke 23:46).

Jesus' mission consisted of dying for the world's sin. John the Baptist grasps this profound concept, exclaiming, "Behold! The Lamb of God who takes away the sin of the world!" (John 1:29). Jesus died in our behalf to pay the price for sin and offer us eternal life. Perhaps Paul says it best: "For He made Him who knew no sin to be sin for us, that we might become the righteousness of God in Him" (2 Corinthians 5:21). God's Lamb sacrificed Himself that we could have a relationship with Him!

EMPLOYMENT POINT: *Receive Jesus' full payment for your sin, to receive the gift of eternal life.*

JUNE 13

EZRA 3–5, WITH
JOHN 20

———◆———

Rejoice Always (1 Thessalonians 5:16).

WHAT THREE RESULTS WILL YOU EXPERIENCE FROM JESUS' PRESENCE?

Thomas is not present at this post-resurrection appearance of Jesus (John 20:19–25). Yet we learn three key principles from His emergence. When Jesus first appears, He says, "Peace be with you" (John 20:19). First, His presence brings peace. "When He had said this, He showed them His hands and His side. Then the disciples were glad when they saw the Lord" (John 20:20).

Next, Jesus' presence brings joy. He imparts to them a temporary filling of the Holy Spirit, which would help sustain them spiritually until the day of Pentecost. Subsequently He states, "If you forgive the sins of any, they are forgiven them; if you retain the sins of any, they are retained" (John 20:23).

Third, Jesus presence brings power to witness; Christ's calling is His enabling. Paul gives the principle the following way: "He who calls you is faithful, who also will do it" (1 Thessalonians 5:24).

EMPLOYMENT POINT: *Walk with Jesus for peace, joy, and power to witness.*

———◆———

JUNE 14

EZRA 6–8, WITH JOHN 21

But be doers of the word (James 1:22).

DOES YOUR BIBLE STUDY GO THIRD PERSON (HE), FIRST PERSON (I), AND THEN SECOND PERSON (YOU)?

Ezra is a practitioner of this method. "Ezra had prepared his heart to seek the Law of the LORD, and to do it, and to teach statutes and ordinances in Israel" (Ezra 7:10). Bible study begins in the third person with the author's message. We learn, "Ezra had prepared his heart to seek the Law of the LORD." Next, it goes to first person (I), which is communicated by the words "and to do it." *I* must personally employ the Word as Ezra did before moving to stage three. The final part of this paradigm shows us the second person (you) through the words "and to teach statutes and ordinances in Israel." In other words, what you've learned from the author (third person) and applied (first person) gets shared to others (second person).

Peter didn't practice what he preached. He claimed to love Jesus more than the other disciples (John 21:15), which leads to Jesus' public correction.

EMPLOYMENT POINT: *Study your Bible, employ what you learn, and then teach others.*

JUNE 15

EZRA 9–10, WITH
ACTS 1

———◦———

You shall receive power when the Holy Spirit has come upon you (Acts 1:8).

WHAT ENABLING POWER DOES THE BAPTISM OF THE HOLY SPIRIT IMPART TO THE BELIEVER?

The Holy Spirit during the Old Testament could come upon and leave the saints. After David sins, he prays, "And do not take Your Holy Spirit from me" (Psalm 51:11). Shortly after Jesus' ascension, the Spirit permanently remains in believers. Jesus states the purpose of the baptism of the Spirit in Acts 1:8, "But you shall receive power when the Holy Spirit has come upon you; and you shall be witnesses to Me in Jerusalem, and in all Judea and Samaria, and to the end of the earth."

The Spirit's power to witness for Jesus is manifest in Acts 2; Peter, who formerly denied the Lord three times, preaches with power after being baptized by the Spirit and three thousand men are saved. Peter's audience "when they heard this [his preaching], they were cut to the heart, and said to Peter and the rest of the apostles, 'Men and brethren, what shall we do?'" (Acts 2:37).

EMPLOYMENT POINT: *Boldly proclaim Jesus' death, burial, and resurrection through the indwelling Holy Spirit.*

———◦———

JUNE 16

NEHEMIAH 1–3, WITH ACTS 2:1–13

I sat down and wept, and mourned for many days (Nehemiah 1:4).

WHAT DO BROKENNESS AND BEING USED BY GOD HAVE IN COMMON?

Nehemiah receives the report about the brokenness of his own people (the Jews) and the walls in Jerusalem (Nehemiah 1:2–3). This leads to Nehemiah's brokenness, which prepares him to be used greatly by the Lord. Isaiah depicts the person that God employs. He writes, "But on this one will I look; on him who is poor and of a contrite spirit, and who trembles at My word" (Isaiah 66:2). Similarly, the greatest sermon ever preached from a mountain, which shows what happens when God's Word is lifted up, begins by Jesus expressing, "Blessed are the poor in spirit, for theirs is the kingdom of heaven" (Matthew 5:3).

After Peter denies the Lord three times, Jesus looks him in the eye. "So Peter went out and wept bitterly" (Luke 22:62). The former proud fisherman would subsequently be used to become a fisher of men. Jesus fills this broken man with His Spirit, and great things happen (Acts 2).

EMPLOYMENT POINT: *Anticipate God doing great things through your brokenness.*

JUNE 17

NEHEMIAH 4–6, WITH
ACTS 2:14–47

They perceived that this work was done by our God (Nehemiah 6:16).

HOW IMPORTANT IS UNITY AMONG GOD'S PEOPLE?

Nehemiah and his fellow Jews encounter great opposition during the rebuilding of the wall; however, they sacrificially worked together and did the impossible. "So the wall was finished on the twenty-fifth day of Elul, in fifty-two days" (Nehemiah 6:15). The Lord's people work together, and by His strength accomplish the impossible.

The early church also had a seemingly impossible mission: to reach the world with the gospel (Acts 1:8). They similarly exhibit unity and see God do great things. Luke writes, "And they continued steadfastly in the apostles' doctrine and fellowship, in the breaking of bread, and in prayers" (Acts 2:42). Amazingly these dynamic saints grew in their knowledge of the Bible and then sacrificially "sold their possessions and goods, and divided them among all, as anyone had need" (Acts 2:45). No wonder that "the Lord added to the church daily those who were being saved" (Acts 2:47).

EMPLOYMENT POINT: *Humbly and sacrificially work together to accomplish great things for God.*

JUNE 18

NEHEMIAH 7–8, WITH ACTS 3

For the joy of the LORD is your strength (Nehemiah 8:10).

WHERE DO YOU DERIVE YOUR STRENGTH?

God energizes His people and the wall around Jerusalem is built in just fifty-two days (Nehemiah 6:15). Now that the city is protected, it is time for the peoples' spiritual renovation. The reading of God's Word humbles the Israelites. "For all the people wept, when they heard the words of the Law" (Nehemiah 8:9). Nehemiah reminds the saints to celebrate because of their newfound obedience. He says, "Do not sorrow, for the joy of the Lord is your strength" (Nehemiah 8:10).

Peter and John come upon an impoverished man who was "lame from his mother's womb" (Acts 3:2). Peter supernaturally heals the beggar. Luke records the healed man's response, "So he, leaping up, stood and walked and entered the temple with them—walking, leaping, and praising God" (Acts 3:8). His newfound ability to walk led to jubilant adoration for God. "And all the people saw him walking and praising God" (Acts 3:9).

EMPLOYMENT POINT: *Celebrate God's goodness, and allow His joy to energize you.*

JUNE 19

NEHEMIAH 9–11, WITH ACTS 4:1–22

Nor is there salvation in any other (Acts 4:12).

ARE YOU FOLLOWING THE RIGHT LEADER?

Nehemiah reviews how God faithfully led the Israelites. "Yet in Your manifold mercies You did not forsake them in the wilderness. The pillar of the cloud did not depart from them by day, to lead them on the road; nor the pillar of fire by night, to show them light, and the way they should go" (Nehemiah 9:19). The Lord longs for His children to travel the well-lit path behind Him.

In Acts 4, Peter and John seek to guide the rebellious religious leaders to Jesus (Acts 4:5–21). Although they reject Jesus who alone can save them, Peter and John keep pointing others to Him. Similarly Jesus challenges a group of disciples in John 6 to fully follow Him, but they turn away (John 6:53–66). "Then Jesus said to the twelve, 'Do you also want to go away?' But Simon Peter answered Him, 'Lord, to whom shall we go? You have the words of eternal life'" (John 6:67–68).

EMPLOYMENT POINT: *Follow Jesus, who alone is the way to God.*

JUNE 20

NEHEMIAH 12–13, WITH ACTS 4:23–37

Remember me, O my God, for good! (Nehemiah 13:31).

HOW CAN YOU BECOME BOLD FOR JESUS?

The Book of Nehemiah begins (Nehemiah 1:5–11) and ends (Nehemiah 13:31) with prayer. The bookends of prayer reveal that Nehemiah continued steadfastly in prayer and would launch missile prayers when needed. Four times in the closing chapter he asks God to remember either him or others (Nehemiah 13:14, 22, 29, 31). Nehemiah lives up to Paul's exhortation, "Pray without ceasing" (1 Thessalonians 5:17). Let's consider Nehemiah's prayer life to be exhibit one.

Jesus' apostles are also given to prayer. Luke describes a time when the religious leaders are persecuting them. "And when they had prayed, the place where they were assembled together was shaken; and they were all filled with the Holy Spirit, and they spoke the word of God with boldness" (Acts 4:31). Both Nehemiah (exhibit one) and the apostles (exhibit two) model great boldness as a result of powerful praying. Prayer is a conduit that moves the hand of God to embolden us!

EMPLOYMENT POINT: *Maintain a consistent prayer life, to receive boldness from Jesus.*

JUNE 21

ESTHER 1–3, WITH ACTS 5:1–16

Be filled with the Spirit (Ephesians 5:18).

WHO CONTROLS YOUR LIFE?

The saints in Jerusalem suffer from poverty. For this reason Barnabas, and saints like him, sell their property and give the money to the apostles to distribute to the needy (Acts 4:32–37). Ananias and Sapphira covet the attention that some of these believers receive for their generosity; therefore, they concoct a lie that they gave all their money from selling their land to the apostles. Peters calls out Ananias on his hypocrisy, and asks, "Why has Satan filled your heart to lie to the Holy Spirit and keep back part of the price of the land for yourself?" (Acts 5:3).

Sapphira follows in the steps of her husband and experiences a similar demise. The Lord strikes both Ananias and Sapphira dead for their duplicity. These children of God permit Satan to control this decision and it cost them their lives. The term "filled" in Acts 5:3 is the same Greek word that appears in Ephesians 5:18.

EMPLOYMENT POINT: *Permit God to control your life, not Satan.*

JUNE 22

ESTHER 4–6, WITH
ACTS 5:17–42

Do not fear those who kill the body but cannot kill the soul (Matthew 10:28).

ARE YOU WILLING TO RISK YOUR LIFE FOR JESUS?

Haman is a Jew-hater; he wants to see them exterminated. Mordecai recognizes that God has sovereignly placed Esther in favor with the king and challenges the queen to sacrifice her life if necessary to protect His chosen people. He understands, "The king's heart is in the hand of the LORD, like the rivers of water; He turns it wherever He wishes" (Proverbs 21:1). That is why Mordecai asks Esther, "Yet who knows whether you have come to the kingdom for such a time as this?" (Esther 4:14).

Then we have Peter and the apostles who were commanded to stop preaching the gospel. They respond, "We ought to obey God rather than men" (Acts 5:29). The religious hierarchy desires permanently to silence the apostles. Yet Gamaliel speaks up about their effort, "but if it is of God, you cannot overthrow it—lest you even be found to fight against God" (Acts 5:39).

EMPLOYMENT POINT: *Risk your life for Jesus, because He gave His life for you.*

JUNE 23

ESTHER 7–10, WITH ACTS 6

But we will give ourselves continually to prayer and to the ministry of the word (Acts 6:4).

HOW IMPORTANT IS IT TO KEEP THE MAIN THING THE MAIN THING?

When Esther is challenged by Mordecai to reveal her ethnicity and petition the king for protection, she instructs others to fast, which includes prayer (Esther 4:15–17). God honors the fasting and prayer with victories over the enemies. By God's grace Mordecai and Esther triumphed by maintaining the right priority.

As the church grows, the needs of the people increase. Although the Lord had instructed the disciples to care for the brethren, as illustrated by His washing their feet in John 13, the apostles understand the necessity to keep the main thing the main thing. Luke writes, "Then the twelve summoned the multitude of the disciples and said, 'It is not desirable that we should leave the word of God and serve tables'" (Acts 6:2). God significantly honors their priorities, "Then the word of God spread, and the number of the disciples multiplied greatly in Jerusalem" (Acts 6:7).

EMPLOYMENT POINT: *Maintain your spiritual priorities, for the church to flourish.*

JUNE 24

JOB 1–3, WITH
ACTS 7:1–19

———◦———

And that man [Job] was blameless and upright, and one who feared
God and shunned evil (Job 1:1).

HOW WOULD GOD SUMMARIZE YOUR CHARACTER?

Job is a rare man. Twice he is described as having stellar character like
Noah and Daniel (Ezekiel 14:14, 20). Furthermore God sums up his
life as having integrity, walking uprightly, being a God-fearing man,
and who turns away from evil. Job determines that he would not
compromise his life by allowing himself to be tempted needlessly. He
describes his commitment to God in Job 31:1, "I have made a covenant with my eyes; why then should I look upon a young woman?"

Like David, Job determines not to gaze upon worthless and
wicked things and chooses not to know wickedness experientially.
The psalmist writes, "I will set nothing wicked [worthless] before my
eyes; I hate the work of those who fall away; it shall not cling to me.
A perverse heart shall depart from me; I will not know wickedness"
(Psalm 101:3–4). Let's imitate Noah, Daniel, David, and Job.

EMPLOYMENT POINT: *Commit to habitually turn away from evil
and to God.*

———◦———

JUNE 25

JOB 4–6, WITH
ACTS 7:20–43

———◆———

For he [Moses] supposed that his brethren would have understood that God would deliver them by his hand, but they did not understand (Acts 7:25).

ARE YOU SURPRISED WHEN PEOPLE DON'T UNDERSTAND YOUR ACTIONS?

Stephen shares how the Israelites didn't initially grasp God raising up Moses to deliver them. Similarly, Job's friends jump to the wrong conclusion about his suffering. Eliphaz asks, "Remember now, who ever perished being innocent? Or where were the upright ever cut off?" (Job 4:7). The so-called friends of Job don't fathom both the person and work of the Lord.

God's ways are higher than our ways and most people will not fathom them. For instance, do you think anyone perceived why Joshua and the Israelites march around the walls of Jericho? Or did it make sense to either army why David approaches Goliath with a sling and a stone, not wearing armor? Paul astutely writes, "But he who is spiritual judges all things, yet he himself is rightly judged by no one" (1 Corinthians 2:15). Great heroes of the faith take God at His Word and act upon it; it doesn't matter what people may think.

EMPLOYMENT POINT: *Follow God, even if it means being misunderstood.*

———◆———

JUNE 26

JOB 7–9, WITH
ACTS 7:44–60

Look! I see the heavens opened and the Son of Man standing at the right hand of God! (Acts 7:56).

WHY IS JESUS DEPICTED AS STANDING?

Jesus sat down when He ascended to God's right hand. This posture characterizes our Lord's completed work. Conversely, the Old Testament high priest's work is never done. One article of furniture that isn't in the Holy of Holies is a chair, because yearly the high priest on the Day of Atonement (Yom Kippur) offers a sacrifice for his sins, and then for the nation (Leviticus 16). The missing piece of furniture communicates that the high priest's work isn't permanently done.

Josephus, a Jewish historian, recorded that there were eighty-three high priests who served from the time of Aaron (the first high priest) to the destruction of the temple in AD 70. Now, why is Jesus cited twice by Luke as "standing at the right hand of God" (Acts 7:55–56)? He is standing to receive the church's first martyr into heaven. We should boldly serve the Lord even in the face of death!

EMPLOYMENT POINT: *Fiercely serve Jesus until death, anticipating His personal greeting.*

JUNE 27

JOB 10–12, WITH
ACTS 8:1–25

———◦———

Therefore those who were scattered went everywhere preaching the word (Acts 8:4).

WHAT ARE YOU DOING TO EVANGELIZE THE WORLD?

Our Lord both equips His disciples for witnessing and also formulates a plan to reach the world. "But you shall receive power when the Holy Spirit has come upon you; and you shall be witnesses to Me in Jerusalem, and in all Judea and Samaria, and to the end of the earth" (Acts 1:8). His disciples evangelize Jerusalem (Acts 2–7), but need a loving shove to get them to Judea and Samaria. "At that time a great persecution arose against the church which was at Jerusalem; and they were all scattered throughout the regions of Judea and Samaria" (Acts 8:1).

Great men and women of God prayerfully develop a plan to reach the lost. Paul shares, "And so I have made it my aim to preach the gospel, not where Christ was named" (Romans 15:20). God's apostle established a plan and thrived on His grace. Paul attributes his mission accomplishments to grace (1 Corinthians 15:10).

EMPLOYMENT POINT: *Develop a God-given strategy to reach the lost.*

———◦———

JUNE 28

JOB 13–15, WITH
ACTS 8:26–40

———— ◦ ————

Preach the word! Be ready in season and out of season (2 Timothy 4:2).

ARE YOU ALWAYS READY TO PROCLAIM JESUS?

Philip had a fruitful ministry in Samaria. "And the multitudes with one accord heeded the things spoken by Philip, hearing and seeing the miracles which he did" (Acts 8:6). Nonetheless he quickly leaves the populated area at the direction of the Lord to go to Gaza, which is desert. The submissive evangelist understands Jesus' words to His disciples, "Follow Me, and I will make you fishers of men" (Matthew 4:19). Jesus enables us to catch souls when we are dedicated followers.

God's servant is not only an obedient evangelist, but also a student of the Word. When the man of Ethiopia was perplexed about Isaiah 53, "Then Philip opened his mouth, and beginning at this Scripture, preached Jesus to him" (Acts 8:35). Philip imitates His Lord who spoke to two disciples on the road to Emmaus. "And beginning at Moses and all the Prophets, He expounded to them in all the Scriptures the things concerning Himself" (Luke 24:27). Let's do likewise!

EMPLOYMENT POINT: *Always be ready to proclaim Jesus.*

———— ◦ ————

JUNE 29

JOB 16–18, WITH
ACTS 9:1–22

———◦◦◦———

Whoever desires to come after Me, let him deny himself, and take up his cross, and follow Me (Mark 8:34).

"LORD, WHAT DO YOU WANT ME TO DO?" (ACTS 9:6).

Jesus confronts Paul and he's saved. The new convert yields to Jesus' will, as shown by the following eight-word question: "Lord, what do You want me to do?" (Acts 9:6). Jesus has plans for Paul. He says to Ananias about Paul, "Go, for he is a chosen vessel of Mine to bear My name before Gentiles, kings, and the children of Israel" (Acts 9:15).

Jesus also has a blueprint for us (Mark 8:34). Our Lord gives three nonnegotiable commands to His disciples. The first two imperatives are given in the aorist tense, which means a once-and-for-all action, and the last is put forth in the present tense, which shows continual motion. First, we must deny self. That is, we are to practice our position of being co-crucified with Jesus (Galatians 2:20). Next, we must be willing to suffer for the One who suffered for us by taking up the cross. Finally, we are to habitually follow Him.

EMPLOYMENT POINT: *Ask not what Jesus can do for you, but what you can do for Him.*

———◦◦◦———

JUNE 30

JOB 19–20, WITH
ACTS 9:23–43

———◦———

How long will you torment my soul, and break me in pieces with words? (Job 19:2).

WHERE SHOULD YOU TURN WHEN THREATENED VERBALLY OR PHYSICALLY?

Job's so-called friends slice and dice him with words. He lacks human encouragement because even his wife suggested, "Curse God and die!" (Job 2:9). (The Hebrew term for "curse" literally means "bless," but Job's wife uses the word sarcastically, as reflected in the English translation.) Job responds by looking beyond his wife and friends to the Almighty. "For I know that my Redeemer lives, and He shall stand at last on the earth; and after my skin is destroyed, this I know, that in my flesh I shall see God" (Job 19:25–26).

Similarly Paul is threatened, but his attackers seek his demise. Luke writes, "The Jews plotted to kill him" (Acts 9:23). Paul rightly turns to Jesus' disciples, but they reject him; therefore, Barnabas, whose name means "son of encouragement," latches onto the recent convert and he's finally accepted. Job and Paul experience the encouragement and protection that comes only through the Lord.

EMPLOYMENT POINT: *Trust in Jesus, who can secure you physically and spiritually.*

———◦———

JULY 1

JOB 21–22, WITH
ACTS 10:1–23

———◆———

I am the way, the truth, and the life (John 14:6).

HOW THEN CAN YOU COMFORT ME WITH EMPTY WORDS, SINCE FALSEHOOD REMAINS IN YOUR ANSWERS? (JOB 21:34).

Job's insensitive friends fail to help him because they do not convey God's truth. Conversely Peter, the apostle to the Jews, is given clarity concerning God's heart for the Gentiles salvation, and is subsequently commissioned to bring Cornelius the gospel. The apostle to the Jews receives a divine dispatch to cross ethnic lines and bring the good news to Gentiles.

As Job's miserable comforters misunderstand the nature of God, so Peter needs to be shown that Jesus died for the Gentiles too. He is told about the Gentiles, whom the Jews considered unclean scavenger dogs, "What God has cleansed you must not call common" (Acts 10:15). When Jesus died the veil of the temple was torn from top to bottom, signifying that everyone now has access to God (Matthew 27:51). Paul writes, "But now in Christ Jesus you [Gentiles] who once were far off have been brought near by the blood of Christ" (Ephesians 2:13).

EMPLOYMENT POINT: *Bring the gospel of truth to all people.*

———◆———

JULY 2

JOB 23–25, WITH
ACTS 10:24–48

———◦———

In truth I perceive that God shows no partiality (Acts 10:34).

WITH WHOM SHOULD YOU SHARE THE GOSPEL?

The Lord calls some people to reach a particular ethnicity. Paul writes, "God shows personal favoritism to no man . . . the gospel for the uncircumcised [Gentiles] had been committed to me, as the gospel for the circumcised [Jews] was to Peter" (Galatians 2:6–7). Although you might be given a target group for Jesus, you are to proclaim Him to everyone who comes upon your path because salvation is universally available through faith in Jesus' finished work.

Luke, who is a Gentile, articulates that Jesus died for all people: "To Him all the prophets witness that, through His name, whoever believes in Him will receive remission of sins" (Acts 10:43). As Peter who is called to reach the Jews leads the Gentile Cornelius to Jesus, seek to bring anyone who will come to Him. Paul reveals the heart of God "who desires all men to be saved and to come to the knowledge of the truth" (1 Timothy 2:4).

EMPLOYMENT POINT: *Lead all people to the impartial Savior.*

———◦———

JULY 3

JOB 26–28, WITH
ACTS 11

———◦———

Indeed these are the mere edges of His ways (Job 26:14).

ARE YOU STRENGTHENING YOUR FAITH THROUGH VIEWING THE FRINGES OF GOD'S WAYS?

Job responds to Bildad and points out the observable vast power of God (Job 26:11–14). The suffering servant expresses that the visible manifestation of the Lord's might are "the mere edges" or "the fringes of His ways." In other words, the extraordinary awesomeness of those things we can see testifies that they are merely the tip of the iceberg when it comes to the omnipotent (all-powerful) God. We should consider the greatness of God's handiwork through creation.

David often viewed the clear sky in Bethlehem while tending his father's flock; he is awed at the Lord's creation. He pens, "The heavens declare the glory of God; and the firmament shows His handiwork. Day unto day utters speech, and night unto night reveals knowledge" (Psalm 19:1–2). As you consider God's might through creation, remember that this is just "the mere edges of His ways." We get a glimpse of the Father's glory through our senses to perceive His unfathomable majesty.

EMPLOYMENT POINT: *Marvel at God's revealed magnificence.*

———◦———

JULY 4

JOB 29–30, WITH ACTS 12

———————

Are they not all ministering spirits sent forth to minister for those who will inherit salvation? (Hebrews 1:14).

WHAT IS A KEY ROLE FOR ANGELS IN THE BOOK OF ACTS?

The question from Hebrews 1:14 expects an answer of "yes." God regularly used angels in the Old Testament to rescue His saints. He used them to deliver Lot (Genesis 19), Daniel (Daniel 6), and Elisha (2 Kings 6:13–17). These ministering spirits were regularly dispatched to do the work of the Lord.

Luke's first use of the term "angel" in the book of Acts points to the apostles being set free from prison by an angel of the Lord (Acts 5:19). God uses angels not only to give a physical deliverance of His saints, but also emancipation from sin through their direction. This is the case with Philip (Acts 8:26) and Cornelius (Acts 10:3, 7; 11:13). An angel of the Lord is sent to free Peter from prison as a response to the church's prayers (Acts 12:7–11). Furthermore, God uses an angel to smite Herod (Acts 12:23), whom earlier executed James (Acts 12:2).

EMPLOYMENT POINT: *Know that God uses angels for physical and spiritual deliverance.*

———————

JULY 5

JOB 31–32, WITH
ACTS 13:1–23

———◦———

I have made a covenant with my eyes; why then should I look upon a young woman? (Job 31:1).

TO WHOM DOES GOD REVEAL HIS WAYS?

Job's reverence for God is displayed by his commitment to holiness (Job 31:1, 9–11). Our Lord's servants must lead consecrated lives to receive His direction. "Pursue peace with all people," the writer of Hebrews pens, "and holiness, without which no one will see the Lord" (Hebrews 12:14). Leading a sanctified life to the Master avails us the privilege to receive His guidance.

Luke introduces us to a diverse group of dedicated Christians, among whom are Barnabas and Paul. The latter receive direction when "the Holy Spirit said, 'Now separate to Me Barnabas and Saul for the work to which I have called them'" (Acts 13:2). It is not just any spirit that gives particular guidance, but the Holy Spirit. Our gracious Father governs His set-apart children by a Divine Escort, who also enables us to know Him intimately. Jesus says, "Blessed are the pure in heart, for they shall see God" (Matthew 5:8).

EMPLOYMENT POINT: *Live a holy life to God and receive His guidance.*

———◦———

JULY 6

JOB 33–34, WITH ACTS 13:24–52

But God raised Him from the dead (Acts 13:30).

DO YOU INCLUDE THE RESURRECTION OF JESUS IN YOUR GOSPEL PRESENTATIONS?

Years ago, I taught a Christian Life and Witness class at a local Bible college. I asked the students to evaluate the gospel tracts at their church to see if the resurrection was included. My surprised students returned and reported that the resurrection isn't even mentioned in a portion of the tracts. Sadly, only half a gospel is given within these defective tracts, which isn't a full gospel presentation.

You will not find, as you read through the Book of Acts, Jesus' resurrection being omitted in the frequent gospel proclamations given. Perhaps the clearest text on the gospel of Jesus Christ is found in 1 Corinthians 15:3–4, which is worthy of memorization. Paul states, "For I delivered to you first of all that which I also received: that Christ died for our sins according to the Scriptures, and that He was buried, and the He rose again the third day according to the Scriptures."

EMPLOYMENT POINT: *Include Jesus' death and resurrection in your gospel presentations.*

July 7

Job 35–37, with Acts 14

———◆———

Yes, and all who desire to live godly in Christ Jesus will suffer persecution (2 Timothy 3:12).

Do you view the Christian life as a playground or battleground?

No person ever modeled godliness like Jesus. Yet He suffered spiritual separation from His Father because He took our sin upon Himself (Matthew 27:46) and physical excruciating pain as He was scourged and crucified. Peter writes, "Therefore, since Christ suffered for us in the flesh, arm yourselves also with the same mind" (1 Peter 4:1). Speaking about suffering, Peter also pens, "For to this you were called, because Christ also suffered for us, leaving us an example, that you should follow His steps" (1 Peter 2:21). We will also face persecution for walking with the Lord.

Paul imitates Jesus and after being stoned in Lystra (Acts 14:19) returns to minister in that very city (Acts 14:21). Our suffering for identifying with Jesus demonstrates our authenticity—as it did for Paul (2 Corinthians 11:16–33). Let's put our armor on, and anticipate spiritual warfare for identifying with Jesus.

EMPLOYMENT POINT: *Expect to experience suffering when you live a godly existence for Jesus.*

———◆———

JULY 8

JOB 38–39, WITH
ACTS 15:1–21

———◆———

Oh, send out Your light and Your truth! (Psalm 43:3).

WHO IS THIS WHO DARKENS COUNSEL BY WORDS WITHOUT KNOWLEDGE? (JOB 38:2).

The primary meaning of "darkens" is *to obscure*. God corrects Job's deluded friends. He says, "You have not spoken of Me what is right, as My servant Job has" (Job 42:8). We must always strive to accurately represent the Lord.

In Acts 15 the apostles and elders are gathered together; they are seeking clarity on God's truth. Certain people were seeking to add elements of the Law to the gospel of grace. Peter says to the council in Acts 15:11, "But we believe that through the grace of the Lord Jesus Christ we [Jews] shall be saved in the same manner as they" [Gentiles]. Pay careful attention to Paul's words to his protégé Timothy. "Be diligent to present yourself approved to God, a worker who does not need to be ashamed, rightly dividing the word of truth" (2 Timothy 2:15). The Lord's servants must strive to understand truth through the Bible, which communicates God's nature and standard of truth to us.

EMPLOYMENT POINT: *Represent God accurately by studying His Word diligently.*

———◆———

JULY 9

JOB 40–42, WITH
ACTS 15:22–41

I know that You can do everything, and that no purpose of Yours can be withheld from You (Job 42:2).

HAVE YOU LIMITED GOD IN YOUR THINKING?

God graciously imparts to Job what he needs: a fresh perspective on His greatness. We have a choice to make when our omnipotent Lord shows us His might. The Israelites witness ten plagues upon the Egyptians and the parting of the Red Sea. They even see His supernatural provision during the wilderness wanderings. How did they react? "Yes, again and again they tempted God, and limited the Holy One of Israel" (Psalm 78:41). Israel chose to ignore the powerful deeds of the Lord.

Paul is under house arrest. He writes about the eternally blessed Father who blesses us abundantly (Ephesians 1:3; 2:6). His response to God's greatness is given in Ephesians 3:20. "Now to Him who is able to do exceedingly abundantly above all that we ask or think, according to the power that works in us." Let's meditate upon the vast ability of God as displayed in the Scriptures and trust Him for great things.

EMPLOYMENT POINT: *Ponder God's power, and trust Him for great things.*

July 10

Psalms 1–3, with
Acts 16:1–15

———————

He who abides in Me, and I in him, bears much fruit (John 15:5).

How can you thrive for Jesus?

Our Lord commands His disciples, "Abide in Me, and I in you" (John 15:4). When we obediently walk with Jesus we go from bearing fruit (John 15:4), to producing "much fruit" (John 15:5, 8), which glorifies God (John 15:8). Jesus desires His followers to produce fruit as we remain in Him.

Equally the Father is pleased when we avoid the company of sinners. The psalmist describes this individual, "But his delight is in the law of the Lord, and in His law he meditates day and night. He shall be like a tree planted by the rivers of water, that brings forth its fruit in its season, whose leaf also shall not wither; and whatever he does shall prosper" (Psalm 1:2–3). The Hebrew uses the *hiphil* (causative) form at the end of Psalm 1:3. This means that God causes the success for the individual who regularly meditates on the Word.

Employment Point: *Walk with Jesus through remaining in His Word and He will cause you to thrive.*

———————

JULY 11

PSALMS 4–6, WITH
ACTS 16:16–40

⸺◈⸺

Return, O LORD, deliver me! Oh, save me for Your mercies' sake! (Psalm 6:4).

TO WHOM DO YOU TURN WHEN YOU SUFFER?

David and Paul experience suffering and persecution. Being like-minded they pivot toward God in times of turmoil. David cries out, "Hear me when I call, O God of my righteousness!" (Psalm 4:1). Often the man after God's own heart faces peril and turns to the Lord.

Paul and Silas are beaten with rods and put in the stocks, which only contributes to their physical misery. "But at midnight Paul and Silas were praying and singing hymns to God, and the prisoners were listening to them" (Acts 16:25). Did you notice that Paul and Silas are singing hymns *to* God, and not *about* God? Moreover, David and Paul thrive walking with God and simultaneously display their faith to others during the trials. Paul lives what he preaches: "Rejoice always, pray without ceasing, in everything give thanks" (1 Thessalonians 5:16–18). Let's imitate David and Paul by trusting in our heavenly Father during turbulent times.

EMPLOYMENT POINT: *Display your faith in God, despite your circumstances.*

⸺◈⸺

JULY 12

PSALMS 7–9, WITH
ACTS 17:1–15

What is man that You are mindful of him? (Psalm 8:4).

ARE YOU CAUSING THE WORLD TO STAND ON ITS HEAD?

God uses the weak for His glory. The Hebrew term for "man" in Psalm 8:4 refers to *mortal man* or *man in his weakness*. Yet God can use the weakness of man to bring Him glory.

It is said of Paul and Silas, "These who have turned the world upside down have come here too" (Acts 17:6). God's missionaries understand their own frailty, and communicate the powerful good news about Jesus' death and resurrection. Paul concludes his message to those at Thessalonica, "This Jesus whom I preach to you is the Christ" (Acts 17:3). The Thessalonians that come to Christ also turn the world on its head. Paul writes to these saints, "For from you the word of the Lord has sounded forth, not only in Macedonia and Achaia, but also in every place. Your faith toward God has gone out" (1 Thessalonians 1:8). We should follow in their steps!

EMPLOYMENT POINT: *Proclaim the crucified and resurrected Lord, to turn this world upside-down.*

JULY 13

PSALMS 10–12, WITH
ACTS 17:16–34

For no other foundation can anyone lay than that which is laid, which is Jesus Christ (1 Corinthians 3:11).

IF THE FOUNDATIONS ARE DESTROYED, WHAT CAN THE RIGHTEOUS DO (PSALM 11:3)?

Paul attempts to teach the Athenians that, "He [God] has made from one blood every nation" (Acts 17:26). That is, all people come from Adam. The wise apostle strives to show the blind Greeks that everyone has strayed from God and subsequently will be judged. Paul the prosecutor continues, "because He has appointed a day on which He will judge the world in righteousness by the Man whom He has ordained. He has given assurance of this to all by raising Him from the dead" (Acts 17:31).

Ever since Adam sinned the world has been on shaky ground and needs a Savior. The apostle to the Gentiles directs his audience to the stability that is found in Jesus Christ, who conquered death. Similarly we need to point people to Jesus our Judge; He lived a perfect life, died as our substitute on the cross, defeated death, and will return as Judge.

EMPLOYMENT POINT: *Direct the lost to Jesus, who alone is the soul's firm foundation.*

JULY 14

PSALMS 13–16, WITH ACTS 18

And that from childhood you have known the Holy Scriptures [the Old Testament], which are able to make you wise for salvation through faith which is in Christ Jesus (2 Timothy 3:15).

COULD YOU LEAD SOMEONE TO JESUS FROM THE OLD TESTAMENT?

Apollos learns this skill. Luke writes, "For he vigorously refuted the Jews publicly, showing from the Scriptures [the Old Testament] that Jesus is the Christ" (Acts 18:28). Similarly Peter possesses the same ability as Apollos. In Acts 2:27 he preaches about Jesus; Peter quotes Psalm 16:10, which says, "For You will not leave my soul in Sheol, nor will You allow Your Holy One to see corruption." Both Apollos and Peter display a facility of the Old Testament worthy of imitation.

Paul likewise uses the Old Testament as a witness to Jesus' death, burial, and resurrection. "For I delivered to you first of all that which I also received: that Christ died for our sins according to the Scriptures, and that He was buried, and that He rose again the third day according to the Scriptures" (1 Corinthians 15:3–4). Skillful witnesses to Christ utilize the Old Testament to direct people to Jesus.

EMPLOYMENT POINT: *Be able to guide people to Jesus from the Old Testament.*

July 15

Psalms 17–18, with
Acts 19:1–20

———————

For by You I can run against a troop, by my God I can leap over a wall (Psalm 18:29).

Has the Lord's arm been shortened (Numbers 11:23)?

Our question derives from God's promise to feed Israel with meat in the wilderness. Moses thought initially that the Lord's promise is impossible. (After all, there were more than two million people!) How could anyone satisfy those craving meat? Isn't that the point? Only God could supply the large quantity of meat that the children of Israel longed for.

Psalm 18 pertains to David escaping from Saul's army. The omnipotent Father who previously enables David to fell Goliath continues to equip him to do the improbable. He does the same for Paul. "Now God worked unusual miracles by the hands of Paul" (Acts 19:11). The Lord is not limited like we are. He even chose to offer salvation to the world by placing His Son into Mary's womb. The angel then reminds her, "For with God nothing will be impossible" (Luke 1:37). Let's keep our eyes of faith upon the Almighty Father.

Employment Point: *Walk with God and allow Him to do the impossible through you.*

———————

JULY 16

PSALMS 19–21, WITH
ACTS 19:21–41

———

Little children, keep yourselves from idols (1 John 5:21).

HOW DO YOU GUARD YOURSELF FROM IDOLATRY?

An idol is sort of like a proper noun: It can be a particular person, place, or thing. In the case of the worshipers of Diana, it is a thing. The temple of Diana, which is one of the seven ancient wonders of the world, allegedly fell from the sky. Imagine this colossal structure—239 feet wide and 418 feet long—just falling to the earth. Thankfully, Paul has the courage to proclaim the living God to the idol-worshipers at Ephesus.

Indeed, David isn't enlightened by an idol but by the heavens and God's Word. He writes about the Father's revelation through creation, "The heavens declare the glory of God; and the firmament shows His handiwork" (Psalm 19:1). Moreover, he testifies to God's revelation through His Word. "The law of the LORD is perfect, converting the soul" (Psalm 19:7). Moreover David adds, "And in keeping them [the commandments] there is great reward" (Psalm 19:11).

EMPLOYMENT POINT: *Employ God's Word, to protect your heart from idols.*

———

JULY 17

PSALMS 22–24, WITH
ACTS 20:1–16

The LORD is my shepherd; I shall not want (Psalm 23:1).

ARE YOU CONFIDENT IN GOD'S ABILITY TO CARE FOR YOU PHYSICALLY AND SPIRITUALLY?

David and Paul are not strangers to danger. David's confidence shines when he writes, "Yea, though I walk through the valley of the shadow of death, I will fear no evil; for You are with me" (Psalm 23:4). The sweet psalmist of Israel knew danger many times and repeatedly experienced God's protective hand upon his life.

Paul lives in constant danger. Yet during one of his "killer sermons," which lasts all night, Eutychus falls asleep from the third story to his death. (The amount of people in the building coupled with the "many lamps" sucked up much oxygen, promoting slumber.) The Lord then supernaturally uses Paul to raise him from the dead. David and Paul experientially know: "The LORD is my shepherd; I shall not want." The Hebrew word "want" carries the idea of *lack*. Our Lord is equipped to meet all our needs; like David and Paul, we should trust in His provision!

EMPLOYMENT POINT: *Rely upon the Shepherd's provision, both physically and spiritually.*

JULY 18

PSALMS 25–27, WITH ACTS 20:17–38

For to me, to live is Christ, and to die is gain (Philippians 1:21).

HOW PASSIONATE ARE YOU FOR THE LORD?

David and Paul lack no small challenges. Nonetheless their hearts beat to please God. Although David's foes seek his demise, he writes, "One thing I have desired of the LORD, that will I seek: That I may dwell in the house of the LORD all the days of my life, to behold the beauty of the LORD, and to inquire in His temple" (Psalm 27:4). No wonder David is labeled a man after God's own heart.

Similarly, Paul who faces grave opposition, says, "But none of these things move me; nor do I count my life dear to myself, so that I may finish my race with joy, and the ministry which I received from the Lord Jesus, to testify to the gospel of the grace of God" (Acts 20:24). An intimate knowledge of God will motivate you to pursue His presence and serve Him well. Both David and Paul derive their purpose and satisfaction in life from the Lord.

EMPLOYMENT POINT: *Actively seek and serve the living God.*

JULY 19

PSALMS 28–30, WITH ACTS 21:1–14

The LORD will give strength to His people; the LORD will bless His people with peace (Psalm 29:11).

ARE YOU EXPERIENCING PEACE DURING ADVERSITY?

David becomes a paradox to the world; he comes to know God's peace in the midst of trials. He writes, "Yea, though I walk through the valley of the shadow of death, I will fear no evil; for You are with me" (Psalm 23:4). Furthermore, David encounters joy when his enemies pursue him. He writes, "You prepare a table before me in the presence of my enemies; You anoint my head with oil; my cup runs over" (Psalm 23:5). The man after God's heart knows both adversity and peace.

Agabus predicts Paul's suffering in Jerusalem. How does the apostle to the Gentiles respond to his friends? "What do you mean by weeping and breaking my heart? For I am ready not only to be bound, but also to die at Jerusalem for the name of the Lord Jesus" (Acts 21:13). Paul senses peace, which comes from dedication to God. He declares, "For to me, to live is Christ, and to die is gain" (Philippians 1:21).

EMPLOYMENT POINT: *Anticipate Jesus' peace, because He is with you as you suffer.*

July 20

Psalms 31–33, with Acts 21:15–40

He who covers his sins will not prosper, but whoever confesses and forsakes them will have mercy (Proverbs 28:13).

IS CONFESSION GOOD FOR THE SOUL?

Many Bible scholars believe that David, in Psalm 32, is describing his experience relating to committing adultery with Bathsheba and having Uriah killed. David portrays the *weightiness* (the literal meaning of the Hebrew term translated "heavy") of his unconfessed sin. "For day and night Your hand was heavy upon me; my vitality was turned into the drought of summer" (Psalm 32:4).

The Lord pressured David until he confessed his sin. Initially he attempted to cover up these transgressions, but encountered oppressive opposition from his soul's maker. The man after God's own heart learns a valuable lesson. "He who covers his sins will not prosper, but whoever confesses and forsake them will have mercy" (Proverbs 28:13). Centuries later John would write, "If we confess our sins, He is faithful and just to forgive us our sins and to cleanse us from all unrighteousness" (1 John 1:9). Don't delay your confession.

EMPLOYMENT POINT: *Abstain from covering up your sin and confess it quickly, to avoid God's heavy hand.*

JULY 21

PSALMS 34–35, WITH ACTS 22

I will bless the LORD at all times; His praise shall continually be in my mouth (Psalm 34:1).

HOW CONSISTENTLY DO YOU PRAISE THE LORD?

David is in a precarious position, according to the title of Psalm 34. He acts like a madman before the king of Gath in order to preserve his life (1 Samuel 21:10–15). How could David praise God at a time like this? On many prior occasions he experienced the protective hand of God. The Lord had rescued him from a bear, a lion, and the clutches of Goliath. This is why he says, "Oh, taste and see that the LORD is good; blessed is the man who trusts in Him!" (Psalm 34:8).

Jesus is fully dependable; His loving nature is unchanging. "Jesus Christ" pens the writer of Hebrews "is the same yesterday, today, and forever" (Hebrews 13:8). For this reason, "by Him [Jesus] let us continually offer the sacrifice of praise to God, that is, the fruit of our lips, giving thanks to His name" (Hebrews 13:15). Jesus eternally remains the same, and should receive our praise regardless of our circumstances.

EMPLOYMENT POINT: *Unceasingly praise the unchanging God.*

JULY 22

PSALMS 36–37, WITH
ACTS 23:1–11

Delight yourself also in the LORD, and He shall give you the desires of your heart (Psalm 37:4).

WHAT IS YOUR HEART'S DESIRE?

The Lord's will for Paul is communicated to Ananias, "Go, for he is a chosen vessel of Mine to bear My name before Gentiles, kings, and the children of Israel" (Acts 9:15). God's heart soon becomes Paul's heart. Has the Lord's mission for your life become your heart's pleasure? If so, the Lord will strengthen you to represent Him well. He longs to bless those whose hearts find their fulfillment in Him.

Observe how the Lord affirms Paul after a difficult encounter with the Pharisees and Sadducees. "But the following night the Lord stood by him and said, 'Be of good cheer, Paul; for as you have testified for Me in Jerusalem, so you must also bear witness at Rome'" (Acts 23:11). Like Paul, Jesus also embraces God's will. His mindset is predicted in Psalm 40:8, "I delight to do Your will, O my God" (see Hebrews 10:5–9). The Father delights in those who delight doing His will.

EMPLOYMENT POINT: *Find your satisfaction in God, and receive your heart's desire.*

July 23

Psalms 38–40, with Acts 23:12–35

He has put a new song in my mouth—praise to our God; many will see it and fear, and will trust in the LORD (Psalm 40:3).

Are people coming to Jesus because of your new song?

David is rescued from a dangerous situation and blesses the Lord with a new song (Psalm 40). Time and time again the man of God experiences the Father's protection and deliverance, which leads to songs of praise.

Paul also knows the ability of God to deliver him from a precarious place (Acts 23:12–35). Moreover, were Paul and Silas anticipating the Lord releasing them from prison in Acts 16? Even before being set free (after having been beaten with rods and put in the stocks) "Paul and Silas were praying and singing hymns to God" and Luke adds, "and the prisoners were listening to them" (Acts 16:25). Subsequently the prison guard and his family come to Jesus after God intervenes for this dynamic duo (Acts 16:34). Because our heavenly Father has saved us, people need to hear our new song. The world desperately needs to hear heaven's tune through us!

Employment Point: *Let the unsaved experience the saving power of your new song.*

JULY 24

PSALMS 41–43, WITH ACTS 24

As the deer pants for the water brooks, so pants my soul for You, O God (Psalm 42:1).

DO YOU LONG FOR GOD?

We sing a song at church derived from Psalm 42:1. One day a young man asked me with all seriousness, "What are deer pants?" Although today I won't address clothing for deer, let me explain the meaning of "pants." The term refers to a strong and audible thirsting. As a parched deer strongly and loudly pants for water, we should equally desire the Lord.

Psalm 63:1–2 characterizes a panting after the Lord: "O God, You are my God; early will I seek You; my soul thirsts for You; my flesh longs for You in a dry and thirsty land where there is no water. So I have looked for You in the sanctuary, to see Your power and Your glory." We are to cultivate a passion for the Father's presence. "My soul thirsts for God," writes the psalmist, "for the living God" (Psalm 42:2). Let's seek after the Lord with every fiber in our being.

EMPLOYMENT POINT: *Long for the Lord's presence, as the dehydrated deer pants for water.*

JULY 25

PSALMS 44–46, WITH ACTS 25

———◆———

Your throne, O God, is forever and ever (Psalm 45:6).

WHO IS SITTING UPON THE THRONE OF YOUR HEART?

God the Father is characterized as sitting upon the throne in Revelation 4. The heavenly choir praises Him, and proclaims, "Who was and is and is to come!" (Revelation 4:8). John captures the eternal nature and rulership of the Almighty by writing that He has always existed in the past, resides in the present, and will return in the future. Just knowing that our eternal Father habitually exists and rules should calm and remind us to let Him have the rightful place on the throne of our hearts.

Hebrews 1:8 shows like Father like Son when the Father says to the Son, "Your throne, O God, is forever and ever." Clearly the Father calls Jesus, God. Jesus doesn't hesitate to claim equality with His Father. He tells a group of angry Jews, "I and My Father are one" (John 10:30). He is equally worthy to govern our lives; let's bow down to the Father and Son!

EMPLOYMENT POINT: *Offer God the Father, and God the Son, the throne of your heart.*

———◆———

JULY 26

PSALMS 47–49, WITH ACTS 26

Go into all the world and preach the gospel to every creature (Mark 16:15).

IS YOUR HEART ALIGNED WITH GOD'S?

Paul seeks to lead Agrippa to Jesus. The king replies, "You almost persuade me to become a Christian" (Acts 26:28). Paul's heart beats like Jesus'. He shares, "I would to God that not only you, but also all who hear me today, might become both almost and altogether such as I am" (Acts 26:29). Although Paul, whose name means "small," might be little in stature, yet he has a large heart for the lost.

The psalmist also understands the value of souls. Concerning those who trust in riches, he says, "For the redemption of their souls is costly, and it shall cease forever" (Psalm 49:8). Consider Jesus' piercing question, "For what will it profit a man if he gains the whole world, and loses his own soul?" (Mark 8:36). Jesus was on a search-and-rescue mission. Let's imitate Him who said, "For the Son of Man has come to seek and to save that which was lost" (Luke 19:10).

EMPLOYMENT POINT: *Align your heart with Jesus' by seeking to reach the lost.*

JULY 27

PSALMS 50–52, WITH ACTS 27:1–25

The LORD is my light and my salvation; whom shall I fear? The LORD is the strength of my life; of whom shall I be afraid? (Psalm 27:1).

HOW CONFIDENT ARE YOU IN GOD'S ABILITY TO DELIVER YOU FROM DANGER?

The root meaning of "salvation" in Psalm 27:1 is *deliverance*. This same Hebrew term appears in Psalm 50:23, which says, "Whoever offers praise glorifies Me; and to him who orders his conduct aright I will show the salvation of God." Fearing God puts us on safety's path. Our Lord honors those who trust in Him by fearing His name.

Paul receives similar assurance in Acts 27:24–25 from an angel of the Lord. He is told, "Do not be afraid, Paul; you must be brought before Caesar; and indeed God has granted you all those who sail with you" (Acts 27:24). Let the Lord bolster your confidence as He did for Paul in Acts 27:25. "Therefore take heart, men, for I believe God that it will be just as it was told me." We should follow in the steps of God-fearing men like David and Paul, who experienced His protective hand.

EMPLOYMENT POINT: *Trust solely in God's delivering power during times of danger.*

JULY 28

PSALMS 53–55, WITH
ACTS 27:26–44

Friend, why have you come? (Matthew 26:50).

HOW SHOULD YOU RESPOND TO YOUR BETRAYER?

David is betrayed, and reveals his shock and hurt in Psalm 55:13–14. "But it was you, a man my equal, my companion and my acquaintance. We took sweet counsel together, and walked to the house of God in the throng." We are not sure who David refers to, but he is clearly a dear friend. You most likely have suffered at least one betrayal in your life by someone whom you trusted.

Jesus similarly has a close companion betray Him. Judas sells out the Lord Jesus for thirty pieces of silver (the price for a slave) after Jesus has loved Him and provided for his needs. There are two things you should do after being betrayed. First, thank God when you suffer like Jesus. Paul not only wants to know the power of Jesus' resurrection, but also "the fellowship of His sufferings" (Philippians 3:10). Second, thank God that you were betrayed and not vice versa.

EMPLOYMENT POINT: *Enter into Jesus' sufferings when betrayed, and give Him your burden to bear.*

JULY 29

PSALMS 56–58, WITH
ACTS 28:1–15

And we know that all things work together for good to those who love God, to those who are the called according to His purpose (Romans 8:28).

HOW WELL DO YOU APPLY ROMANS 8:28?

The title to Psalm 57 informs us that David is hiding in a cave from Saul. His confidence in God does not waver during this trying time. He writes in Psalm 57:2, "I will cry out to God Most High, to God who performs all things for me." Knowing that God "performs all things for me" has a New Testament counterpart. Paul testifies, "And we know that all things work together for good to those who love God, to those who are the called according to His purpose" (Romans 8:28).

Moreover because David understands that he serves "God Most High" (Psalm 57:2), he remains undaunted. He continues, "My heart is steadfast, O God, my heart is steadfast; I will sing and give praise" (Psalm 57:7). Our Lord gives us stability in the midst of normally unstable circumstances. Are you currently having a "cave experience"? Know that the Most High rules and oversees "all things" in your life.

EMPLOYMENT POINT: *Believe that God works all things together for your good.*

JULY 30

PSALMS 59–61, WITH
ACTS 28:16–31

———— ◆ ————

For You have been a shelter for me, a strong tower from the enemy (Psalm 61:3).

CAN GOD ACCOMPLISH GREAT THINGS IN YOUR LIFE WHEN YOU ARE LIMITED GEOGRAPHICALLY OR ON THE RUN?

David is on the lam; he hides in a cave from his enemies. What good can come from this? The Lord guides David to pen Psalms 57 and 142 out of his cave experience. David's place of shelter in a remote location leads to an expansion of his ministry. Only God could do this; He can expand our outreach while limiting us.

We find Paul under house arrest at the end of Acts 28. Remember that he is the man who wants to preach Christ where He has never been proclaimed (Romans 15:20). What good can come from the limitation placed upon him? First and foremost, he's ultimately God's prisoner and not Rome's (Ephesians 3:1; 4:1). From this remote location Paul writes Ephesians, Philippians, Colossians, and Philemon. Think about the global impact from Paul's isolation; God can do the same for you!

EMPLOYMENT POINT: *Trust God to broaden your ministry when He has limited you geographically.*

———— ◆ ————

JULY 31

PSALMS 62–64, WITH ROMANS 1

Now in the morning, having risen a long while before daylight, He went out and departed to a solitary place; and there He prayed (Mark 1:35).

DO YOU DAILY PENCIL JESUS INTO YOUR PLANNER FOR AN EARLY MORNING MEETING?

Jesus has a conference call scheduled with His Father during a busy time of ministry (Mark 1:32–39). He leaves a thriving ministry to meet with His Dad and subsequently receives direction from Him. The Lord successfully serves the Father as He daily waits upon His guidance. Indeed, from these sacred times together Jesus derives what to teach and what to do, which pleased His Father (John 8:28–29).

David also prioritizes early morning meetings with his heavenly Father. "O God," writes the psalmist, "You are my God; early will I seek You" (Psalm 63:1). Unbelievers have regularly shunned God through the ages. Paul writes, "although they knew God, they did not glorify Him as God" (Romans 1:21). Yet only the Almighty Father satisfies the soul's greatest longings. Jesus says, "Blessed are those who hunger and thirst for righteousness, for they shall be filled" (Matthew 5:6). Let's pursue Him passionately and regularly!

EMPLOYMENT POINT: *Seek God early and experience His direction and blessing.*

AUGUST 1

PSALMS 65–67, WITH ROMANS 2

———◦———

Let the peoples praise You, O God; let all the peoples praise You (Psalm 67:3).

DOES YOUR LIFE BRING PRAISE TO GOD?

Paul makes the argument that all people are sinners (Romans 1:18–3:20). He confronts the Jews for not living according to the very Law they proclaim (Romans 2:17–27). The title "Jew" derives from "Judah" and means *praise*. God desires His people to bring praise unto Him. This is a consistent theme throughout the Bible. Centuries before Paul writes, the poet shares: "Let the peoples praise You, O God; let all the peoples praise You" (Psalm 67:3).

Indeed, Paul shows that being a "true Jew" involves lifestyle more than ethnicity, and that all God's people are to bring praise to Him. Paul argues, "For he is not a Jew who is one outwardly, nor is circumcision that which is outward in the flesh; but he is a Jew who is one inwardly; and circumcision is that of the heart, in the Spirit, not in the letter; whose praise is not from men but from God" (Romans 2:28–29).

EMPLOYMENT POINT: *Live in such a way that your life brings praise to God.*

———◦———

AUGUST 2

PSALMS 68–69, WITH ROMANS 3

Save me, O God! (Psalm 69:1).

ARE YOU DROWNING IN SIN?

Once again David faces a dangerous situation. He equates the perilous environment to drowning. He cries out to the Deliverer, "For the waters have come up to my neck" (Psalm 69:1). Wisely David turns to the great Liberator.

Mankind is similarly drowning spiritually, "for all have sinned and fall short of the glory of God" (Romans 3:23). The good news is that the same God who emancipates David from the wicked will save all those who by faith turn to Him. God's rescue operation consists of imputing (putting into one's account) His righteousness to all who turn from their sin and place their faith in Jesus, who died for their sin and rose from the dead. Paul clearly affirms that imputed righteousness is freely given "through faith in Jesus Christ, to all and on all who believe" (Romans 3:22). The gift is available to all who will receive it by faith!

EMPLOYMENT POINT: *Receive freely God's righteousness, through believing on Jesus' finished work.*

AUGUST 3

PSALMS 70–72, WITH ROMANS 4

Blessed be the LORD God, the God of Israel, who only does wondrous things! (Psalm 72:18).

HOW GREAT IS THE OBJECT OF YOUR FAITH?

Our faith is only as good as its object. Solomon writes Psalm 72; he recognizes God's unparalleled ability to do the impossible. The Hebrew term "wondrous" used in Psalm 72:18 means *to do something wonderful, extraordinary,* or *difficult.* Solomon grasps the unique nature and power of God; he attributes to the Father an unprecedented and unrivaled capacity.

The Lord promises something impossible to Abraham; he would become the father of a nation, which he still believes as he enters the century mark. Paul writes, "He did not waver at the promise of God through unbelief, but was strengthened in faith, giving glory to God, and being fully convinced that what He promised He was also able to perform" (Romans 4:20–21). Romans 4 shows that only God does wondrous things. He alone could bring Isaac into the world when Abraham was approximately one hundred years old, and He alone can save our souls.

EMPLOYMENT POINT: *Embrace God's promises, knowing that He alone can fulfill them.*

August 4

Psalms 73–74, with Romans 5

For by one man's disobedience many were made sinners, so also by one Man's obedience many will be made righteous (Romans 5:19).

WHO ARE THE TWO MOST IMPORTANT PERSONS IN HISTORY?

Daniel, my second-born son, has a PhD in history. Frankly, he knows more about key historical personages than I'll ever know. Yet there are only two key historical people we must know. First, there is Adam; his act of disobedience caused us to receive his sinful nature, which brings death and eternal separation from God. The second notable character is Jesus. Paul gives us a stark contrast between the two: "For as in Adam all die, even so in Christ all shall be made alive" (1 Corinthians 15:22).

Like my son, we should want to teach history. Children of God should have the primary emphasis placed upon Jesus undoing Adam's transgression, by His death and resurrection. Knowing the correct history of both Adam and Jesus, as revealed in Scripture, will give you the necessary information that the unsaved world desperately needs to know. Will you be their history teacher?

EMPLOYMENT POINT: *Proclaim Jesus' death, burial, and resurrection as the solution to Adam's disobedience.*

AUGUST 5

PSALMS 75–77, WITH ROMANS 6

You are the God who does wonders; You have declared Your strength among the peoples (Psalm 77:14).

ARE YOU DAILY EXPERIENCING GOD'S STRENGTH IN YOUR LIFE?

You and I sit in a privileged seat. We have been raised with Jesus positionally to be situated in heavenly places (Ephesians 1:3; 2:6). Moreover, because of Jesus' death, we are crucified positionally with Him. For this reason Paul writes, "I have been crucified with Christ" (Galatians 2:20). As a result of our position in Christ (having been crucified and resurrected with Him), we should daily practice our position and lead victorious Christian lives.

Romans 6:1–4 testifies that we are free from sin because of our union with Jesus, and that we should now "walk in newness of life." In other words, we no longer are slaves to sin. Today, let's personalize Romans 6. Paul advises, "Likewise you also, reckon yourselves to be dead indeed to sin, but alive to God in Christ Jesus our Lord" (Romans 6:11). We should allow the God "who does wonders" to manifest His strength through our set-apart lives.

EMPLOYMENT POINT: *Walk in newness of life through your union with Jesus.*

AUGUST 6

PSALM 78, WITH ROMANS 7

Yes, again and again they tempted God, and limited the Holy One of Israel (Psalm 78:41).

ARE THOSE WHO DON'T LEARN FROM HISTORY DOOMED TO REPEAT THE SAME MISTAKES?

Asaph, the writer of Psalm 78, gives us a regrettable history on Israel. Yet they are God's chosen people and He repeatedly provides for them. What's their response? "And [they] forgot His works," writes Asaph, "and His wonders that He had shown them" (Psalm 78:11). The Lord continually extends mercy toward His special treasure (Israel) by guiding them in the wilderness—where they regularly murmur and complain. Asaph explains, "In the daytime also He led them with the cloud, and all the night with a light of fire" (Psalm 78:14). Patiently the Lord worked with His people despite their hardheartedness and independent spirit.

Paul, being aware of Old Testament history, reminds the New Testament saints that the ancient Scriptures "were written for our admonition" (1 Corinthians 10:11) and that "therefore let him who thinks he stands take heed lest he fall" (1 Corinthians 10:12). Let's learn from Israel's sins and not repeat them!

EMPLOYMENT POINT: *Don't grieve God by unbelief, and limit His vast power.*

AUGUST 7

PSALMS 79–81, WITH ROMANS 8:1–18

Restore us, O God; cause Your face to shine, and we shall be saved! (Psalm 80:3, 7, 19).

HOW SHOULD YOU RESTORE AND MAINTAIN A RIGHT RELATIONSHIP WITH GOD?

The writer of Psalm 80 pleads with his heavenly Father to return the blessing of the Lord upon a disobedient people. Confession of sin begins the restorative process. "He who covers his sins will not prosper, but whoever confesses and forsakes them will have mercy" (Proverbs 28:13). Moses also understands the importance of God's special presence. After Israel sinned with the golden calf, Moses petitions God. He pleads, "If Your Presence does not go with us, do not bring us up from here" (Exodus 33:15).

Even the great apostle Paul stumbled in his walk with God (Romans 7:15). He proclaims that the key to victory is found in walking by the Spirit's power. (The Spirit is mentioned nineteen times in Romans 8.) He writes, "For if you live according to the flesh you will die; but if by the Spirit you put to death the deeds of the body, you will live" (Romans 8:13).

EMPLOYMENT POINT: *Confess your sin, and depend upon the Spirit's power for victory over the flesh.*

AUGUST 8

PSALMS 82–84, WITH
ROMANS 8:19–39

For the LORD God is a sun and shield; the LORD will give grace and glory; no good thing will He withhold from those who walk uprightly (Psalm 84:11).

HOW CONFIDENT ARE YOU THAT GOD IS FOR YOU AND WILL COMPLETE HIS WORK IN YOU?

Paul uses five verbs to describe God's work of salvation: foreknew, predestined, called, justified, and glorified (Romans 8:29–30). He chose all past tense verbs—even "glorified." From God's vantage point, we will have a glorified body, which completes His work in us. Elsewhere Paul writes, "being confident of this very thing, that He who has begun a good work in you will complete it until the day of Jesus Christ" (Philippians 1:6).

Moreover, our heavenly Father did not spare His Son to bring us into a right relationship with Him. What greater sacrifice could He have offered? For this reason Paul asks, "If God is for us, who can be against us?" (Romans 8:31). Furthermore, consider "that neither death nor life, nor angels nor principalities nor powers, nor things present nor things to come . . . shall be able to separate us from the love of God which is in Christ Jesus our Lord" (Romans 8:38–39).

EMPLOYMENT POINT: *Embrace that God is for you and will complete His work in you.*

AUGUST 9

PSALMS 85–87, WITH ROMANS 9

Teach me Your way, O LORD; I will walk in Your truth; unite my heart to fear Your name (Psalm 86:11).

ARE YOUR DESIRES UNITED WITH GOD'S?

Paul is the apostle to the Gentiles (Romans 11:13). Yet he longs for all people to be saved. He shares, "For I could wish that I myself were accursed from Christ for my brethren, my countrymen according to the flesh" (Romans 9:3). Jesus directed Paul to the Gentiles; however, he is willing to be condemned eternally for the Jews to be saved. His heart beats with God's holy heart because Paul would be willing to offer himself for the lost (as did Jesus).

Paul expresses God's nature when he writes to Timothy, "who desires all men to be saved and to come to the knowledge of the truth" (1 Timothy 2:4). We have a high calling: "For to this end we both labor and suffer reproach," writes the apostle, "because we trust in the living God, who is the Savior of all men, especially of those who believe" (1 Timothy 4:10).

EMPLOYMENT POINT: *Unite your heart with Jesus' heart, and willingly lay down your life for the salvation of others.*

AUGUST 10

PSALMS 88–89, WITH ROMANS 10

———◦———

I will sing of the mercies of the LORD forever; with my mouth will I make known Your faithfulness to all generations (Psalm 89:1).

HOW RELIABLE ARE THE PROMISES OF GOD?

The Lord promises David an eternal house, throne, and kingdom (2 Samuel 7:12–16). Psalm 89:4 confirms this promise to David. The psalmist writes, "Your seed I will establish forever, and build up your throne to all generations." Although the nation of Israel rejected their Messiah, He will again nationally work with them in the future (Romans 11:1–2).

However, the Lord will be saving individual souls in the interim whether Jews or Gentiles. Paul pens, "For there is no distinction between Jew and Greek, for the same Lord over all is rich to all who call upon Him. For 'whoever calls on the name of the LORD shall be saved'" (Romans 10:12–13). Israel's rejection of the Messiah led to the birth of the church, so that individual Jews and Gentiles alike could be saved.

EMPLOYMENT POINT: *Proclaim God's faithfulness to all generations because His Word is trustworthy; the gospel of Jesus Christ should be heralded to Jew and Gentile alike.*

———◦———

AUGUST 11

PSALMS 90–92, WITH ROMANS 11:1–21

So teach us to number our days, that we may gain a heart of wisdom (Psalm 90:12).

HOW GOOD ARE YOU WITH THE ARITHMETIC OF LIFE?

The eternal God is our "dwelling place," which term means *refuge* or *security* (Psalms 90:1; 91:9–10). Moses, who writes the oldest psalm in the book of Psalms, gives a contrast between the eternal God as our security (Psalm 90:1–2) and frail man (Psalm 90:3–11). Moses understands man's mortality because he led the nation of Israel during the wilderness wanderings where all the men twenty and above died, except Joshua and Caleb (Numbers 14:29–32). This means that under his watch, there were more than 600,000 funerals (Number 1:46).

James tells us that our lives are like a vapor that appear and quickly vanish (James 4:14). Paul, who personally understands the frailty of life because of his plethora of enemies, writes, "Redeeming the time, because the days are evil" (Ephesians 5:16). Enroll in the "arithmetic of life" class, with God as your professor, because your stay on planet earth is brief.

EMPLOYMENT POINT: *Serve God diligently while you can, because life passes quickly.*

AUGUST 12

PSALMS 93–95, WITH ROMANS 11:22–36

Oh, the depth of the riches both of the wisdom and knowledge of God! How unsearchable are His judgments and His ways past finding out! (Romans 11:33).

WHEN WAS THE LAST TIME YOU STOOD IN AWE OF GOD?

When we read Romans 8 we learned that not only is God for us, but also that He will complete the good work that He had begun in us (Romans 8:28–39). Yet an objector to God's ability might ask, "Well, since God hasn't completed His work with Israel, how do we know that He'll finish what He's begun with us?" Paul's doxology in Romans 11:33–36 results from his contemplation of God's past, present, and future work with Israel (Romans 9:1–11:32). This is why he heaps praise upon the Almighty.

Similarly the psalmist recognizes the awesomeness of God's person and work. For this reason he writes, "Oh come, let us worship and bow down; let us kneel before the LORD our Maker. For He is our God, and we are the people of His pasture, and the sheep of His hand" (Psalm 95:6–7). Let us worship our Maker!

EMPLOYMENT POINT: *Praise the Lord, who masterfully will finish His work with us.*

AUGUST 13

PSALMS 96–98, WITH ROMANS 12

———◆———

I beseech you therefore, brethren, by the mercies of God, that you present your bodies a living sacrifice, holy, acceptable to God, which is your reasonable service (Romans 12:1).

WHAT IS THE "THEREFORE" THERE FOR, IN ROMANS 12:1?

I grew up watching the TV music-video series *Schoolhouse Rock*. One of the songs asks the question, "Conjunction junction, what's your function?" The "therefore" of Romans 12:1 is a conjunction—one which Paul uses to draw upon the previous eleven chapters to give the weighty exhortation in Romans 12:1–2.

The apostle argues that all people are sinners (Romans 1:18–3:20) and that God justifies the sinner by faith (Romans 3:21–5:21) and then explains that we are set apart for Him (Romans 6–8) and subsequently transitions to his masterful synopsis about Israel (Romans 9–11). Paul then deliberately instructs those for whom Christ died to get on the altar and stay there. He follows this admonition with the warning not to be squeezed into the mold of this world's system (Romans 12:2).

EMPLOYMENT POINT: *Dedicate yourself permanently to God's service.*

———◆———

AUGUST 14

PSALMS 99–102, WITH ROMANS 13

But put on the Lord Jesus Christ, and make no provision for the flesh, to fulfill its lusts (Romans 13:14).

WHAT IS YOUR PLAN TO BE LIKE JESUS AND NOT PROVIDE FOR THE FLESH?

Both David and Paul have a prescription for godliness: The holy tandem chooses to deliberately avoid wickedness. Paul advises to "make no provision for the flesh" (Romans 13:14). That is, the apostle decides that he will "walk properly, as in the day, not in revelry and drunkenness, not in lewdness and lust, not in strife and envy" (Romans 13:13).

David concurs with Paul's choice: "I will set nothing wicked before my eyes; I hate the work of those who fall away; it shall not cling to me. A perverse heart shall depart from me; I will not know wickedness" (Psalm 101:3–4). Our Lord desires us to be holy, and not to experientially know wickedness. Wisdom cries out not only to sidestep the path of evil, but also to "put on the Lord Jesus Christ." Carrying His Word in our hearts, with continual prayers on our lips, will help us to maintain this godly stance.

EMPLOYMENT POINT: *Discard the old sinful paths and put on Jesus.*

AUGUST 15

PSALMS 103–104, WITH ROMANS 14

For we shall all stand before the judgment seat of Christ (Romans 14:10).

IS GOD AN EXTREMIST WHEN IT COMES TO SIN REMOVAL?

David uses a merism (a figure of speech showing two extremes, encompassing its entirety) to make a point about God's mercy. He writes, "As far as the east is from the west, so far has He removed our transgressions from us" (Psalm 103:12). The sweet psalmist of Israel uses the merism "east from the west" to express that our sin is totally eliminated. No wonder he adds, "But the mercy of the LORD is from everlasting to everlasting on those who fear Him" (Psalm 103:17). In other words, God's mercy to us is beyond comprehension and incalculable.

The Father's love for His children is extraordinary; He placed the sin of the world upon His own Son in order that we could know forgiveness of sins and enjoy an intimate relationship with Him. Paul articulates this beautifully in 2 Corinthians 5:21: "For He made Him who knew no sin to be sin for us."

EMPLOYMENT POINT: *Praise God for His mercy that is lavished upon us through Jesus.*

AUGUST 16

PSALMS 105–106, WITH ROMANS 15:1–20

———◦———

So I sought for a man among them who would make a wall, and stand in the gap before Me on behalf of the land, that I should not destroy it; but I found no one (Ezekiel 22:30).

WHO HAVE YOU KEPT ALIVE THROUGH YOUR PRAYERS?

God was displeased with Israel because they made a golden calf and attributed the nation's deliverance from Egypt to an idol. "Therefore He said that He would destroy them, had not Moses His chosen one stood before Him in the breach" (Psalm 106:23). Furthermore, God would have killed Aaron too if Moses hadn't mediated for him after the incident with the golden calf (Deuteronomy 9:20). Prayer warriors who intercede for others might make the difference between life and death.

Life isn't about us fulfilling our fallen nature's desires through idolatry. John writes, "Little children, keep yourselves from idols" (1 John 5:21). Rather, we should be consumed with loving the Lord with every fiber in our being and demonstrating that love by caring for our neighbor. Paul writes, "We then who are strong ought to bear with the scruples of the weak, and not to please ourselves" (Romans 15:1).

EMPLOYMENT POINT: *Stand in the gap for others through intercessory prayer.*

———◦———

AUGUST 17

PSALMS 107–108, WITH ROMANS 15:21–33

They wandered in the wilderness in a desolate way; they found no city to dwell in (Psalm 107:4).

ARE YOU WANDERING AIMLESSLY?

Israel often strayed from God, so they lacked direction. Once they repented of their independent spirit (Psalm 107:6), God again directed them: "And He led them forth by the right way, that they might go to a city for a dwelling place" (Psalm 107:7). The Lord longs to direct His saints, but He patiently waits upon them to cry out to Him for help.

Paul, by way of contrast consistently walks with the Lord and enjoys His guidance. He writes, "But now I am going to Jerusalem to minister to the saints" (Romans 15:25). Why did Paul and his fellow laborers experience the Father's guiding light? He shares their holy ambition in 2 Corinthians 5:9. "Therefore we make it our aim, whether present or absent, to be well pleasing to Him." Paul and his associates practice Proverbs 3:6, which says, "In all your ways acknowledge Him, and He shall direct your paths."

EMPLOYMENT POINT: *Walk with God, to be led down the right path.*

AUGUST 18

PSALMS 109–111, WITH ROMANS 16

———————

The works of the LORD are great, studied by all who have pleasure in them (Psalm 111:2).

ARE YOU FAITHFULLY STUDYING THE LORD'S GREAT WORKS?

Psalm 111:2 begins in the Hebrew text with the word "great" because "great are the works of the LORD." David is a student of God's breathtaking handiwork. He writes, "The heavens declare the glory of God; and the firmament shows His handiwork" (Psalm 19:1). God's creative hand has given us an amazing world in which we live with many wonders to be contemplated.

We have the privilege not only to study God's great work of creation, but the inspired Word, which also reveals His awesomeness. The Bible is a progressive revelation. Paul refers to "the mystery kept secret since the world began but now made manifest, and by the prophetic Scriptures made known to all nations" (Romans 16:25–26). Biblically, the term "mystery" points to a sacred secret that once was unknown but now is revealed. It's our privilege to deeply probe these uncovered treasures; let's be committed students of His handiwork!

EMPLOYMENT POINT: *Study God's works and words, and marvel at His majesty.*

———————

August 19

Psalms 112–115, with
1 Corinthians 1

But our God is in heaven; He does whatever He pleases (Psalm 115:3).

Who is your source for wisdom?

Sadly, many from Israel had turned to idols for their supply of wisdom; they looked to inanimate objects for their guidance and blessing. The psalmist exposes their folly: "Those who make them [idols] are like them; so is everyone who trusts in them" (Psalm 115:8). Individuals who fashion idols are as ignorant as those who believe in them.

The Corinthian saints are exposed to a history of renowned philosophers whose stream of wisdom is limited to their own intelligence. Paul asks a question that shows the vanity of pursuing this world's wisdom. He rhetorically asks in 1 Corinthians 1:20, "Has not God made foolish the wisdom of this world?" True wisdom doesn't derive from idols or man's philosophy. Rather, it is to be found in a person: Jesus Christ. Paul writes about Him, "in whom are hidden all the treasures of wisdom and knowledge" (Colossians 2:3). Let's seek wisdom from its true source!

EMPLOYMENT POINT: *Pursue the Almighty God's wisdom through Jesus Christ.*

AUGUST 20

PSALMS 116–118, WITH 1 CORINTHIANS 2

For I determined not to know anything among you except Jesus Christ and Him crucified (1 Corinthians 2:2).

HOW RESOLVED ARE YOU TO STAY ON THE RIGHT MESSAGE?

Paul went to Corinth during his second missionary journey and founded this local church (Acts 18:1–17). Homer described Corinth as a wealthy but immoral city. When Plato referred to a prostitute, he used the term "Corinthian girl." Much of the immorality centered on the temple of Aphrodite, and its one thousand prostitutes. In essence, Corinth was a cesspool of immorality based upon idolatry.

The great apostle knows that only one thing could penetrate such a sin-laden people: the gospel of Jesus Christ. He calls it "the power of God" in 1 Corinthians 2:5. "For I am not ashamed of the gospel of Christ," Paul adds in Romans 1:16, "for it is the power of God to salvation for everyone who believes." Once Paul received the right message from Jesus, he vigorously heralded it everywhere that he traveled. We likewise, with great boldness, should trumpet the message of God to a darkened world embedded in sin.

EMPLOYMENT POINT: *Proclaim the gospel to the lost, trusting in its saving power.*

AUGUST 21

PSALM 119:1–48, WITH
1 CORINTHIANS 3

But he who is spiritual judges all things, yet he himself is rightly judged by no one (1 Corinthians 2:15).

ARE YOU A SPIRITUAL CHRISTIAN?

Paul founded the church at Corinth about AD 51, and writes this epistle to them around AD 56. They had five years to become spiritual, yet he assesses them as follows: "For you are still carnal" (1 Corinthians 3:3). He then adds continuing in the same verse, "For where there are envy, strife, and divisions among you, are you not carnal and behaving like mere men?" The apostle must have been heartbroken that the Corinthian saints had not become spiritually mature.

Similarly, the psalmist asks a penetrating question in Psalm 119:9. He queries, "How can a young man cleanse his way?" Subsequently he shows that the path to spiritual maturity is to obey God's Word, seek Him wholeheartedly, and to deposit His Word deeply within (Psalm 119:9–11). The believers at Corinth should have heeded the teachings of the Book of Psalms to please their spiritual father (Paul) and heavenly Father.

EMPLOYMENT POINT: *Apply what you've learned from the Bible, to become mature.*

August 22

Psalm 119:49–104, with 1 Corinthians 4

Your faithfulness endures to all generations; You established the earth, and it abides 119:90).

What does God expect from His servants?

Paul commands the saints at Corinth to "consider us, as servants of Christ and stewards of the mysteries of God" (1 Corinthians 4:1). The Greek term for "servants" later came to be used of galley slaves who rowed in the bottom tier of a ship. With humility, Paul describes himself and his fellow apostles in this manner. Is that your mindset?

The bondservant of Christ continues, "Moreover it is required in stewards that one be found faithful" (1 Corinthians 4:2). As God spectacularly created the earth and continually cares for it, we should humbly attend to the things of the Lord. Peter builds upon Paul's analogy when he writes, "As each one has received a gift [spiritual gift], minister it to one another, as good stewards of the manifold grace of God" (1 Peter 4:10). God has graced each believer with at least one spiritual gift; now we are to serve others as recipients of His grace.

Employment Point: *Serve the Lord faithfully, and with humility.*

AUGUST 23

PSALM 119:105–176, WITH 1 CORINTHIANS 5

My soul keeps Your testimonies, and I love them exceedingly (Psalm 119:167).

DO YOU LOVE GOD'S WORD AND DELIGHT TO OBEY ITS COMMANDS?

Paul receives a report that unfettered immorality has permeated the church at Corinth. Sadly, the church is not broken over the activity within, but rather embraces the sin and sinner. The apostle writes, "And you are puffed up, and have not rather mourned, that he who has done this deed might be taken away from among you" (1 Corinthians 5:2). Sin, like a festering wound, corrupts the church.

Apparently the man involved in the sin attends the church and is a believer, because Paul focuses only upon his removal (1 Corinthians 5:2–5). In this letter, Paul describes the church as a temple that houses the Holy Spirit (1 Corinthians 3:16). Moreover, he characterizes the individual believer the same way (1 Corinthians 6:19–20). The Almighty Father requires both to be holy because "without which [holiness] no one will see the Lord" (Hebrews 12:14). All saints should strive for personal holiness and church purity.

EMPLOYMENT POINT: *Love and obey God's Word, to maintain a holy life.*

AUGUST 24

PSALMS 120–123, WITH
1 CORINTHIANS 6

I will lift up my eyes to the hills—from whence comes my help? My help comes from the LORD, who made heaven and earth (Psalm 121:1–2).

DO YOU NOT KNOW THAT WE SHALL JUDGE ANGELS? (1 CORINTHIANS 6:3).

Paul's question from the Greek text expects the answer "yes." The Corinthian saints were going to secular law courts to have their church matters litigated. How sad! The embarrassed apostle reminds them that they should be able as God's children to resolve their issues in-house. Moreover, one day they will judge the evil angels, so they as Christians should be able to settle their disputes internally. These carnally minded saints displayed their "envy, strife, and divisions" (1 Corinthians 3:3) to an unbelieving world.

What is at the heart of their problem? They didn't look skyward for help. James declares, "But the wisdom that is from above is first pure, then peaceable, gentle, willing to yield, full of mercy and good fruits, without partiality and without hypocrisy" (James 3:17). Tragically, the Corinthians displayed worldly and not godly wisdom!

EMPLOYMENT POINT: *Seek heaven's wisdom to settle internal conflicts.*

AUGUST 25

PSALMS 124–127, WITH
1 CORINTHIANS 7:1–24

Behold, children are a heritage from the LORD, the fruit of the womb is a reward (Psalm 127:3).

DO YOU APPRECIATE THE GIFTS THAT GOD HAS GIVEN TO YOU?

There is a natural order to life; generally speaking, parents leave an inheritance to children. The writer of Proverbs concurs, "Houses and riches are an inheritance from fathers" (Proverbs 19:14). Additionally the verse concludes with, "but a prudent wife is from the LORD." Both a wise wife and children are presents from the Lord. We would do well to meditate upon these gifts from the Father of lights and regularly thank Him.

Speaking about gifts, God has given the blessing of sex to married couples. Marriage is the appropriate venue to enjoy the Lord's provision. This is why the apostle writes, "Nevertheless, because of sexual immorality, let each man have his own wife, and let each woman have her own husband" (1 Corinthians 7:2). These gifts are to be celebrated. James writes, "Every good gift and every perfect gift is from above" (James 1:17). Truly God is good, and has displayed His goodness to us.

EMPLOYMENT POINT: *Celebrate the gifts of a godly spouse and children.*

August 26

Psalms 128–131, with
1 Corinthians 7:25–40

Blessed is every one who fears the LORD, who walks in His ways (Psalm 128:1).

DO YOU WALK DAILY IN THE FEAR OF THE LORD?

Our heavenly Father doesn't show partiality. He pronounces His blessing upon each individual who chooses to revere Him and walk with Him. If you are single and walk with Him, then He promises to bless you too. Paul shows the advantage of being single in 1 Corinthians 7. He writes, "you may serve the Lord without distraction" (1 Corinthians 7:35). Daniel is one such biblical example; he is a single man who brings great glory to God. Indeed, he dedicates himself to God (Daniel 1:8) maintaining a close walk with Him through daily scheduled prayer (Daniel 6:10).

Whether single or married, the Lord desires to put His blessing upon those who choose to honor Him with their lives. Consider these blessings: "When you eat the labor of your hands, you shall be happy, and it shall be well with you" (Psalm 128:2). Since the Lord is eternally blessed (Romans 9:5), He loves to bless.

EMPLOYMENT POINT: *Fear God, who desires to bless those who walk with Him.*

AUGUST 27

PSALMS 132–135, WITH
1 CORINTHIANS 8

Let each of us please his neighbor for his good, leading to edification (Romans 15:2).

DO YOU PLACE YOUR BROTHERS AND SISTERS IN CHRIST ABOVE YOUR CHRISTIAN LIBERTY?

The Corinthian saints are saved out of a pagan lifestyle. Previously they worshiped idols and frequented the local temple. Excess meat from these sacrifices could be purchased at the temple. Paul's concern is that as Christians gathered for fellowship that someone would see the meat at the table from the temple and would not understand that "the earth is the LORD's, and all its fullness" (1 Corinthians 10:26). In other words, God created meat to be eaten, and there is nothing inherently wrong with enjoying His provision.

However, a new or immature believer might not grasp that "the earth is the LORD's, and all its fullness" and stumble as a result. In this case, Paul writes, "Therefore, if food makes my brother stumble, I will never again eat meat, lest I make my brother stumble" (1 Corinthians 8:13). The psalmist concurs that brethren should "dwell together in unity!" (Psalm 133:1). Let love govern your decisions.

EMPLOYMENT POINT: *Sacrifice your rights, in order not to cause a believer to stumble.*

August 28

Psalms 136–138, with 1 Corinthians 9

———◦———

I have fought the good fight, I have finished the race, I have kept the faith (2 Timothy 4:7).

How disciplined are you for Jesus?

The Greeks had both the Olympic and Isthmian games. Strict training standards were imposed upon the competitors; any contestant was disqualified to compete if he broke the rules leading up to the event. Paul's question in 1 Corinthians 9:24, therefore, expects an answer of "yes": "Do you not know that those who run in a race all run, but one receives the prize? Run in such a way that you may obtain it."

Athletes and Christians must focus upon the prize. The former strives for a temporal reward and the latter for an eternal. Paul explains, "And everyone who competes for the prize is temperate in all things. Now they do it to obtain a perishable crown, but we for an imperishable crown" (1 Corinthians 9:25). Let's anticipate the Lord's courage and strength. David exclaims, "In the day when I cried out, You answered me, and made me bold with strength in my soul" (Psalm 138:3).

Employment Point: *Sacrifice self-indulgence for Jesus, and await His reward.*

———◦———

August 29

Psalms 139–141, with
1 Corinthians 10:1–13

Search me, O God, and know my heart (Psalm 139:23).

Are you closely following the One who formed you in your mother's womb?

David is amazed by God's omniscience; He knows everything about David (Psalm 139:1–6). Then the man after God's own heart marvels at the Lord's omnipresence; He is everywhere (Psalm 139:7–12). Next, the sweet psalmist of Israel is astonished by the omnipotence of the Lord; He is all-powerful (Psalm 139:13–18). The Lord wove David in his mother's womb. No wonder David exclaims, "I will praise You, for I am fearfully and wonderfully made; marvelous are Your works; and that my soul knows very well" (Psalm 139:14).

God had called Israel to Himself; Moses' generation had great privileges. Paul uses "all" five times in 1 Corinthians 10:1–4 showing "all" that God did for them. Yet they rebelled. He warns the Corinthian saints, "Therefore let him who thinks he stands take heed lest he fall" (1 Corinthians 10:12). Similarly, we should be cautious not to imitate the same sinful patterns of the Israelites.

Employment Point: *Marvel at God's majesty, and submit to His design for your life.*

August 30

Psalms 142–144, with
1 Corinthians 10:14–33

Therefore, my beloved, flee from idolatry (1 Corinthians 10:14).

Where is your security?

David cries out to God for help from a cave (Psalm 142). Perhaps he is hiding from Saul or Absalom. He enjoys a straightforward relationship with the Lord. "I pour out my complaint before Him," writes David, "I declare before Him my trouble" (Psalm 142:2). Are you similarly transparent with your Father? To whom we turn in times of trouble reveals where our faith lies.

The man after God's own heart doesn't rely upon idols for protection. Rather, "I cried out to You, O LORD: I said, 'You are my refuge, my portion in the land of the living'" (Psalm 142:5). The root term for "refuge" occurs fifty-six times in the Old Testament and means *refuge* or *shelter*. Unlike Israel who many times in the past depended upon idols for their needs, David completely trusts in the living God. As David believes God will intervene in his behalf (Psalm 142:7), so should we.

Employment Point: *Cry out to the living God as your shelter in a time of storm.*

AUGUST 31

PSALMS 145–147, WITH
1 CORINTHIANS 11:1–15

How unsearchable are His judgments and His ways past finding out! (Romans 11:33).

HAS GOD EVER ASKED YOU FOR COUNSEL?

David writes, "Great is the LORD, and greatly to be praised; and His greatness is unsearchable" (Psalm 145:3). No mind will ever fully comprehend the vastness of the Lord's greatness; it is beyond finding out. Job is awed by God's knowledge. He exclaims, "He does great things past finding out, yes, wonders without number" (Job 9:10). Isaiah asks and then replies, "Have you not known? Have you not heard? The everlasting God, the LORD, the Creator of the ends of the earth, neither faints nor is weary. His understanding is unsearchable" (Isaiah 40:28).

Similarly, as Paul ponders the depth of God's wisdom and knowledge, he writes, "Oh, the depth of the riches both of the wisdom and knowledge of God! How unsearchable are His judgments and His ways past finding out!" (Romans 11:33). This leads to the apostle's following questions: "For who has known the mind of the LORD? Or who has become His counselor?" (Romans 11:34).

EMPLOYMENT POINT: *Pursue the greatness of God, and stand amazed at its vastness.*

September 1

Psalms 148–150, with
1 Corinthians 11:16–34

But let a man examine himself, and so let him eat of the bread and drink of the cup (1 Corinthians 11:28).

Are you regularly examining your life?

Socrates said that the unexamined life is not worth living. The Corinthian saints are not heeding this admonition. In the context of the Lord's Supper, Paul warns his spiritual children at Corinth about the danger of having unconfessed sin before participating in the ordinance. Because they are careless in handling the sacred, Paul writes, "For this reason many are weak and sick among you, and many sleep" (1 Corinthians 11:30). It should be noted that not only is the unexamined life not worthy living, but it also can kill you!

Believers should strive not to sin; however, we should quickly confess our sin when we fall short of God's standards. "If we confess our sins," writes John, "He is faithful and just to forgive us our sins and to cleanse us from all unrighteousness." Consider the following: "He who covers his sins will not prosper, but whoever confesses and forsakes them will have mercy" (Proverbs 28:13).

Employment Point: *Regularly examine yourself before God, and confess any known sin.*

September 2

Proverbs 1–2, with 1 Corinthians 12

The fear of the LORD is the beginning of knowledge (Proverbs 1:7).

Are you seeking the right kind of unity?

Proverbs 1:11–19 reveals the danger from the wrong kind of unity. The wicked cry out, "Cast in your lot among us, let us all have one purse" (Proverbs 1:14). Underline or highlight all the references to "we" and "us" from Proverbs 1:11–14 in your Bible. This kind of unity produces death; negative socialization takes an individual down the corridor of destruction (1 Corinthians 15:33).

Sadly, the Corinthian saints are not imitating the right kind of unity: the Trinity. Although the believers at Corinth lack no spiritual gift (1 Corinthians 1:7), they are selfishly using their gifts seeking to draw attention to themselves. Observe how Paul uses the Trinity as a model for diversity through unity in 1 Corinthians 12:4–6. "There are diversities of gifts, but the same Spirit. There are differences of ministries, but the same Lord. And there are diversities of activities, but it is the same God who works all in all."

EMPLOYMENT POINT: *Strive for spiritual unity through diversity, like the Trinity.*

September 3

Proverbs 3–4, with 1 Corinthians 13

And now abide faith, hope, love, these three; but the greatest of these is love (1 Corinthians 13:13).

Why is love more important than spiritual gifts?

Spiritual gifts are to be administered in love. Paul gives a series of overstatements (hyperboles) in 1 Corinthians 13:1–3, expressing that you can have great giftedness, but that if you don't exercise your gifts in love, it lacks substance. Spiritual gifts are temporal assets, but "love never fails" (1 Corinthians 13:8) because it is eternal. The Corinthian saints lacked no spiritual gift (1 Corinthians 1:7); yet they didn't focus on that which is eternal: love.

Our service for the Lord and life in general must be carried out in faith, which still remains (1 Corinthians 13:13). The wise man commands, "Trust in the LORD with all your heart, and lean not on your own understanding; in all your ways acknowledge Him, and He shall direct your paths" (Proverbs 3:5–6). We are not to be a self-supporting people and "lean" upon our own wisdom. *Knowing* [God] *intimately*, the literal meaning of "acknowledge," assures His direction in our lives.

Employment Point: *Love and trust God wholeheartedly while serving others.*

SEPTEMBER 4

PROVERBS 5–6, WITH
1 CORINTHIANS 14:1–20

Whoever commits adultery with a woman lacks understanding; he who does so destroys his own soul (Proverbs 6:32).

ARE YOU A PURSUER OF LUST OR LOVE?

The believers at Corinth are reminded by Paul to prioritize spiritual gifts in the church (1 Corinthians 12:28–31) and to use them lovingly (1 Corinthians 13). They are then commanded, "Pursue love, and desire spiritual gifts, but especially that you may prophesy" (1 Corinthians 14:1). These selfish saints place the speaking in tongues (foreign languages not previously learned by the speaker) above prophesying (both the foretelling and forth-telling of God's Word). Hence the admonition is given to "pursue love" by using the gifts properly, which edifies others. In essence, shows Paul, love "does not seek its own" (1 Corinthians 13:5).

Similarly, all believers need to protect their hearts. About the immoral woman, wisdom shouts out, "Do not lust after her beauty in your heart" (Proverbs 6:25). Don't give your heart to an evil woman: "Keep your heart with all diligence, for out of it spring the issues of life" (Proverbs 4:23).

EMPLOYMENT POINT: *Pursue loving God and your spouse, while guarding your heart.*

September 5

Proverbs 7–8, with
1 Corinthians 14:21–40

Say to wisdom, "you are my sister," and call understanding your nearest kin (Proverbs 7:4).

Are you closely related to wisdom and understanding?

During the Old Testament period, a sister was viewed as an intimate relative—the term was even used at times for one's wife (Song of Solomon 4:9–10, 12; 5:1–2). God's wisdom should become your intimate friend. Speaking about intimacy, the Lord's wisdom and understanding will protect you morally. These twins must be kept in close proximity. Proverbs 7:5 shows their value: "That they may keep you from the immoral woman, from the seductress who flatters with her words." Daily we should pursue these twin virtues; like buried treasure, they are to be sought with all diligence.

Paul relays the value of digging deeply into God's Word, which reveals Christ. About Him, Paul writes, "in whom are hidden all the treasures of wisdom and knowledge" (Colossians 2:3). Children of God are to "grow in the grace and knowledge of our Lord and Savior Jesus Christ" (2 Peter 3:18). Let's pursue wisdom through knowing Jesus!

Employment Point: *Foster intimacy with Jesus, and find wisdom and understanding.*

SEPTEMBER 6

PROVERBS 9–10, WITH
1 CORINTHIANS 15:1–32

The fear of the LORD is the beginning of wisdom, and the knowledge of the Holy One is understanding (Proverbs 9:10).

HAVE YOU BELIEVED IN THE ONE WHO POSSESSES ALL WISDOM AND KNOWLEDGE?

Proverbs 9:10 parallels Proverbs 1:7, with one difference. "The fear of the LORD is the beginning of knowledge," reveals Proverbs 1:7; whereas Proverbs 9:10 states, "The fear of the LORD is the beginning of wisdom." Both virtues (wisdom and knowledge) are found in Jesus Christ. Paul writes about Jesus, "in whom are hidden all the treasures of wisdom and knowledge" (Colossians 2:3). Jesus, the eternal Son of God, has forever inherently carried these twin traits, and desires to impart both wisdom and knowledge to His children.

The Corinthians needed to know Jesus personally, so that they could also have true wisdom and knowledge. This is why Paul travels to Corinth and preaches Christ's death, burial, and resurrection to them. "Moreover, brethren," writes Paul to the Corinthian saints approximately five years after first visiting them, "I declare to you the gospel which I preached to you, which also you received and in which you stand" (1 Corinthians 15:1).

EMPLOYMENT POINT: *Receive the gospel, to know God's wisdom and knowledge.*

September 7

Proverbs 11–12, with
1 Corinthians 15:33–58

—◆—

He who heeds counsel is wise (Proverbs 12:15).

HOW BRIGHTLY WILL YOU SHINE ETERNALLY?

Paul is the Corinthian saints' spiritual father (1 Corinthians 4:14–15). He longs for them to receive a full reward. In the context of the resurrection, Paul reports, "There is one glory of the sun, another glory of the moon, and another glory of the stars; for one star differs from another star in glory. So also is the resurrection of the dead" (1 Corinthians 15:41–42). As there are varying degrees of glory for the stellar bodies, will there also be differences in glorified bodies? The apostle implies that some saints will have a greater degree of glory.

Daniel agrees with Paul's teaching: "Those who are wise shall shine like the brightness of the firmament, and those who turn many to righteousness like the stars forever and ever" (Daniel 12:3). The prophet concurs with Paul by using a similar analogy. He shows that the saints who loyally serve God receive a greater eternal glory.

EMPLOYMENT POINT: *Zealously serve the Lord now, to shine brightly forever.*

—◆—

SEPTEMBER 8

PROVERBS 13–14, WITH
1 CORINTHIANS 16

There is one who makes himself rich, yet has nothing; and one who makes himself poor, yet has great riches (Proverbs 13:7).

HAVE YOU MADE YOURSELF POOR TO BECOME RICH?

Paul feels deeply for the impoverished saints in Jerusalem; therefore, he collects money from the churches to meet their needs. A weekly offering had already been established. The apostle to the Gentiles writes, "as I have given orders to the churches of Galatia, so you must do also. On the first day of the week let each one of you lay something aside, storing up as he may prosper, that there be no collections when I come" (1 Corinthians 16:1–2). Guided by the Holy Spirit, Paul set the precedence for regular giving through the local church to support the ministry.

Moreover, Paul elaborates on the command for the saints to give to their church in 2 Corinthians 8–9. He offers up Jesus as a pattern for sacrificial giving because He left heavenly riches becoming poor to make us rich. "For you know the grace of our Lord Jesus Christ, that though He was rich, yet for your sakes He became poor, that you through His poverty might become rich" (2 Corinthians 8:9).

EMPLOYMENT POINT: *Imitate Jesus and make yourself poor, to become rich.*

September 9

Proverbs 15–16, with 2 Corinthians 1

There is a way that seems right to a man, but its end is the way of death (Proverbs 16:25).

Whom do you depend upon for safety?

Proverbs 28:26 reveals, "He who trusts in his own heart is a fool, but whoever walks wisely will be delivered." Fools live dangerously by self-reliance. The wise man reveals this in Proverbs 16:25 and also similarly in Proverbs 14:12. Twice the proverb is given to emphasize to us the importance of its lesson.

Conversely Paul trusts in the Lord. Yet his life is in constant danger. Nonetheless the apostle relies upon the Lord's ability to rescue him. Observe the three tenses in 2 Corinthians 1:10. Let's consider the context, beginning with 2 Corinthians 1:9: "Yes, we had the sentence of death in ourselves, that we should not trust in ourselves but in God who raises the dead, who delivered [past tense] us from so great a death, and does deliver [present tense] us; in whom we trust that He will still deliver [future tense] us." God's past and present deliverance assures Paul that He'd do the same in the future.

Employment Point: *Depend upon God's protective hand always.*

SEPTEMBER 10

PROVERBS 17–18, WITH 2 CORINTHIANS 2

For we are to God the fragrance of Christ among those who are being saved and among those who are perishing (2 Corinthians 2:15).

ARE YOU EMITTING THE FRAGRANCE OF CHRIST TO ALL WHO GET A WHIFF OF YOU?

Paul carries a heavy burden because his associate Titus cannot be found. Yet he writes, "Now thanks be to God who always leads us in triumph in Christ, and through us diffuses the fragrance of His knowledge in every place" (2 Corinthians 2:14). Mature saints display wisdom that grasps the Lord's sovereignty and boasts that He victoriously leads His saints to triumph regardless of the circumstances.

The imagery Paul describes consists of a Roman general who has just experienced triumph over his enemies, and then leads a victorious procession. For Paul, Jesus leads the march as a conquering general. Furthermore, the Roman parade would be accompanied by the release of sweet smells from burning spices. Likewise, our witness for Jesus should waft the aroma of His presence!

EMPLOYMENT POINT: *Glorify God by emitting the fragrance of Christ wherever He leads you.*

September 11

Proverbs 19–20, with 2 Corinthians 3

———⸺◈⸺———

The discretion of a man makes him slow to anger, and his glory is to overlook a transgression (Proverbs 19:11).

Who equips you to be a minister of the New Testament?

Paul's integrity suffers reproach by false teachers in 2 Corinthians. They are influencing the saints at Corinth to rebel against their spiritual father. The much-maligned pastor could easily walk away from the Corinthians whom he sacrificed greatly to reach with the gospel. He doesn't because the Lord is the One who brought Him to Corinth—and continues to strengthen his resolve to shepherd them.

How does a minister of the new covenant (New Testament) continue in the face of great opposition? Paul writes, "Not that we are sufficient of ourselves to think of anything as being from ourselves, but our sufficiency is from God, who also made us sufficient as ministers of the new covenant" (2 Corinthians 3:5–6). As ministers of the New Testament we must also continue to serve Jesus faithfully despite tremendous resistance, by deriving our inner strength via the Holy Spirit.

Employment Point: *Trust in God's sufficiency for you, as a minister of the New Testament.*

———⸺◈⸺———

SEPTEMBER 12

PROVERBS 21–22, WITH 2 CORINTHIANS 4

———◦———

Therefore, since we have this ministry, as we have received mercy, we do not lose heart (2 Corinthians 4:1).

HAVE YOU CHOSEN TO BE DISCOURAGED?

Challenges and difficulties are part of life, but to be discouraged is a choice. Paul and his associates are given the ministry of the new covenant. Along with the calling comes God's mercy. That is, He equips us to endure every obstacle because His calling is His enabling. In other words, since the Lord calls us to ministry, He strengthens us to continue in the face of opposition.

Paul has a thorn in the flesh. Three times he seeks God to remove the pain. The Lord's response to Paul's impassioned pleas, "My grace is sufficient for you, for My strength is made perfect in weakness" (2 Corinthians 12:9). As Paul learns to boast about his infirmities, so should we. He continues in the same verse, "Therefore most gladly I will rather boast in my infirmities, that the power of Christ may rest upon me." Bravery and non-discouragement come with God's mercy.

EMPLOYMENT POINT: *Receive God's mercy and grace, instead of discouragement.*

———◦———

September 13

Proverbs 23–24, with
2 Corinthians 5

Apply your heart to instruction, and your ears to words of knowledge (Proverbs 23:12).

Are you living up to your new capacity in Christ?

Paul reminds the Corinthian saints about their God-given ability to walk according to the Lord's standards: "Therefore, if anyone is in Christ, he is a new creation; old things have passed away; behold, all things have become new" (2 Corinthians 5:17). Positionally, we are seated with Christ in heavenly places and have His enablement upon us to live victorious Christian lives.

The moment you believe in Jesus, He imparts to you His righteousness (2 Corinthians 5:21), and a redeemed nature that positions you to be co-crucified with Him (Galatians 2:20) and to have a "newness of life" because of His resurrection (Romans 6:4). As recipients of "the righteousness of God in Him," we should strive to embrace His wisdom daily through the Word, while leading others to Him (2 Corinthians 5:18–20). You are Jesus' ambassador; represent Him well!

Employment Point: *Maximize your new capacity in Jesus by finding the lost and training the found.*

SEPTEMBER 14

PROVERBS 25–27, WITH
2 CORINTHIANS 6

Open rebuke is better than love carefully concealed (Proverbs 27:5).

SHOULD WE QUIETLY LOVE THOSE WHO ARE INFLUENCED BY BAD DOCTRINE?

The church at Corinth suffers infiltration by savage wolves. They are unclean false teachers who preach another Jesus. Paul isn't silenced or intimidated; he confronts the situation boldly. He uses the present imperative, which means *stop being yoked*, when he writes, "Do not be unequally yoked together with unbelievers. For what fellowship has righteousness with lawlessness? And what communion has light with darkness?" (2 Corinthians 6:14). The apostle by God's authority demands that the saints immediately separate from the purveyors of heresy.

Paul asks five rhetorical questions in 2 Corinthians 6:14–16, which makes the point that Jesus and Satan don't mix. Bad doctrine leads to bad living. Paul understands this and gives the following three commands and a promise: "Come out from among them and be separate, says the Lord. Do not touch what is unclean, and I will receive you" (2 Corinthians 6:17). Obedience will facilitate God's blessing.

EMPLOYMENT POINT: *Boldly and lovingly confront those influenced by false teachers, to separate from them.*

267

SEPTEMBER 15

PROVERBS 28–29, WITH
2 CORINTHIANS 7

The wicked flee when no one pursues, but the righteous are bold as a lion (Proverbs 28:1).

DO YOU BOLDLY MINISTER FOR JESUS?

Paul's reputation is besmirched. False teachers with a barrage of attempted character assassinations attack Paul by spreading misinformation to the Corinthian saints. Does Paul abandon his post? Does he flee to find an easier place for ministry? No! Rather, he makes an appeal to his children in the faith. The much-maligned apostle pleads, "Open your hearts to us. We have wronged no one, we have corrupted no one, we have cheated no one" (2 Corinthians 7:2). Paul's integrity enables him to be bold as a lion.

Furthermore, he longs for his children's doctrinal and moral purity. They must separate from bad doctrine and living. He testifies, "Therefore, having these promises [see 2 Corinthians 6:17–18], beloved, let us cleanse ourselves from all filthiness of the flesh and spirit, perfecting holiness in the fear of God" (2 Corinthians 7:1). Rightly, the apostle exposes the corruption of the false teachers and exhorts his flock to abandon them and embrace God's promises.

EMPLOYMENT POINT: *Live with integrity, to boldly minister for Jesus.*

September 16

Proverbs 30–31, with 2 Corinthians 8

For you know the grace of our Lord Jesus Christ, that though He was rich, yet for your sakes He became poor, that you through His poverty might become rich (2 Corinthians 8:9).

Do you serve others with your strength?

The lady of strength in Proverbs 31:10–31 is traditionally called "the virtuous woman." "Virtuous" derives from the Hebrew term meaning *strength*. The sacrificial woman uses both her inner and outer strength to serve her family. Both husband and children know that their wife and mother possess enormous character, accompanied by an exemplary work ethic.

Spotting and praising a virtuous woman occurs in the story of Boaz and Ruth. He pegs her with the following accolade: "for all the people of my town know that you are a virtuous woman" (Ruth 3:11). Boaz heaps praise upon Ruth because she sacrifices to serve her mother-in-law Naomi. Similarly, we should display an inner and outer strength by serving others like the virtuous woman, Ruth, and Jesus.

EMPLOYMENT POINT: *Sacrificially serve others with your inner and outer strength, to be virtuous in God's eyes.*

SEPTEMBER 17

ECCLESIASTES 1–3, WITH
2 CORINTHIANS 9

To everything there is a season, a time for every purpose under heaven (Ecclesiastes 3:1).

DO YOU UNDERSTAND YOUR PURPOSE FOR THIS SEASON OF LIFE?

The saints in Jerusalem are experiencing a financial drought. For this reason, Paul coordinates an offering to meet their needs. He holds up the Macedonian saints as models of sacrificial giving. God lavishes them with His grace, and because of this, "in a great trial of affliction the abundance of their joy and their deep poverty abounded in the riches of their liberality" (2 Corinthians 8:2). Although the Macedonian believers are themselves deeply impoverished, they give generously. Could the Lord hold *you* up as a model of sacrificial giving?

Now is the Corinthian saints' season to give; they should take advantage of the privilege to lay up treasures in heaven. "Therefore, as we have opportunity [literally "season"]," writes Paul, "let us do good to all, especially to those who are of the household of faith" (Galatians 6:10). Exhorting believers to meet the need of other saints is not only biblical, but also helps givers to lay up treasures in heaven.

EMPLOYMENT POINT: *Fulfill your God-given purpose in this season of life.*

September 18

Ecclesiastes 4–6, with 2 Corinthians 10

―――◦◦◦―――

Bringing every thought into captivity to the obedience of Christ (2 Corinthians 10:5).

Are you capturing every thought to obey Jesus?

There exists a connection between our minds and mouths. Jesus says, "For out of the abundance of the heart the mouth speaks" (Matthew 12:34). It's good to police your speech. "Set a guard, O Lord, over my mouth; keep watch over the door of my lips" (Psalm 141:3). Jesus' greatest descendant David wisely cautions individuals to protect their speech, whereas, the Lord pointed to the root of conversation: the heart.

David's biological son Solomon concurs with his father. He writes, "Do not be rash with your mouth, and let not your heart utter anything hastily before God. For God is in heaven, and you on earth; therefore let your words be few" (Ecclesiastes 5:2). Guard your heart if you don't want to sin with your lips. Let's heed the following advice from the psalmist: "Your word I have hidden in my heart, that I might not sin against You" (Psalm 119:11).

Employment Point: *Let God's Word captivate your thinking, to capture every thought in obedience to Jesus.*

―――◦◦◦―――

SEPTEMBER 19

ECCLESIASTES 7–9, WITH 2 CORINTHIANS 11:1–15

For such are false apostles, deceitful workers, transforming themselves into apostles of Christ (2 Corinthians 11:13).

HOW SHOULD YOU PROTECT YOURSELF FROM DECEIVERS?

Satan solicits the help of corrupt ambassadors to carry out his dastardly work. It isn't hard for him to do this since "there is not a just man on earth who does good and does not sin" (Ecclesiastes 7:20). Solomon decries fallen mankind by saying, "Truly, this only I have found: That God made man upright, but they have sought out many schemes" (Ecclesiastes 7:29). The wise man captures the essence of Adam's sin with its implications to all men.

Satan keeps his emissaries on a short leash and directs them according to his wishes. The master deceiver led false apostles to Corinth to manipulate the saints. They have a "different spirit" and preach a "different gospel" (2 Corinthians 11:4). The way to guard your heart from trickery is to evaluate everyone and everything by God's Word, which leads to your spiritual maturity (1 Corinthians 2:15–16).

EMPLOYMENT POINT: *Study your Bible daily to discern the truth from Satan's manifold lies.*

SEPTEMBER 20

ECCLESIASTES 10–12, WITH
2 CORINTHIANS 11:16–33

Remember now your Creator in the days of your youth (Ecclesiastes 12:1).

ARE YOU LIVING AS IF ETERNITY IS JUST AROUND THE CORNER?

Youth should not be squandered frivolously, but lived for the Designer. ("Creator" in the Hebrew is plural, and suggests more than one member of the Godhead.) Life is a gift from God; however, it is brief. James asks and then answers, "For what is your life? It is even a vapor that appears for a little time and then vanishes away" (James 4:14). Solomon, the wise man, desires us to fear God and use our fleeting moments for Him, since judgment looms (Ecclesiastes 12:13–14).

Paul experiences Solomon's words (Ecclesiastes 12) and calls himself "the aged" (Philemon 9) and lives closely to death (2 Corinthians 11:23–33). He exists in the danger zone and grasps the frailty of life. Both Solomon and Paul would heartily concur with the sage advice of Moses: "So teach us to number our days, that we may gain a heart of wisdom" (Psalm 90:12).

EMPLOYMENT POINT: *Live for Jesus, since you are one heartbeat away from eternity.*

September 21

Song of Solomon 1–3, with 2 Corinthians 12

Do not stir up nor awaken love until it pleases (Song of Solomon 2:7).

Do you understand your season in life?

Solomon is courting. Apparently the Shulamite maiden is his first true love. Great advice gets offered to the couple to be wedded. "Catch us the foxes, the little foxes that spoil the vines, for our vines have tender grapes" (Song of Solomon 2:15). Stated otherwise, work through any issues prior to marriage that need to be ironed out. This can only be applied if you "do not stir up nor awaken love until it pleases" (Song of Solomon 2:7; 3:5; 8:4). The repeated lesson conveys the wisdom not to become physically involved with the one you are courting or else you won't be able to objectively resolve any tensions.

Paul has a different season of life; God graced him to be celibate (1 Corinthians 7:7). The apostle's singleness permits him to focus solely upon his spiritual children: "For the children ought not to lay up for the parents, but the parents for the children" (2 Corinthians 12:14).

Employment Point: *Use your season of life wisely for God's glory.*

SEPTEMBER 22

SONG OF SOLOMON 4–5, WITH 2 CORINTHIANS 13

Examine yourselves as to whether you are in the faith. Test yourselves. Do you not know yourselves, that Jesus Christ is in you?—unless indeed you are disqualified (2 Corinthians 13:5).

WHEN WAS THE LAST TIME YOU EXAMINED YOUR SOUL?

The believers at Corinth are quick to scrutinize Paul's life, driven by the misinformation of the false teachers; however, they don't seem to want to look into the mirror. Jesus also rebuked the religious leaders of His day, using a bit of humor to make His point in Matthew 7:3: "And why do you look at the speck in your brother's eye, but do not consider the plank in your own eye?" Clearly Jesus desires all people to perform regular self-examinations.

It is interesting that Solomon and the Shulamite give each other a physical examination from head to toe, and lavish praise upon the other after the inspection (Song of Solomon 4–5). Conversely, the saints at Corinth look at Paul not to praise or encourage him, but rather to condemn him.

EMPLOYMENT POINT: *Regularly inspect your life, and correct whatever doesn't please the Lord.*

SEPTEMBER 23

SONG OF SOLOMON 6–8, WITH GALATIANS 1

———◦———

I marvel that you are turning away so soon from Him who called you in the grace of Christ, to a different gospel (Galatians 1:6).

HOW ARE YOU PROTECTING THOSE WHOM YOU LOVE?

The older siblings say about their younger sister, "If she is a wall, we will build upon her a battlement of silver; and if she is a door, we will enclose her with boards of cedar" (Song of Solomon 8:9). Simply stated, if their sister has strong moral values, the family will build upon them; however, if she seems morally vulnerable, then they are going to lock her up in her room. Godly families seek to build up and secure their own.

Paul wants to similarly watch over and guard his spiritual family. False teachers have infiltrated the church at Galatia, and he warns his children in the faith about the danger of another gospel. He understands the unadulterated gospel consisting of Jesus' death, burial, and resurrection; therefore, adding anything to the gospel of grace destroys its message. So, whether it is a younger sister or a member of your congregation, seek to protect them.

EMPLOYMENT POINT: *Safeguard those entrusted to your care, morally and spiritually.*

———◦———

SEPTEMBER 24

ISAIAH 1–3, WITH GALATIANS 2

Knowing that a man is not justified by the works of the law but by faith in Jesus Christ (Galatians 2:16).

WHAT CAN WASH AWAY MY SIN?

Jesus doesn't come "to destroy the Law or the Prophets" (Matthew 5:17). He emerges to fulfill Bible prophecy. Only Jesus could meet the requirements of the Law and that is why He appears as the Lamb of God. Salvation isn't secured by attempting to keep the Law, but in believing in the One who did. Thus Paul writes, "For I through the law died to the law that I might live to God" (Galatians 2:19).

"Come now, and let us reason together," writes Isaiah seven hundred years before Jesus is born, "though your sins are like scarlet, they shall be as white as snow; though they are red like crimson, they shall be as wool" (Isaiah 1:18). Both Paul and Isaiah refer to salvation as ultimately accomplished through the finished work of Jesus. The blood of Christ washes away the sin of all who come to God through faith, whether before or after the cross.

EMPLOYMENT POINT: *Believe in Jesus' finished work that washes away sin.*

September 25

Isaiah 4–6, with Galatians 3

———⊙———

And one cried to another and said: "Holy, holy, holy is the LORD of hosts; the whole earth is full of His glory!" (Isaiah 6:3).

Whom shall I send, and who will go for Us? (Isaiah 6:8).

God reveals His glory to Isaiah. The seraphim—a classification of angels whose title means *burning ones*—proclaim the Lord's holiness three times. This is the convention in the Hebrew language to depict God's perfect holiness, since superlatives are not used. Isaiah witnesses God's splendor, repents of his own sin, and offers himself to God. He responds, "Here am I! Send me" (Isaiah 6:8).

Similarly, Abraham receives the call of God. Paul writes, "And the Scripture, foreseeing that God would justify the Gentiles by faith, preached the gospel to Abraham beforehand, saying, 'In You all the nations shall be blessed'" (Galatians 3:8). The father of faith obeys the call of God and the Lord sovereignly uses the Seed of Abraham (Jesus) to bring the blessing of salvation to Jew and Gentile alike.

Employment Point: *Marvel at God's majesty, and honor your holy calling by proclaiming salvation through Jesus.*

———⊙———

SEPTEMBER 26

ISAIAH 7–9, WITH GALATIANS 4

———

For unto us a Child is born, unto us a Son is given; and the government will be upon His shoulder. And His name will be called Wonderful, Counselor, Mighty God, Everlasting Father, Prince of Peace (Isaiah 9:6).

WHY IS THE PREDICTED SON BORN?

The Son, to be born more than six centuries after Isaiah's prophetic words, is called "Everlasting Father," which literally means *father of eternity*. That is, the "Mighty God" possesses eternity, since He is its Father. Jesus created time; He is not controlled by it, but chooses to enter time. God the Father, God the Son, and God the Holy Spirit purposed in eternity past that Jesus would step (with literal feet) into time, offering eternal life (Titus 1:2).

Paul captures the perfect timing of the Trinity: "But when the fullness of the time had come, God sent forth His Son, born of a woman, born under the law" (Galatians 4:4). Jesus enters the world through Mary (the virgin) at the appointed time. The reason for His coming is now given: "To redeem those who were under the law, that we might receive the adoption as sons" (Galatians 4:5). Our Redeemer arrived right on schedule, with the invitation to eternal life!

EMPLOYMENT POINT: *Receive the Father of Eternity, to be given everlasting life.*

———

SEPTEMBER 27

ISAIAH 10–12, WITH GALATIANS 5

———

For we through the Spirit eagerly wait for the hope of righteousness by faith (Galatians 5:5).

WHAT ARE YOU EAGERLY EXPECTING?

The two English words "eagerly wait" translate from one term that occurs seven times in the Greek New Testament (Romans 8:19, 23, 25; 1 Corinthians 1:7; Galatians 5:5; Philippians 3:20; Hebrews 9:28). Each reference pertains to the return of our Lord. The word has the root idea "to expect" and has a preposition affixed to it, which shows an intense expectation. We are to eagerly desire Jesus to return.

He will return to the earth at His Second Coming to establish the kingdom. Isaiah gives us a taste of Jesus' future rule: "The wolf also shall dwell with the lamb, the leopard shall lie down with the young goat, the calf and the young lion and the fatling together; and a little child shall lead them" (Isaiah 11:6). Jesus, the Prince of Peace, will return after the Tribulation (Revelation 6–19) and reestablish the tranquil environment that was experienced by Adam and Eve before the Fall.

EMPLOYMENT POINT: *Live passionately for Jesus, as you anticipate His return.*

———

September 28

Isaiah 13–15, with Galatians 6

———◦◉◦———

Do not be deceived, God is not mocked; for whatever a man sows, that he will also reap (Galatians 6:7).

WHERE ARE YOU LAYING UP TREASURES?

Believers have an obligation to meet the needs of the man of God. Paul gives the following command in Galatians 6:6: "Let him who is taught the word share in all good things with him who teaches." The apostle states the right of the preacher to be compensated for his ministry. Robbing God is a fool's bargain on this side of eternity (Malachi 3:8), which will bring shame when you meet Jesus (1 John 2:28).

Those who preach the gospel are given the right to have their needs met by the saints. Paul writes, "Even so the Lord has commanded that those who preach the gospel should live by the gospel" (1 Corinthians 9:14). The apostle gives a graphic picture when he points out that "God is not mocked." "Mocked" conveys *to turn up one's nose*. Don't snub God; your current finances and future reward are connected to your church giving.

EMPLOYMENT POINT: *Lay up treasures in heaven by meeting the physical needs of your pastors.*

———◦◉◦———

SEPTEMBER 29

ISAIAH 16–18, WITH EPHESIANS 1

———◦———

Christ came, who is over all, the eternally blessed God. Amen (Romans 9:5).

ARE YOU LIVING YOUR ELEVATED STATUS?

Paul characterizes Jesus as the "eternally blessed God." His very nature is blessed, and therefore He desires to bless others. Positionally you are seated with the One who conquered death, ascended to the right hand of God, and sat down (Colossians 3:1). For this reason we are to bless God, "who has blessed us with every spiritual blessing in the heavenly places in Christ" (Ephesians 1:3).

Moreover, we are "heirs of God and joint heirs with Christ" (Romans 8:17). In essence, all the spiritual blessings that Jesus possesses are made available to us. God's mercy (Ephesians 2:4) and grace (Ephesians 2:6–9) are at our disposal continually because of our heavenly seating. It is time for us to revel in all our spiritual treasures and manifest to this fallen world the glories of being a child of the King. Jesus sacrificed His life so that we can experience these blessings through Him!

EMPLOYMENT POINT: *Practice your position, and enjoy your riches in Christ.*

———◦———

SEPTEMBER 30

ISAIAH 19–21, WITH EPHESIANS 2

And He came and preached peace to you who were afar off and to those who were near (Ephesians 2:17).

ARE YOU AN INDISCRIMINATE PREACHER?

Paul evangelizes the predominantly Gentile city of Ephesus in a spectacular way (Acts 19:11–20). Luke records, "Now God worked unusual miracles by the hands of Paul" (Acts 19:11). Our sovereign Father chose Israel during the Old Testament era to be His universal light. Initially, Gentiles were on the outside looking in. When Jesus died the veil of the temple was torn from top to bottom, signifying worldwide approachability to Him.

The apostle to the Gentiles states, "For through Him [Jesus] we both [Jew and Gentile] have access by one Spirit to the Father" (Ephesians 2:18). Jesus calls us to proclaim His death, burial, and resurrection to all people. He explicitly commands, "Go into all the world and preach the gospel to every creature" (Mark 16:15). Jesus has made the way; Paul has set the example. Now it is time that we honor Jesus' command to us, by following the apostle Paul's universal heart for all people!

EMPLOYMENT POINT: *Proclaim the gospel to Jew and Gentile alike.*

October 1

Isaiah 22–23, with Ephesians 3

———◦———

To me, who am less than the least of all the saints, this grace was given, that I should preach among the Gentiles the unsearchable riches of Christ (Ephesians 3:8).

What are you communicating to men and angels?

Paul receives God's call "to make all see what is the fellowship of the mystery" (Ephesians 3:9). The mystery, which is a sacred secret that once was hidden but revealed now, is that the Jews and Gentiles would become one body comprising the church. God's great apostle and missionary to the Gentiles embraces his stewardship to show the glories of this mystery, which causes him to marvel.

Moreover, not only are we to do the same, but "now the manifold wisdom of God might be made known by the church to the principalities and powers in the heavenly places" (Ephesians 3:10). Angels are to witness the mystery of Christ's one body, the church, through us. Since they are desirous to investigate the things of the gospel (1 Peter 1:12), let's display the Lord's glorious wisdom even to the angels.

Employment Point: *Model well the glory of Christ's one body the church to men and angels alike.*

———◦———

OCTOBER 2

ISAIAH 24–26, WITH EPHESIANS 4

You will keep him in perfect peace, whose mind is stayed on You, because he trusts in You (Isaiah 26:3).

WHAT IS YOUR PLAN FOR PERSONAL PEACE?

Paul teaches us how to keep our minds upon the Father, which enables us to experience His peace: "put off, concerning your former conduct, the old man . . . and that you put on the new man which was created according to God" (Ephesians 4:22, 24). As nature fills empty spaces like water filling a hole on a rainy day, so we are not just to "put off" the old, but also "put on the new." God's wisdom, displayed to Paul, instructs biblical counselors about the life-changing principle of putting off the old and putting on the new, which I've personally used regularly over three decades of counseling.

Putting off the old and replacing it with the new begins with a commitment. Knowing this, Paul guides the saints, "be renewed in the spirit of your mind" (Ephesians 4:23). Let's make that commitment!

EMPLOYMENT POINT: *Be renewed daily in your mind by replacing the old with the new, to experience God's perfect peace.*

October 3

Isaiah 27–28, with Ephesians 5

And do not be drunk with wine, in which is dissipation; but be filled with the Spirit (Ephesians 5:18).

Who or what controls you?

Twice Isaiah condemns the "drunkards of Ephraim" (Isaiah 28:1, 3). These wayward children of Israel are likened to alcoholics; they are renowned for their pride and drunkenness. How sad when individuals identified with the Almighty adopt the sinful ways of the world; it must break His holy heart!

We should be known for being governed by God's Spirit—not by unclean spirits. How do you know if you are a Spirit-filled Christian? Paul shares three characteristics of those who are filled or controlled by His Spirit in Ephesians 5:19–21: They are joyful, thankful, and submissive, "speaking to one another in psalms and hymns and spiritual songs, singing and making melody in your heart to the Lord, giving thanks always for all things to God the Father in the name of our Lord Jesus Christ, submitting to one another in the fear of God."

Employment Point: *Seek Jesus daily, and obey His Word, to be controlled by the Holy Spirit.*

OCTOBER 4

ISAIAH 29–30, WITH EPHESIANS 6

Be strong in the Lord and in the power of His might (Ephesians 6:10).

WHOM DO YOU TRUST FOR PROTECTION FROM THE ENEMY?

The Assyrians threaten the Israelites. Instead of relying upon the Lord they seek an alliance for protection with Egypt. Isaiah describes the situation, "Who walk to go down to Egypt, and have not asked My advice, to strengthen themselves in the strength of Pharaoh, and to trust in the shadow of Egypt!" (Isaiah 30:2). Israel depends upon the arm of flesh, instead of the strength of the Lord, for protection from the Assyrians.

Paul speaks about the archenemy Satan in Ephesians 6. No human alliance will produce victory over the Wicked One. The apostle uses the imagery of a Roman soldier, whom he sees daily because of his house arrest, to depict how the Christian warrior should be outfitted for battle. Paul, an experienced combatant commands, "Put on the whole armor of God, that you may be able to stand against the wiles of the devil" (Ephesians 6:11). Soldier, don ever piece without exception!

EMPLOYMENT POINT: *Dress for spiritual success by putting on the whole armor of God.*

October 5

Isaiah 31–33, with Philippians 1

———◦◦◦———

I am appointed for the defense of the gospel (Philippians 1:17).

What are you defending based upon your words and deeds?

As Israel receives threats by the Assyrians, they desire to flee to Egypt for protection. The Lord warns the nation, "Now the Egyptians are men, and not God" (Isaiah 31:3). Regrettably, the children of Israel quickly forget the works God had performed for them and misplace their trust.

Conversely, Paul wholeheartedly places his confidence upon the Lord. While under house arrest, he writes, "being confident of this very thing, that He who has begun a good work in you will complete it until the day of Jesus Christ" (Philippians 1:6). Twice Paul testifies that he had been commissioned to defend the gospel (Philippians 1:7, 17). Peter reminds believers that we have a similar calling, "But sanctify the Lord God in your hearts, and always be ready to give a defense to everyone who asks you a reason for the hope that is in you" (1 Peter 3:15). Let's be obedient apologists (defenders of the faith) for the Lord.

Employment Point: *Rely upon God and defend the gospel by your words and actions.*

———◦◦◦———

October 6

Isaiah 34–36, with Philippians 2

———◆———

Let this mind be in you which was also in Christ Jesus (Philippians 2:5).

Do you think like Jesus?

Paul commands us to embrace the attitude of Jesus and become the servant of all. Our Lord chose not to exercise some of His attributes while on earth, but "He humbled Himself and became obedient to the point of death, even the death of the cross" (Philippians 2:8). Paul follows in Jesus' footsteps. "Yes, and if I am being poured out as a drink offering on the sacrifice and service of your faith, I am glad and rejoice with you all" (Philippians 2:17). As a drink offering is poured out to the ground, Paul willingly sacrifices his life for others.

Timothy also exemplifies this mindset. Paul writes about his protégé in the faith, "For I have no one like-minded [literally "like-souled"], who will sincerely care for your state" (Philippians 2:20). Epaphroditus follows suit "for the work of Christ he came close to death" (Philippians 2:30). We should also pursue the path of these courageous and godly men!

Employment Point: *Adopt Jesus' mindset and sacrificially serve others.*

———◆———

OCTOBER 7

ISAIAH 37–38, WITH PHILIPPIANS 3

———

For many walk, of whom I have told you often, and now tell you even weeping, that they are the enemies of the cross of Christ (Philippians 3:18).

WHAT SHOULD WE WAIT FOR WHEN THE ENEMY RAGES?

Sennacherib, king of Assyria, is seeking to overthrow the southern kingdom of Judah. Arrogantly he threatens both king and kingdom. God miraculously thwarted him by striking the army. This is a result of godly king Hezekiah humbling himself and seeking the Lord's protection. "Then the angel of the LORD went out, and killed in the camp of the Assyrians one hundred and eighty-five thousand" (Isaiah 37:36). Wisely Judah's king sought *the* King for protection from the enemy.

Paul understands the outcome of the wicked opposed to Jesus, "whose end is destruction, whose god is their belly, and whose glory is their shame—who set their mind on earthly things" (Philippians 3:19). What should keep us motivated in the midst of a world that opposes Jesus and those belonging to Him? Paul answers, "For our citizenship is in heaven, from which we also eagerly wait for the Savior, the Lord Jesus Christ" (Philippians 3:20).

EMPLOYMENT POINT: *Expect Jesus' protection when evil abounds, and await His return.*

———

OCTOBER 8

ISAIAH 39–40, WITH PHILIPPIANS 4

———◦◦◦———

I can do all things through Christ who strengthens me (Philippians 4:13).

ARE YOU WAITING UPON GOD FOR YOUR PROVISION?

Paul pens Philippians 4:13 while under house arrest and depends upon God to provide for him through others. Previously his needs were met through two offerings from the saints at Philippi (Philippians 4:16). The imprisoned apostle assures these believers of the Lord's care: "And my God shall supply all your need according to His riches in glory by Christ Jesus" (Philippians 4:19).

Paul, an Old Testament scholar, understands God's power, which is revealed through five rhetorical questions in Isaiah 40:12–14. "Who has measured the waters in the hollow of His hand, measured heaven with a span and calculated the dust of the earth in a measure? Weighed the mountains in scales and the hills in a balance? Who has directed the Spirit of the LORD, or as His counselor has taught Him? With whom did He take counsel, and who instructed Him, and taught Him in the path of justice? Who taught Him knowledge, and showed Him the way of understanding?"

EMPLOYMENT POINT: *Trust the all-powerful God to supply your needs.*

———◦◦◦———

OCTOBER 9

ISAIAH 41–42, WITH COLOSSIANS 1

———⋄———

Fear not, for I am with you, be not dismayed, for I am your God. I will strengthen you. Yes, I will help you, I will uphold you with My righteous right hand (Isaiah 41:10).

DOES JESUS TAKE FIRST PLACE IN YOUR LIFE?

God is omnipresent; He is everywhere. Also, the Lord is omnipotent; He is all-powerful. His attributes should cause us never to fear. We can trust our heavenly Father who has "conveyed us into the kingdom of the Son of His love" (Colossians 1:13). Furthermore, we can rely upon Jesus who "is before all things, and in Him all things consists" (Colossians 1:17). Jesus exists forever, and continues manifesting His omnipresence and omnipotence by maintaining the universe. We can depend upon Him, since He creates all things and governs the globe by His infinite resources.

Not only did Jesus exist before creation; He created all things, and sustains the universe. After Paul teaches us about the depth of our Creator and Sustainer, he writes, "that in all things He may have the preeminence" (Colossians 1:18). Jesus rightly deserves first place in our lives; let's bow before Him!

EMPLOYMENT POINT: *Give the Creator and Sustainer of your life first place in all matters.*

———⋄———

October 10

Isaiah 43–44, with Colossians 2

And you are complete in Him, who is the head of all principality and power (Colossians 2:10).

What completes you?

God masterfully designed you. David writes, "For You formed my inward parts; You covered me in my mother's womb" (Psalm 139:13). The Hebrew text emphasizes that our heavenly Father wonderfully designed David in the womb. Twice the word "You" refers to God emphatically. For this reason David exclaims, "I will praise You, for I am fearfully and wonderfully made, marvelous are Your works, and that my soul knows very well" (Psalm 139:14). David understands that the Almighty Father uniquely and lovingly designed him to offer praise to the Lord.

Furthermore, God weaved you in your mother's womb; He also redeemed you. "Thus says the LORD, your Redeemer, and He who formed you from the womb: 'I am the LORD, who makes all things'" (Isaiah 44:24). Imagine, the heavenly Designer formed you in the womb, redeemed you through His Son, and makes you complete. Why should you ever turn to anyone or anything else for completion?

EMPLOYMENT POINT: *Marvel that God created and recreated you for His glory!*

OCTOBER 11

ISAIAH 45–47, WITH COLOSSIANS 3

———◦———

Set your mind on things above, not on things on the earth (Colossians 3:2).

ARE YOU TRYING TO SERVE TWO MASTERS?

God asks the idolatrous nation of Israel, "To whom will you liken Me, and make Me equal and compare Me, that we should be alike?" (Isaiah 46:5). Isaiah gives similar statements in Isaiah 40:18, 25, which appear in the context of idolatry. Israel ignores the Almighty who created them; they choose to worship handcrafted idols instead of the living God.

Paul describes the saints as being positionally raised with Christ and commands them to "seek those things which are above" (Colossians 3:1). Then he lists several things that should not be pursued since believers are co-crucified with Jesus. The apostle to the Gentiles gives the last one as "covetousness," and qualifies, "which is idolatry" (Colossians 3:5). Our hearts should not house idols, but God's Word. Once again, Paul writes, "Let the word of Christ dwell in you richly in all wisdom" (Colossians 3:16). The present imperative "dwell" means *to be at home*.

EMPLOYMENT POINT: *Serve Jesus, and make your heart His home.*

———◦———

OCTOBER 12

ISAIAH 48–49, WITH COLOSSIANS 4

Oh, that you had heeded My commandments! Then your peace would have been like a river, and your righteousness like the waves of the sea (Isaiah 48:18).

ARE YOU OBEYING GOD'S COMMANDMENTS AND FULFILLING YOUR GOD-GIVEN ROLE?

The Lord delights in us when we willingly obey Him. "For this is the love of God," writes John, "that we keep His commandments. And His commandments are not burdensome" (1 John 5:3). Our gracious Father has saved us, gifted us spiritually, and calls us to faithfully serve Him. God floods our hearts with His peace and righteousness when we please Him by keeping His commandments.

Paul has many wonderful things to say to the Colossian saints. Yet he reserves these words for Archippus: "Take heed to the ministry which you have received in the Lord, that you may fulfill it" (Colossians 4:17). By way of contrast, Paul describes another servant, "Epaphras, who is one of you, a bondservant of Christ, greets you, always laboring fervently for you in prayer" (Colossians 4:12). Let's fervently serve the Lord like Epaphras, so that the Lord would never need to have a letter sent to our church correcting us for slothfulness.

EMPLOYMENT POINT: *Serve Jesus, and make your heart His home.*

OCTOBER 13

ISAIAH 50–52, WITH 1 THESSALONIANS 1

—◦—

And you became followers of us and of the Lord, having received the word in much affliction, with joy of the Holy Spirit (1 Thessalonians 1:6).

DO YOU IMITATE PAUL AND JESUS BY OBEYING GOD DESPITE PERSECUTION?

Isaiah 50:4–11 gives us the third of four servant songs (Isaiah 42:1–9; 49:1–13; 52:13–53:12). They refer to Jesus, the suffering servant: "The Lord God has opened My ear; and I was not rebellious, nor did I turn away. I gave My back to those who struck Me, and My cheeks to those who plucked out the beard; I did not hide My face from shame and spitting" (Isaiah 50:5–6). Jesus submitted to the Father's will, and received abject humiliation from those He came to save.

Similarly, the Thessalonian saints suffered; however, they experience joy for following the Lord. The church at Thessalonica becomes a model church. Paul gives the result of their obedience in 1 Thessalonians 1:7: "so that you became examples to all in Macedonia and Achaia who believe." We also are called to follow in the steps of the Lord and His persecuted children (1 Peter 2:21; Philippians 1:29).

EMPLOYMENT POINT: *Walk persecution's path like Jesus, Paul, and the Thessalonian saints, to please God.*

—◦—

OCTOBER 14

ISAIAH 53–55, WITH
1 THESSALONIANS 2

———

So, affectionately longing for you, we were well pleased to impart to you not only the gospel of God, but also our own lives, because you had become dear to us (1 Thessalonians 2:8).

ARE YOU WILLING TO LAY DOWN YOUR LIFE FOR OTHERS?

Isaiah predicts the Lord Jesus' sacrifice. Observe in Isaiah 53:4–6 all the references to "we," "our," and "us." This prophetic passage powerfully proclaims Jesus' substitutionary atonement—that is, Jesus took *our* place upon the cross, bearing the sin of the world. The prophet pens, "All we like sheep have gone astray; we have turned, every one, to his own way; and the LORD has laid on Him the iniquity of us all" (Isaiah 53:6). Today, praise the Lord for Jesus' willingness to be the Lamb of God who became the perfect sacrifice and substitute for *our* sin.

The apostle Paul and his associates display Christlikeness by freely giving themselves to the Thessalonian saints. They imitate Jesus in their actions. Let's consider the "we" and "us" in 2 Corinthians 5:21: "For He made Him who knew no sin to be sin for us, that we might become the righteousness of God in Him."

EMPLOYMENT POINT: *Give your life away to others, as Jesus did.*

———

October 15

Isaiah 56–58, with 1 Thessalonians 3

Then you shall call, and the LORD will answer; you shall cry, and He will say, "Here I am" (Isaiah 58:9).

ARE YOUR PRAYERS BEING ANSWERED?

Praying and fasting are a dynamic duo. Yet the children of Israel are just going through the motions, so God ignored their prayers. The Israelites exploited their workers (Isaiah 58:3) and were not meeting the needs of the poor (Isaiah 58:7). If they would repent, God would honor their prayers with fasting and guide them. "The LORD will guide you continually," writes Isaiah, "and satisfy your soul in drought" (Isaiah 58:11). God the Father delights honoring the prayers accompanied with fasting of His children when they are simultaneously caring for the needy.

Paul also regularly comes before the throne of grace (1 Thessalonians 3:8–9). As a result of seeking the Lord, he writes, "Now may our God and Father Himself, and our Lord Jesus Christ, direct our way to you" (1 Thessalonians 3:11). Furthermore, he prays for the Thessalonians to increase in love and holiness (1 Thessalonians 3:12–13).

EMPLOYMENT POINT: *Fast and pray with a righteous life, and receive answered prayer.*

October 16

Isaiah 59–61, with 1 Thessalonians 4

The Spirit of the Lord God is upon Me, because the LORD has anointed Me to preach good tidings to the poor (Isaiah 61:1).

Are you focused upon Jesus' imminent return?

Jesus reads Isaiah 61:1–2 at His hometown of Nazareth. He finishes the reading with, "To proclaim the acceptable year of the LORD" (Luke 4:19). He chooses not to continue to the next line: "And the day of vengeance of our God" (Isaiah 61:2). Why? Jesus came the first time to offer salvation; His Second Coming will be to enact vengeance (Revelation 19:11–21). The Lamb of God will return as the lion from the tribe of Judah.

Paul writes about the Rapture in 1 Thessalonians 4:13–18, which occurs before the Tribulation and Second Coming of Jesus. "For if we believe that Jesus died and rose again, even so God will bring with Him those who sleep in Jesus" (1 Thessalonians 4:14). The verbs "died" and "rose" are active. In other words, Jesus deliberately died and raised Himself up. Knowing that Jesus can return at any moment for us should bring encouragement to the soul (1 Thessalonians 4:18).

EMPLOYMENT POINT: *Believe upon Jesus' finished work, and await His return.*

October 17

Isaiah 62–64, with
1 Thessalonians 5

For since the beginning of the world men have not heard nor perceived by the ear, nor has the eye seen any God besides You, who acts for the one who waits for Him (Isaiah 64:4).

Are you waiting upon God to act?

Years ago I heard the following pronouncement: Patience is a virtue. Possess it if you can. Seldom found in a woman, and never in a man. The Bible teaches that waiting upon the Lord displays a life of dependence. Paul reminds us to stay focused upon the Lord. "Rejoice always, pray without ceasing, in everything give thanks; for this is the will of God in Christ Jesus for you" (1 Thessalonians 5:16–18). The Greek modifier is placed first in each of these verses. We should "always rejoice," "without ceasing pray," and "in everything give thanks."

Our sovereign Father is working; we need to abide in Him while He works. We are to abide in Jesus, knowing that He is working in us and through us to accomplish His will. After all, "He who calls you is faithful, who also will do it" (1 Thessalonians 5:24).

EMPLOYMENT POINT: *Continually rejoice, pray, give thanks, and know that God is on the move.*

OCTOBER 18

ISAIAH 65–66, WITH
2 THESSALONIANS 1

These shall be punished with everlasting destruction from the presence of the Lord and from the glory of His power (2 Thessalonians 1:9).

DO YOU WARN OTHERS ABOUT THE REALITY OF HELL?

Jesus speaks about hell more than any other biblical figure. He uses eleven out of the twelve Greek New Testament uses of "Gehenna" or "hell." After writing about the new heavens and earth, Isaiah pens, "And they shall go forth and look upon the corpses of the men who have transgressed against Me. For their worm does not die, and their fire is not quenched. They shall be an abhorrence to all flesh" (Isaiah 66:24). The prophet depicts hell as a place of continual internal torment ("their worm does not die") and perpetual external punishment ("their fire is not quenched").

Similarly, Paul reminds the Thessalonians that their persecutors will be punished (2 Thessalonians 1:5–10). The apostle shows the vehemence of "vengeance on those who do not know God . . . these shall be punished with everlasting destruction from the presence of the Lord and from the glory of His power" (2 Thessalonians 1:8–9).

EMPLOYMENT POINT: *Warn the unsaved: Believe in Jesus, or experience hell.*

October 19

Jeremiah 1–2, with
2 Thessalonians 2

Before I formed you in the womb I knew you; before you were born I sanctified you; I ordained you a prophet to the nations (Jeremiah 1:5).

Are you firmly rooted and grounded in your faith?

God calls Jeremiah to proclaim His Word to a rebellious people. His message: The destruction of Jerusalem and the temple are rapidly approaching. Furthermore, the people are to submit to the invading Babylonians because God is chastening the nation through them. Although Jeremiah will look like a traitor to his own people because of his message, yet the Lord calls him to boldly trumpet impending judgment. God's weeping prophet will shed many tears, but thankfully remain loyal to the Almighty.

Similarly Paul warns the Thessalonians; he exposes the future work of the Antichrist (2 Thessalonians 2:1–12). In light of the Man of Sin's rebellion, Paul exhorts the saints, "Therefore, brethren, stand fast and hold the traditions which you were taught, whether by word or our epistle" (2 Thessalonians 2:15). The apostle gives two present-tense commands, showing that believers are to stand fast continually and hold the teachings passed down to them.

Employment Point: *Remain loyal to your God-given call, despite ungodly opposition.*

OCTOBER 20

JEREMIAH 3–4, WITH 2 THESSALONIANS 3

Finally, brethren, pray for us, that the word of the Lord may run swiftly and be glorified, just as it is with you (2 Thessalonians 3:1).

ARE YOU REGULARLY PRAYING FOR THOSE WHO PROCLAIM GOD'S WORD?

God's spokesmen desire the Word of the Lord to be heeded, whether Old Testament prophet or New Testament apostle. Jeremiah is no exception. Yet both he and his message will be rejected. Nonetheless God reveals His heart through the prophet in Jeremiah 4:1. "If you will return, O Israel, says the LORD, return to Me; and if you will put away your abominations out of My sight, then you shall not be moved." The Almighty Father desires His wayward children to repent of their idolatrous ways, so he can once again bless them.

Paul, who is both an apostle and prophet, solicits the saints to pray for preachers to boldly trumpet the Word. "Continue earnestly in prayer, being vigilant in it with thanksgiving; meanwhile praying also for us, that God would open to us a door for the word, to speak the mystery of Christ" (Colossians 4:2–3).

EMPLOYMENT POINT: *Pray for God's heralds to be bold, and to have an open door.*

OCTOBER 21

JEREMIAH 5–6, WITH
1 TIMOTHY 1

———◦———

This is a faithful saying and worthy of all acceptance, that Christ Jesus came into the world to save sinners, of whom I am chief (1Timothy 1:15).

HOW AWARE ARE YOU OF YOUR OWN SINFULNESS?

Paul is not a young man when he writes his first epistle to Timothy. With humility, as his time on earth is coming to a close, he gives a self-assessment. He uses the emphatic present tense, "I am," which shows that he is presently and continually the foremost sinner. Staying close to the Lord produces an awareness of our own sinfulness. This happened also to Isaiah (Isaiah 6:1–8). The Lord works through the humble; in addition, for this reason we should strive to pursue our daily walk with Him not only to know Him better, but also to know ourselves!

Sadly, the nation of Israel ignores their sinful plight, which shows their hearts are far from God. Jeremiah writes, "The prophets prophesy falsely, and the priests rule by their own power; and My people love to have it so" (Jeremiah 5:31). Their pride leads to God's judgment.

EMPLOYMENT POINT: *Daily draw near to God, for a continual awareness of your sinfulness and the need of His mercy and grace.*

———◦———

OCTOBER 22

JEREMIAH 7–8, WITH
1 TIMOTHY 2

The harvest is past, the summer is ended, and we are not saved! (Jeremiah 8:20).

IS YOUR HEART ALIGNED WITH THE SAVIOR'S HEART?

Paul regularly refers to the Father and Son as "Savior" in 1 Timothy, 2 Timothy, and Titus (1 Timothy 1:1; 2:3; 4:10; 2 Timothy 1:10; Titus 1:3, 4; 2:10, 13; 3:4, 6). The Lord's heart longs for "all" people to be saved. "For this is good and acceptable in the sight of God our Savior," writes Paul, "who desires all men to be saved and to come to the knowledge of the truth" (1 Timothy 2:3–4). God the Father and the eternal Son of God have a passion for souls to be saved.

Moreover, Jesus died for "all" people. Observe Paul's use of "all," "who gave Himself a ransom for all" (1 Timothy 2:6). Jesus qualifies to be the world's Savior since He is "our great God and Savior." Permit Paul's following admonition from Titus 2:13 to direct us: "looking for the blessed hope and glorious appearing of our great God and Savior Jesus Christ." Focusing upon Father and Son as Savior should move us to carry out their mission for rescuing souls.

EMPLOYMENT POINT: *Align your heart with the Savior of mankind.*

October 23

Jeremiah 9–10, with 1 Timothy 3

———◦———

And without controversy great is the mystery of godliness: God was manifested in the flesh, justified in the Spirit, seen by angels, preached among the Gentiles, believed on in the world, received up in glory (1 Timothy 3:16).

Do you intimately know the God-Man?

Jesus, although being fully God, is also fully Man. Paul writes, "For there is one God and one Mediator between God and men, the Man Christ Jesus" (1 Timothy 2:5). Even now, Jesus mediates for us in His glorified body in heaven. We are privileged to know Jesus, who had come in flesh. The God-Man represents and unites us to the Father. We can enjoy the privilege of walking with God because the Father receives us through Christ's righteousness!

Five centuries prior to this, Jeremiah writes, "But let him who glories glory in this, that he understands and knows Me" (Jeremiah 9:24). Imagine, since we have the complete revelation of the Bible (both Old and New Testaments), we can now know God's Son intimately through a personal relationship with Him. Because of Jesus we can walk with the living God; we are blessed indeed!

Employment Point: *Cultivate a daily personal walk with the God-Man.*

———◦———

OCTOBER 24

JEREMIAH 11–13, WITH
1 TIMOTHY 4

———❖———

Take heed to yourself and to the doctrine. Continue in them, for
in doing this you will save both yourself and those who hear you
(1 Timothy 4:16).

HOW CAN YOU MAINTAIN PURITY AND IMPACT
OTHERS FOR JESUS IN A WICKED WORLD?

Spiritual seduction is widespread. Paul warns Timothy, "Now the
Spirit expressly says that in latter times some will depart from the
faith, giving heed to deceiving spirits and doctrines of demons, speaking lies in hypocrisy, having their own conscience seared with a hot
iron" (1 Timothy 4:1–2). Paul prescribes for Timothy to protect his
own heart. Centuries earlier the wise man wrote, "Keep your heart
with all diligence" (Proverbs 4:23). Godly men have known through
the ages the importance of keeping a sentinel to protect the heart
from enemy combatants.

Moreover, Paul commands Timothy to pay close attention to
Scripture (1 Timothy 4:16). The imperative "continue" as "continue
in them" consists of a present command, which means *remain* in the
Bible. We are to remain in the Bible and have the Bible continue in
us for spiritual victory, in a world that opposes all things Christian.

EMPLOYMENT POINT: *Guard your heart while remaining in the
Scripture, for a productive life and ministry.*

———❖———

October 25

Jeremiah 14–16, with 1 Timothy 5

———◦◉◦———

Then the LORD said to me, "Do not pray for this people, for their good" (Jeremiah 14:11).

Do you presume upon God's mercy?

We live in a hardened world. So did Jeremiah and Paul and Timothy. Paul instructs his young protégé, "Some men's sins are clearly evident, preceding them to judgment, but those of some men follow later" (1 Timothy 5:24). In his second epistle, Paul informs Timothy, "Alexander the coppersmith did me much harm. May the Lord repay him according to his works" (2 Timothy 4:14). For those of us who care about the things of the Lord, opposition abounds!

Jeremiah ministers to a recalcitrant people. God has enough of the disobedient nation and tells the weeping prophet, "Even if Moses and Samuel stood before Me, My mind would not be favorable toward this people. Cast them out of My sight, and let them go forth" (Jeremiah 15:1). Although God's patience and longsuffering are infinite, He does not permit Israel to indefinitely persist in their obstinate ways. It is dangerous to presume upon God's mercy.

EMPLOYMENT POINT: *Reach out to the lost, before God's mercy expires for them.*

———◦◉◦———

October 26

Jeremiah 17–19, with 1 Timothy 6

He who trusts in his own heart is a fool, but whoever walks wisely will be delivered (Proverbs 28:26).

How can I have my deepest needs met?

Follow your heart is shouted from rooftops and whispered in counseling chambers as the means to find fulfillment. Why doesn't this universal counsel work? God informs Jeremiah: "The heart is deceitful above all things, and desperately wicked" (Jeremiah 17:9). Earlier God speaks about two kinds of lives. He reveals, "Cursed is the man who trusts in man" (Jeremiah 17:5) and adds, "Blessed is the man who trusts in the LORD" (Jeremiah 17:7). Our choice determines whether we experience the path of blessing, which God prefers, or the trail of scourging.

Two essential ingredients for a fulfilled life are godliness and contentment. Paul writes, "Now godliness with contentment is great gain" (1 Timothy 6:6). To find satisfaction in this life, you must be devoted to God and content with His provision for you. Truly God desires to bless you, but obedience to God's Word is the only way!

EMPLOYMENT POINT: *Pursue God and His ways through the Word, to know inner blessedness.*

October 27

Jeremiah 20–22, with 2 Timothy 1

For God has not given us a spirit of fear, but of power and of love and of a sound mind (2 Timothy 1:7).

DOES YOUR SPIRITUAL SPINE NEED STIFFENING?

At times serving the Lord can be frightening. Jeremiah is repeatedly punished for preaching truth. One instance occurs in Jeremiah 20:2, "Then Pashhur struck Jeremiah the prophet, and put him in the stocks." The writer of Hebrews perfectly describes Jeremiah's plight. He pens, "Still others had trial of mockings and scourgings, yes, and of chains and imprisonment" (Hebrews 11:36).

Paul experiences similar treatment. He reminds Timothy, "Therefore do not be ashamed of the testimony of our Lord, nor of me His prisoner, but share with me in the sufferings for the gospel according to the power of God" (2 Timothy 1:8). Satan loves to strike terror in God's servants. That is probably one reason why Paul reminds Timothy to depend upon God's power (2 Timothy 1:7). Let's heed John's words, "There is no fear in love, but perfect love casts out fear" (1 John 4:18).

EMPLOYMENT POINT: *Draw upon God's power to spiritually stiffen your spine during dangerous times.*

OCTOBER 28

JEREMIAH 23–24, WITH 2 TIMOTHY 2

Woe to the shepherds who destroy and scatter the sheep of My pasture! (Jeremiah 23:1).

WHOSE FEET ARE YOU SITTING AT?

Mary, the sister of Martha and brother of Lazarus, regularly is at Jesus' feet. When Lazarus dies, "Mary came where Jesus was, and saw Him, she fell down at His feet" (John 11:32). Subsequently, she sacrificially "anointed the feet of Jesus" with perfume (John 12:3). Also, while her sister Martha was distracted with much service, Mary "sat at Jesus' feet and heard His word" (Luke 10:39). Mary displays vast wisdom by opting to be at the Master's feet, both serving and learning.

Sadly, many gather at the feet of false teachers and prophets in Jeremiah's day. Nothing changes six hundred years later, as Paul writes to Timothy. Yet Paul tells this choice servant, "Be diligent to present yourself approved to God, a worker who does not need to be ashamed, rightly dividing the word of truth" (2 Timothy 2:15). Paul commands Timothy to please the Lord through accurate interpretation of the Bible.

EMPLOYMENT POINT: *Receive systematic biblical instruction from those who regularly sit at Jesus' feet.*

October 29

Jeremiah 25–26, with 2 Timothy 3

All Scripture is given by inspiration of God, and is profitable for doctrine, for reproof, for correction, for instruction in righteousness (2 Timothy 3:16).

How dependent are you upon God's Word?

Jeremiah ministers during dark days in Israel. God had already judged the northern kingdom in 722 BC. He dispatched the Assyrians who invaded and conquered their land. The Lord chastened them because of their disobedient and idolatrous ways. Similarly, the same is occurring in Judah, the southern kingdom, but the attackers are Babylonians. Jeremiah takes heart that the captivity would only last seventy years, according to Jeremiah 25:11. God's Word gives the weeping prophet hope during a period of despair.

Paul and Timothy also minister during fierce times "in the last days" (2 Timothy 3:1). Like Jeremiah, Paul and Timothy are given hope through the Bible. It is inspired, which literally means *God-breathed*. It is given "that the man of God may be complete, thoroughly equipped for every good work" (2 Timothy 3:17). Scripture inherently carries the ability to give comfort to any generation. The living Word revives the downtrodden like no other book ever written.

Employment Point: *Daily derive your hope and strength from God's Word.*

OCTOBER 30

JEREMIAH 27–28, WITH
2 TIMOTHY 4

Be diligent to come to me quickly (2 Timothy 4:9).

WOULD ANYONE ASK YOU FOR HELP IN THEIR TIME OF NEED?

Both Jeremiah and Paul faithfully serve God while being persecuted. Jeremiah proclaims a difficult message to the people; they need to submit to the invading Babylonian soldiers or die. It gets worse because Hananiah inaccurately represents the Lord and tells the Israelites just the opposite (Jeremiah 28:1–3). Jeremiah confronts the lying prophet and pronounces God's death sentence upon him, which is fulfilled verbatim (Jeremiah 28:17).

Also, Paul is about to die and needs assistance. He can't turn to Demas. Why? Second Timothy 4:10 records Paul's heartbreaking words, "for Demas has forsaken me, having loved this present world" (2 Timothy 4:10). Thankfully Paul can depend upon Timothy and dispatches him to "bring the cloak that I left with Carpus at Troas when you come—and the books, especially the parchments" (2 Timothy 4:13). The apostle's true son in the faith can be fully relied upon when he is most needed.

EMPLOYMENT POINT: Be *faithful to God and to His servants in their time of need.*

OCTOBER 31

JEREMIAH 29–30, WITH TITUS 1

For I know the thoughts that I think toward you, says the LORD, thoughts of peace and not of evil, to give you a future and a hope (Jeremiah 29:11).

DO YOU PONDER THE FUTURE OF OTHERS?

The Lord humbles the southern kingdom of Judah to bring them to repentance. After seventy years of captivity (Jeremiah 29:10), they would seek the Lord. "Then you will call upon Me and go and pray to Me, and I will listen to you" (Jeremiah 29:12). God manifests His patience and commitment once again to His people by sharing His future plans for them, which helps keep them optimistic.

Christians need to consider eternity, so that they will be motivated to preach the gospel to all people. Paul reminds Titus, "in hope of eternal life which God, who cannot lie, promised before time began" (Titus 1:2). Before there existed "time," the Greek term for which gives us the English word "chronology," God promised eternal life. It is now the "season," which is the meaning of the word for "time" that emerges in Titus 1:3 to proclaim the gospel to the lost.

EMPLOYMENT POINT: *Consider the future for the unsaved, and proclaim the gospel to them.*

November 1

Jeremiah 31–32, with Titus 2

The LORD has appeared of old to me, saying: "Yes, I have loved you with an everlasting love; therefore with lovingkindness I have drawn you" (Jeremiah 31:3).

How can you and the Lord become inseparable?

God's love attracts and is attractive. Jesus draws you through His sacrifice, "who gave Himself for us, that He might redeem us from every lawless deed and purify for Himself His own special people, zealous for good works" (Titus 2:14). The Father sent the Son as our substitute to redeem us. How costly is our redemption? Jesus' shed blood paid the price for our redemption. Believing on His finished work brings the sinner into a personal relationship with Him. Jesus died to save our souls so that we might experience intimacy with Him through walking daily by His side.

Furthermore, we get close to the Lord through personal holiness. That is, we should abstain from "every lawless deed" even "bringing every thought into captivity to the obedience of Christ" (2 Corinthians 10:5). Our redemption is costly; let's show the Lord our appreciation for His sacrifice by abstaining from sin.

EMPLOYMENT POINT: *Know God personally through His Son's death, and intimately through personal holiness.*

NOVEMBER 2

JEREMIAH 33–35, WITH TITUS 3

Most assuredly, I say to you, he who believes in Me, the works that I do he will do also; and greater works than these he will do, because I go to My Father (John 14:12).

WHAT SHOULD WE ASK GOD FOR AS WE SERVE HIM?

The answer is *great things*, because Jesus prays for us. This is why we can accomplish amazing things—or rather, why He can do incredible things through us. The apostle reminds his coworker Titus that the Lord has redeemed us, so now we should be "zealous for good works" (Titus 2:14). Paul agrees, "For we are His workmanship, created in Christ Jesus for good works, which God prepared beforehand that we should walk in them" (Ephesians 2:10).

Titus builds upon his earlier statement in Titus 2:14. He shares, "that those who have believed in God should be careful to maintain good works" (Titus 3:8). We must pray before, during, and after serving God. The Lord implores Jeremiah, "Call to Me, and I will answer you, and show you great and mighty things, which you do not know" (Jeremiah 33:3). He is able; let's trust Him to do the impossible!

EMPLOYMENT POINT: *Maintain good works, while asking God to display His vast power through you.*

NOVEMBER 3

JEREMIAH 36–37, WITH PHILEMON

———◦◦◦———

I appeal to you for my son Onesimus, whom I have begotten while in my chains (Philemon 10).

HOW WELL DO YOU USE YOUR INFLUENCE?

Your power is determined by your influence. That is, influence is power. Paul is under house arrest. How can he exhibit influence? First, he is an apostle; he could order Philemon to free Onesimus: "Therefore, though I might be very bold in Christ to command you what is fitting" (Philemon 8). Rather, he chooses differently: "yet for love's sake I rather appeal to you—being such a one as Paul, the aged, and now also a prisoner of Jesus Christ" (Philemon 9).

Two rattling sounds are meant to be heard by Philemon: Paul's bones (he's "aged") and his chains (he's a "prisoner"). Did the apostle to the Gentiles appeal free Onesimus? Ignatius reportedly wrote a letter fifty years later to the Ephesian church, and mentions a bishop named Onesimus. The Lord desires that His children use their influence to further the work of the kingdom. In a day when power corrupts, and absolute power corrupts absolutely, let's influence others for Jesus.

EMPLOYMENT POINT: *Skillfully make appeals to others for the Lord.*

———◦◦◦———

November 4

Jeremiah 38–39, with Hebrews 1

Now Jeremiah remained in the court of the prison until the day that Jerusalem was taken. And he was there when Jerusalem was taken (Jeremiah 38:28).

Does the Lord's nature remain the same even when we suffer?

Jeremiah faithfully proclaims the word of the Lord and sees its fulfillment (Babylon capturing Judah) from a prison cell. Be encouraged; the universe changes, but not the Lord. "They will perish, but You remain; and they will all grow old like a garment; like a cloak You will fold them up, and they will be changed. But You are the same, and Your years will not fail" (Hebrews 1:11–12). We derive stability in the midst of a fickle world spiraling out of control from an unvarying God.

Observe that Jesus, the eternal Son of God, does not change. Once again we turn to the anonymous writer of Hebrews, who pens, "Jesus Christ is the same yesterday, today, and forever" (Hebrews 13:8). Dwelling upon the Lord's attributes such as goodness, love, and grace, which He freely shares with us, sustains us during difficult times.

Employment Point: *Focus upon the Lord's unchanging nature, to remain faithful to Him in the midst of suffering.*

NOVEMBER 5

JEREMIAH 40–42, WITH HEBREWS 2

And the captain of the guard took Jeremiah and said to him: "The LORD your God has pronounced this doom on this place. Now the LORD has brought it, and has done just as He said. Because you people have sinned against the LORD, and not obeyed His voice, therefore this thing has come upon you" (Jeremiah 40:2–3).

ARE YOU WARNING THE LOST ABOUT IMPENDING JUDGMENT?

Like Jeremiah warned Israel, the writer of Hebrews warns those affiliated with the church not to put off believing in Jesus. He pens, "how shall we escape if we neglect so great a salvation?" (Hebrews 2:3). Just because Israel or those associated with a church hear the truth, it doesn't excuse their idleness.

Israel suffered a severe judgment in 586 BC because of their disobedience; ignoring the gospel message until it's too late will bring permanent and eternal torment. Consider the following warning from Hebrews 10:28–29: "Anyone who has rejected Moses' law dies without mercy on the testimony of two or three witnesses, of how much worse punishment, do you suppose, will he be thought worthy who has trampled the Son of God underfoot, counted the blood of the covenant by which he was sanctified a common thing, and insulted the Spirit of grace?"

EMPLOYMENT POINT: *Encourage the lost to believe on Jesus, before judgment comes.*

November 6

Jeremiah 43–45, with Hebrews 3

———◆———

Enter by the narrow gate; for wide is the gate and broad is the way that leads to destruction, and there are many who go in by it. Because narrow is the gate and difficult is the way which leads to life, and there are few who find it (Matthew 7:13–14).

Are you choosing the narrow path for a broad future?

Baruch, the scribe, faithfully serves the Lord while the vast majority of the southern kingdom of Judah does not. He remains loyal to God and the prophet Jeremiah. The Almighty says to him, "And do you seek great things for yourself? Do not seek them; for behold, I will bring adversity on all flesh, says the LORD. But I will give your life to you as a prize in all places, wherever you go" (Jeremiah 45:5).

Conversely, more than 600,000 men didn't have the faith to enter the Promised Land, and subsequently die in the wilderness. The anonymous writer of Hebrews writes in Hebrews 3:17, "Now with whom was He angry forty years? Was it not with those who sinned, whose corpses fell in the wilderness? So we see that they could not enter in because of unbelief" (Hebrews 3:19).

EMPLOYMENT POINT: *Walk the narrow path by faith, for the Lord's blessing of life.*

———◆———

NOVEMBER 7

JEREMIAH 46–48, WITH HEBREWS 4

———※———

For we do not have a High Priest who cannot sympathize with our weaknesses, but was in all points tempted as we are, yet without sin (Hebrews 4:15).

WHY SHOULD YOU TRUST JESUS FOR VICTORY OVER SIN?

The Jewish historian Flavius Josephus documented that eighty-three high priests served the Lord from Aaron, the first high priest, until the destruction of the temple in AD 70. The writer of Hebrews uses the present tense verb "we have" in Hebrews 4:14, showing that we currently have a "great High Priest" in Jesus. First, know that Jesus has a *preeminent priesthood*. All other high priests served and died; Jesus lives forever. This is why the author of Hebrews pens, "He always lives to make intercession for them [His saints]" (Hebrews 7:25).

Two, our High Priest is a *perfect person*: "For we do not have a High Priest who cannot sympathize with our weaknesses, but was in all points tempted as we are, yet without sin" (Hebrews 4:15). Finally, Jesus has *punctual provision*; it is perfectly timed. That's why we can "come boldly to the throne of grace" (Hebrews 4:16).

EMPLOYMENT POINT: *Depend upon Jesus as your High Priest because of His preeminent priesthood, perfect person, and punctual provision.*

———※———

NOVEMBER 8

JEREMIAH 49–50, WITH HEBREWS 5

Those who sow in tears shall reap in joy (Psalm 126:5).

WHAT BREAKS YOUR HEART CAUSING YOU TO WEEP?

God's chastening of the entire nation of Israel will produce a sincere repentance. Jeremiah, the weeping prophet writes, "The children of Israel shall come, they and the children of Judah together; with continual weeping they shall come, and seek the LORD their God" (Jeremiah 50:4). Tears often demonstrate genuine repentance; they outwardly manifest an inward brokenness.

The writer of Hebrews depicts our great High Priest, Jesus, broken in the garden of Gethsemane. He pens, "who, in the days of His flesh, when He had offered up prayers and supplications, with vehement cries and tears to Him who was able to save Him from death, and was heard because of His godly fear" (Hebrews 5:7). Almighty God honors tearful prayers from a contrite and broken spirit. The psalmist writes, "He who continually goes forth weeping, bearing seed for sowing, shall doubtless come again with rejoicing" (Psalm 126:6).

EMPLOYMENT POINT: *In brokenness bring your tears, and concerns to God's throne.*

NOVEMBER 9

JEREMIAH 51–52, WITH HEBREWS 6

It is impossible for God to lie (Hebrews 6:18).

DO YOU COMPLETELY TRUST GOD AND THE INTEGRITY OF HIS WORD?

The Lord predicts a future destruction of Babylon through Jeremiah. He writes about a time when Babylon will be destroyed and never inhabited by humans again (Jeremiah 50:39; 51:29). This particular prophecy is not fulfilled in 539 BC when the Medes overthrew the kingdom of Babylon. Daniel gives that prophecy about Babylon, which is fulfilled in the sixth century BC (see Daniel 2 with Daniel 5). Please remember, all of God's Word will be fulfilled (Matthew 5:17–18).

John pens two chapters on the future judgment of Babylon, which will be accomplished during the Tribulation (Revelation 17 and 18). Babylon's final demise is described in Revelation 18:21: "Then a mighty angel took up a stone like a great millstone and threw it into the sea, saying, 'Thus with violence the great city Babylon shall be thrown down, and shall not be found anymore.'" Two different judgments are prophesied. One was fulfilled; the other judgment is pending.

EMPLOYMENT POINT: *Depend upon God and His Word completely.*

NOVEMBER 10

LAMENTATIONS 1–2, WITH HEBREWS 7

But He, because He continues forever, has an unchangeable priesthood (Hebrews 7:24).

WHY IS JESUS A SUPERIOR HIGH PRIEST?

Old Testament priests were mediators between people and God. Yet their service expired eventually because of their mortality. The writer of Hebrews equates Jesus' priesthood with that of Melchizedek. He served as a priest to Salem, which later becomes Jerusalem, and had no recorded genealogy. Melchizedek is described, "without father, without mother, without genealogy, having neither beginning of days nor end of life, but made like the Son of God, remains a priest continually" (Hebrews 7:3). Cleverly, the author uses the lack of a recorded genealogy to compare him with Jesus.

However, Melchizedek does have a genealogy, but not one that is recorded (Hebrews 7:6). Creatively, the author of Hebrews uses Melchizedek as an illustration of Jesus' priesthood. The new covenant (New Testament) is superior to the old covenant (Old Testament) because Jesus shed His blood, conquered death, and "always lives to make intercession" for us (Hebrews 7:25).

EMPLOYMENT POINT: *Rely upon your superior High Priest, who continually intercedes for you.*

NOVEMBER 11

LAMENTATIONS 3–5, WITH HEBREWS 8

———◆———

Great is Your faithfulness (Lamentations 3:23).

ARE YOU FAITHFULLY SEEKING THE FAITHFUL GOD?

Our Lord cannot lie. He set His affection upon Israel and chose them to be His special people. Why? "The LORD did not set His love on you [Israel] nor choose you because you were more in number than any other people, for you were the least of all peoples; but because the LORD loves you, and because He would keep the oath which He swore to your fathers" (Deuteronomy 7:7–8). Almighty God cannot lie and always keeps His promises; this is exactly what He does for His people.

Although Israel turns away from the Lord, He remains faithful to them. Jeremiah writes, "Through the LORD's mercies we are not consumed, because His compassions fail not" (Lamentations 3:22). The faithful God will complete what He's begun with Israel (Hebrews 8:7–13). God has also chosen you for Himself (Ephesians 1:4). Remember, "The LORD is good to those who wait for Him, to the soul who seeks Him" (Lamentations 3:25).

EMPLOYMENT POINT: *Cling faithfully to the faithful God.*

———◆———

NOVEMBER 12

EZEKIEL 1–3, WITH HEBREWS 9

And as it is appointed for men to die once, but after this the judgment (Hebrews 9:27).

ARE YOU GUILTY OF NOT WARNING THE LOST OF IMPENDING JUDGMENT?

The Lord reveals His glory to Ezekiel and then gives him the following warning: "When I say to the wicked, 'You shall surely die,' and you give him no warning, nor speak to warn the wicked from his wicked way, to save his life, that same wicked man shall die in his iniquity; but his blood I will require at your hand" (Ezekiel 3:18). Ezekiel is called to confront his people to repent of their sin. If he doesn't sound the alarm, then he will be held accountable for their bloodshed. The stakes are high because the watchman physically protects the nations, yet Ezekiel has been entrusted with soul care.

Similarly, we are heralds commissioned by Jesus to proclaim His death and resurrection to the lost. Failure to do so will result with more than bloody hands; we will be accountable for their souls! Let's endeavor to share the gospel with everyone we can, so that our conscience will remain clean before the Lord.

EMPLOYMENT POINT: *Warn the lost of their coming judgment.*

NOVEMBER 13

EZEKIEL 4–6, WITH
HEBREWS 10:1–23

But this Man, after He had offered one sacrifice for sins forever, sat down at the right hand of God (Hebrews 10:12).

DO YOU NEED TO SAY "ENCORE" TO JESUS CONCERNING HIS SACRIFICE FOR SIN?

The Lord assesses Israel to Ezekiel, and says, "for all the house of Israel are impudent and hardhearted" (Ezekiel 3:7). Moreover, He uses the prophet in a series of object lessons to the nation depicting their sinfulness (Ezekiel 4 and 5). Ultimately, the temple will soon be destroyed (586 BC), which shows God's dissatisfaction of His people. His presence gradually leaving the temple throughout the Book of Ezekiel symbolizes His displeasure with Israel.

Another temple is eventually built, and priests are still functioning when the Book of Hebrews is written. Once again, the nation will be judged and the temple destroyed (AD 70). Regretfully, the priests stand daily performing their ministry (Hebrews 10:11). They missed the point that decade's prior Jesus offered Himself as the perfect sacrifice and then sat down at God's right hand, showing that He had completed the mission.

EMPLOYMENT POINT: *Draw near to the only High Priest who fully accomplished the work of redemption.*

November 14

Ezekiel 7–9, with Hebrews 10:24–39

It is a fearful thing to fall into the hands of the living God (Hebrews 10:31).

How perilous is it to willfully ignore Jesus' sacrifice?

Peppered throughout the Book of Hebrews are warning passages. They are directed at those who identify with Jesus and His church but have not yet believed on Him for salvation. The author asks, "How shall we escape if we neglect so great a salvation?" (Hebrews 2:3). He again warns them not to put off believing in Jesus, "For if we sin willfully after we have received the knowledge of the truth, there no longer remains a sacrifice for sins, but a certain fearful expectation of judgment" (Hebrews 10:26–27). Turning away from Jesus means certain doom, because bypassing Him cuts off the only path to the Father.

Judah similarly ignores God's ways and plunge into the depth of sin (Ezekiel 8). Because they refuse to repent, the Lord tells Ezekiel, "Therefore I also will act in fury" (Ezekiel 8:18). Let's not forget, "It is a fearful thing to fall into the hands of the living God" (Hebrews 10:31).

Employment Point: *Turn from your sin to Jesus, believing upon His sacrifice for your salvation.*

NOVEMBER 15

EZEKIEL 10–12, WITH HEBREWS 11:1–19

For he waited for the city which has foundations, whose builder and maker is God (Hebrews 11:10).

WHICH CITY WILL YOU LIVE FOR?

Christians have a divine summons: Live not for this world, but for the one to come. Paul reminds the Philippian saints, "our citizenship is in heaven" (Philippians 3:20). Sadly, the Israelites in Ezekiel's day adopt their neighbors' heathen practices. The prophet chides the shortsighted Israelites, "for you have not walked in My statutes nor executed My judgments, but have done according to the customs of the Gentiles which are all around you" (Ezekiel 11:12). They embrace this world's system instead of living for the one where all things will be made new.

Abraham exists differently. "He waited for the city which has foundations" (Hebrews 11:10). Did you notice that the term "foundation" is plural, which implies an unshakeable and permanent foundation? Carefully observe John's description of the New Jerusalem. "Now the wall of the city had twelve foundations" (Revelation 21:14). Abraham's faith produces an unmovable eternal stability.

EMPLOYMENT POINT: *Keep your eyes of faith on the city with foundations.*

NOVEMBER 16

EZEKIEL 13–15, WITH HEBREWS 11:20–40

For we walk by faith, not by sight (2 Corinthians 5:7).

ARE YOU QUALIFIED TO BE IN THE HALL OF FAITH?

Having raised three sons has provided some great perks for dad. It was my privilege to take them to Canton, Ohio, to see the Pro Football Hall of Fame, and to Cooperstown, New York, for the Pro Baseball Hall of Fame. Seeing the memorabilia of great athletes was inspiring. So much more should reading about the heroes of faith stoke us spiritually.

Ezekiel ministers to a faithless Israel, so God points them to three role models: Noah, Daniel, and Job (Ezekiel 14:14, 20). They are exemplary servants because they act upon God's Word despite physical obstacles. The same could be stated about the faithful in Hebrews 11. For instance, Moses survives severe trials "for he endured as seeing Him who is invisible" (Hebrews 11:27). This hero of the faith chose to walk by faith with the invisible God and to forsake the world's system pertaining to the lust of the flesh, the lust of the eyes, and the pride of life. We must do the same!

EMPLOYMENT POINT: *Walk by faith, and not by sight, to qualify for God's Hall of Faith.*

NOVEMBER 17

EZEKIEL 16, WITH
HEBREWS 12

For whom the LORD loves He chastens, and scourges every son whom He receives (Hebrews 12:6).

ARE WE FOLLOWING THE FATHER'S EXAMPLE WITH OUR CHILDREN?

The Canaanites practiced child sacrifices. God warned His people not to imitate this abomination (Leviticus 20:2–5). Ezekiel exposes Israel's sin, "Moreover you took your sons and your daughters, whom you bore to Me, and these you sacrificed to them to be devoured. Were your acts of harlotry a small matter, that you have slain My children and offered them up to them by causing them to pass through the fire?" (Ezekiel 16:20–21).

As the Lord chastens Israel for adopting the practices of the Ammonites who sacrificed their children to Molech, we must do the same with our children. "For whom the LORD loves He corrects, just as a father the son in whom he delights" (Proverbs 3:12). Both the Old Testament and the New Testament testify to God the Father as the ideal model for rearing our children.

EMPLOYMENT POINT: *Imitate the Father's love for His children by disciplining and instructing your own in His ways.*

331

NOVEMBER 18

EZEKIEL 17–19, WITH HEBREWS 13

Repent, and turn from all your transgressions, so that iniquity will not be your ruin (Ezekiel 18:30).

ARE YOU FOLLOWING THOSE ENTRUSTED WITH YOUR SOUL CARE?

We are individuals, and individually we will answer to Jesus on the day of judgment. John Donne rightfully wrote in 1624 that no man is an island. Yet God graciously provides to sinners faithful messengers of the Word whose voices should be honored. Twice the prophet warns Israel, "The soul who sins shall die" (Ezekiel 18:4, 20). The stern warning should have stirred the hearts of Israel to swiftly repent of their sins.

Six centuries later another emissary speaks: "Obey those who rule over you, and be submissive, for they watch out for your souls, as those who must give account. Let them do so with joy and not with grief, for that would be unprofitable for you" (Hebrews 13:17). The dual commands "obey" and "be submissive" should be noted. Soul care has been the mission of God's choice servants through the ages; let their account of you to their Master be a good one!

EMPLOYMENT POINT: *Follow the shepherds entrusted to care for your soul.*

NOVEMBER 19

EZEKIEL 20–21, WITH JAMES 1

But be doers of the word, and not hearers only, deceiving yourselves (James 1:22).

ARE YOU TRULY LIVING ACCORDING TO THE BOOK?

The Lord gives a history lesson to the elders of Israel in Ezekiel 20. They are reminded how God powerfully brought them out of Egyptian captivity, cared for them in the wilderness, and then spoke to the children of those in the wilderness to live differently than their parents. Three times Ezekiel says about obeying the commandments of the Bible, "if a man does, he shall live by them" (Ezekiel 20:11, 13, 21). Truly the Almighty Father consistently governs His people. They are to obediently walk with Him and will be chastened if they go astray. Regretfully they didn't learn from their history, and repeated the sins of former generations.

God is eternally blessed and longs to bless His children; however, they must actively do and not passively hear the Word. James writes, "But he who looks into the perfect law of liberty and continues in it, and is not a forgetful hearer but a doer of the work, this one will be blessed in what he does" (James 1:25).

EMPLOYMENT POINT: *Hear and heed God's Word for His blessing.*

NOVEMBER 20

EZEKIEL 22–23, WITH JAMES 2

If you really fulfill the royal law according to the Scripture, "You shall love your neighbor as yourself," you do well (James 2:8).

HOW DO YOU KNOW IF YOU ARE GIVEN TO PARTIALITY?

Those to whom James writes show partiality. He appeals, "My brethren, do not hold the faith of our Lord Jesus Christ, the Lord of glory, with partiality" (James 2:1). James calls out the saints to whom he addresses because they give preference to the rich while looking down upon the poor. They certainly didn't learn these practices from Scripture!

Ezekiel's readers similarly show partiality. They are not loving their neighbors, but murdering them while committing idolatry (Ezekiel 22:2–4). Also, "they have oppressed the stranger" (Ezekiel 22:7). Indiscriminately loving one's neighbor is the cure for partiality. God is no respecter of persons; we demonstrate our genuine faith by loving our neighbor. Providing for our poor brothers and sisters needs reveals our saving faith and absence of partiality. That is why James pens, "Thus also faith by itself, if it does not have works, is dead" (James 2:17).

EMPLOYMENT POINT: *Love your neighbor, and display your impartiality.*

NOVEMBER 21

EZEKIEL 24–26, WITH JAMES 3

But I say to you that for every idle word men may speak, they will give account of it in the day of judgment (Matthew 12:36).

ARE YOU CAREFULLY WEIGHING EACH WORD THAT YOU ARE ABOUT TO SPEAK?

Each of us will give an account for the words we speak. James warns teachers, "My brethren, let not many of you become teachers, knowing that we shall receive a stricter judgment" (James 3:1). Those who systematically teach God's Word will be held to a higher standard than others. Our speech should be consistent. James continues, "With it [the tongue] we bless our God and Father, and with it we curse men, who have been made in the similitude of God" (James 3:9).

Whether we regularly instruct others from the Scripture or not, David imparts the following wisdom: "Set a guard, O LORD, over my mouth; keep watch over the door of my lips," writes the man after God's own heart in Psalm 141:3. Let's not confuse others with mixed messages. James assesses, "Out of the same mouth proceed blessing and cursing. My brethren, these things ought not to be so" (James 3:10).

EMPLOYMENT POINT: *Carefully choose your words, to glorify God.*

NOVEMBER 22

EZEKIEL 27–28, WITH JAMES 4

Therefore submit to God. Resist the devil and he will flee from you (James 4:7).

DO YOU HAVE SATAN ON THE RUN?

Ezekiel begins by writing about "the prince of Tyre" (Ezekiel 28:2), but transitions to Satan who is called "the king of Tyre" (Ezekiel 28:12). He is depicted as a beautiful cherub. Cherubim are an order of angels who serve God. The Lord assigned cherubim to protect the tree of life in the garden of Eden after Adam and Eve are expelled (Genesis 3:24). Also, twice Ezekiel points out that the Wicked One is "created" (Ezekiel 28:13, 15), which implies that he has limitations. His pride leads to his fall and future attacks on mankind.

Moreover, James despises this world's system, which manifests itself through the lust of the flesh, the lust of the eyes, and the pride of life. As Satan used these allurements on Eve (Genesis 3), he does the same to Jesus (Matthew 4:1–11; Luke 4:1–13). Our author asks a question expecting the answer yes, which reminds us what to withstand: "Do you not know that friendship with the world is enmity with God?" (James 4:4).

EMPLOYMENT POINT: *Resist Satan and this world's system to please the Lord.*

NOVEMBER 23

EZEKIEL 29–31, WITH JAMES 5

Brethren, if a man is overtaken in any trespass, you who are spiritual restore such a one in a spirit of gentleness, considering yourself lest you also be tempted (Galatians 6:1).

AM I MY BROTHER'S KEEPER?

Paul tells mature believers to give a "hand up" to stumbling saints. Seeking to restore sinning brethren testifies to our love for God by loving our neighbor. Paul continues, "Bear one another's burdens, and so fulfill the law of Christ" (Galatians 6:2). Elsewhere Paul shares, "Let each of you look out not only for his own interests, but also for the interests of others" (Philippians 2:4). Keeping an eye on our brethren in Christ and assisting them when necessary shows love for our neighbor.

James agrees with Paul, and writes, "Brethren, if anyone among you wanders from the truth, and someone turns him back, let him know that he who turns a sinner from the error of his way will save a soul from death and cover a multitude of sins" (James 5:19–20). Moreover, Jesus predicts Peter's denials in Luke 22 and also says, "and when you have returned to Me, strengthen your brethren" (Luke 22:32).

EMPLOYMENT POINT: *Seek to restore stumbling saints to Jesus.*

NOVEMBER 24

EZEKIEL 32–33, WITH
1 PETER 1

In whom we have redemption through His blood, the forgiveness of sins (Colossians 1:14).

WHY SHOULD JESUS' SHED BLOOD LEAVE YOU WITHOUT BLOODY HANDS?

Ezekiel is called to be a watchman to the Israelites. His mission consists of warning God's people of impending judgment. Yet the blood of the judged will be upon his hands if he remains silent (Ezekiel 33:6–8). The prophet has the responsibility of sounding the alarm to not have bloody hands and a soiled conscience.

As Christians we need to ponder the price that was paid for our redemption. Peter writes, "knowing that you were not redeemed with corruptible things, like silver or gold, from your aimless conduct received by tradition from your fathers, but with the precious blood of Christ" (1 Peter 1:18–19). How can we remain silent and quietly let the unsaved go into eternity without Jesus after all that He has done for us? Do we want their blood on our hands because we didn't herald the gospel?

EMPLOYMENT POINT: *Value your costly redemption by telling others about Jesus' sacrifice for their salvation.*

NOVEMBER 25

EZEKIEL 34–35, WITH
1 PETER 2

You are My flock, the flock of My pasture (Ezekiel 34:31).

ARE YOU LIVING ACCORDING TO YOUR HOLY CALLING?

The leaders of Israel, called shepherds, fleece the flock instead of nurturing them (Ezekiel 34:1–10); therefore, the Lord will judge them and care for His chosen ones (Ezekiel 34:11–31). Those entrusted with God's flock should do so with care, since the ire of the Good Shepherd will be meted out on abusers of the privilege.

Like Israel, the church is set apart for the Lord. Peter explains, "But you are a chosen generation, a royal priesthood, a holy nation, His own special people, that you may proclaim the praises of Him who called you out of darkness into His marvelous light" (1 Peter 2:9). We have a good God; He pursues us when we stray from Him. "For you were like sheep going astray," writes Peter, "but have now returned to the Shepherd and Overseer of your souls" (1 Peter 2:25). We are a "spiritual house, a holy priesthood" and are "to offer up spiritual sacrifices acceptable to God" (1 Peter 2:5).

EMPLOYMENT POINT: *Live your life as a daily offering to God.*

NOVEMBER 26

EZEKIEL 36–37, WITH
1 PETER 3

And you He made alive, who were dead in trespasses and sins (Ephesians 2:1).

WILL YOU OBEY GOD AND SPEAK TO THE DEAD?

Israel consists of the living dead. Yet God is not finished with the nation and calls Ezekiel to prophesy to a valley of dry bones. Would the prophet obediently preach to the dead? Yes! The man of God prophesies, "Behold, O My people, I will open your graves and cause you to come up from your graves, and bring you into the land of Israel" (Ezekiel 37:12). A stunned Ezekiel then observes a resurrection.

Only the Lord gives life to the dead. On account of this we share the gospel with the spiritually dead and defend its life-giving message. Peter commands the saints, "But sanctify the Lord God in your hearts, and always be ready to give a defense to everyone who asks you a reason for the hope that is in you" (1 Peter 3:15). The Greek term "defense" gives us the English term "apologetics," which means *to give reasonable arguments in the defense of something.*

EMPLOYMENT POINT: *Proclaim the gospel, expecting God to give life to the spiritually dead.*

NOVEMBER 27

EZEKIEL 38–39, WITH
1 PETER 4

But the end of all things is at hand; therefore be serious and watchful in your prayers (1 Peter 4:7).

TO WHOM DO YOU TURN FOR SECURITY?

The Tribulation officially begins with the Antichrist making a covenant of peace with Israel (Daniel 9:24–27). He violates that agreement at the midpoint of the seven years of Tribulation (Daniel 9:27). It seems likely that it is during the first half of the Tribulation that the invasion predicted in Ezekiel 38 and 39 occurs, when there is a false sense of security during the beginning of the Tribulation. God thwarts the attackers, even though Israel turns to the Antichrist for security.

Unlike Israel, we should "be serious and watchful" (1 Peter 4:7). Peter calls believers to be sober-minded and vigilant. He gives us good reason for this in 1 Peter 5:8: "Be sober, be vigilant; because your adversary the devil walks about like a roaring lion, seeking whom he may devour." Let's stay on guard and not trust in man for our protection; he is limited by virtue of his mortality!

EMPLOYMENT POINT: *Remain spiritually alert by prayerfully trusting in Jesus for your security.*

NOVEMBER 28

EZEKIEL 40, WITH
1 PETER 5

———◎———

And when he brings out his own sheep, he goes before them; and the sheep follow him, for they know his voice (John 10:4).

ARE YOU LEADING BY EXAMPLE?

Shepherds in Bethlehem during Jesus' day led the sheep and didn't drive them. These caretakers personal knowledge and sincere concern for the sheep created a secure environment for them, so they willingly followed their shepherd. Jesus shares, "Yet they will be no means follow a stranger, but will flee from him, for they do not know the voice of strangers" (John 10:5). Sheep learned by experience to trust the shepherd for their food, security, and movement.

Peter addresses pastors (shepherds) and says, "nor as being lords over those entrusted to you, but being examples to the flock" (1 Peter 5:3). Godly leaders pave a path of integrity for their followers to tread. Jesus set a standard for those entrusted with soul care to emulate. He says, "I am the good shepherd. The good shepherd gives His life for the sheep" (John 10:11). We are called to do the same for others!

EMPLOYMENT POINT: *Model Christlike character worthy of imitation.*

———◎———

NOVEMBER 29

EZEKIEL 41–42, WITH 2 PETER 1

For prophecy never came by the will of man, but holy men of God spoke as they were moved by the Holy Spirit (2 Peter 1:21).

DO YOU LIVE AS IF GOD WILL FULFILL EVERY PREDICTION IN THE BIBLE?

Just before Jesus ascends to the right hand of God His disciples ask the following question: "Lord, will You at this time restore the kingdom to Israel?" (Acts 1:6). These disciples anticipate a future literal kingdom, which Jesus will establish when He returns to earth the second time (Revelation 19:11–21).

Ezekiel 40–48 describes the millennial temple that will be constructed for the coming kingdom. Jesus' disciples are never corrected for desiring the future kingdom to come; however, they are repeatedly reminded that before the kingdom comes the cross (Mark 8:31; 10:32–45). Regardless of the present suffering, our future is secure because Jesus says, "the Scripture cannot be broken" (John 10:35). Each and every prediction and promise that the Bible makes will be fulfilled because the sacred Word is inerrant (without error) and infallible (never failing).

EMPLOYMENT POINT: *Endure present persecution and suffering, for the kingdom is coming.*

November 30

Ezekiel 43–44, with
2 Peter 2

———◆———

The LORD on high is mightier than the noise of many waters, than the mighty waves of the sea (Psalm 93:4).

Are you reflecting God's glory?

Ezekiel writes just prior to the destruction of the temple in 586 BC. In Ezekiel 10–11 he shows the glory leaving the temple. Yet he also writes about a future millennial temple (Ezekiel 40–48). The prophet describes the return of God's glory in Ezekiel 43:2. "And behold, the glory of the God of Israel came from the way of the east. His voice was like the sound of many waters; and the earth shone with His glory."

Today God chooses His children to display His glory. Paul writes, "But we all, with unveiled face, beholding as in a mirror the glory of the Lord, are being transformed into the same image from glory to glory, just as by the Spirit of the Lord" (2 Corinthians 3:18). The Lord's daily process of sanctification—God conforming us to the image of Jesus Christ—will ultimately be completed, and we'll look like Him!

Employment Point: *Reflect God's glory through godly living.*

———◆———

DECEMBER 1

EZEKIEL 45–46, WITH
2 PETER 3

Nevertheless we, according to His promise, look for new heavens and a new earth in which righteousness dwells (2 Peter 3:13).

ARE YOU STANDING UPON THE PROMISES OF GOD?

The Father has given us promises so that we may lead a victorious Christian life while awaiting Jesus' return. Earlier in 2 Peter, the apostle to the Jews gives one reason to bank upon the Father's promises. He writes, "by which have been given to us exceedingly great and precious promises, that through these you may be partakers of the divine nature, having escaped the corruption that is in the world through lust" (2 Peter 1:4). Anticipating the fulfillment of God's promises keeps us motivated not to embrace this world's values, but to await that which is to come.

Moreover, Jesus tells the parable about ten minas (Luke 19:11–27). The master doles out one mina (equivalent to about three months wages for the average day laborer) and commands each servant, "Do business till I come" (Luke 19:13). God's servants who believe Jesus will return act faithfully and are rewarded. Let's be about the King's business until Jesus comes again.

EMPLOYMENT POINT: *Embrace God's promises by living daily for Him.*

DECEMBER 2

EZEKIEL 47–48, WITH
1 JOHN 1

———◆———

You are the light of the world. A city that is set on a hill cannot be hidden (Matthew 5:14).

DOES YOUR WALK MATCH YOUR TALK?

John exposes the false teachers' inconsistencies by the words "if we say" (1 John 1:6, 8, 10). They claim to walk in God's light, not have a sin nature, and never to sin. The apostle of love uncovers their hypocrisy—saying one thing and doing another. He enlightens us positively and negatively about God's nature from 1 John 1:5. (Essentially, he reveals God's perfect nature by a positive and negative observation.) "This is the message which we have heard from him and declare to you, that God is light [positively stated] and in Him is no darkness at all" [negatively stated].

Since God exists as our perfect standard, he writes, "But if we walk in the light as He is in the light, we have fellowship with one another, and the blood of Jesus Christ His Son cleanses us from all sin" (1 John 1:7). What a privilege we have to remain in the light of the Unblemished One!

EMPLOYMENT POINT: *Fellowship with God by remaining in His light.*

———◆———

DECEMBER 3

DANIEL 1–2, WITH
1 JOHN 2

———◦———

But he who is spiritual judges all things, yet he himself is rightly judged by no one (1 Corinthians 2:15).

ARE YOU A SPIRITUAL FATHER, YOUNG MAN, OR CHILD?

The apostle John gives a statement pertaining to all of God's children. "I write to you, little children, because your sins are forgiven you for His name's sake" (1 John 2:12). Then he transitions to the spiritually mature (fathers). Fathers have walked with the Lord for an extended period of time; they thoroughly know God's Word and make all their decisions based upon its content (1 John 2:13).

Next, we meet the young men. They are not old enough to be fathers, but are strong in God's Word. Daniel is an Old Testament example of a young man moving toward spiritual fatherhood. In Daniel 1, he "purposed in his heart that he would not defile himself" (Daniel 1:8). Truly his life testifies to reaching the status of a mature father. He cultivated an intimacy with God and never compromised his values (Daniel 6:10). Finally, there are the children, whether recently saved or still spiritually immature (1 John 2:13).

EMPLOYMENT POINT: *Purpose to become a spiritual father in the faith.*

———◦———

December 4

Daniel 3–4, with
1 John 3

Pride goes before destruction, and a haughty spirit before a fall (Proverbs 16:18).

Have your accomplishments gone to your head?

Nebuchadnezzar has a dream of a great image, with its head made of fine gold. The image as interpreted by Daniel represents world powers and the fine head of gold symbolizes Babylon, which is the kingdom that Nebuchadnezzar rules. Apparently the interpretation to the king goes to his head and he sets up an idol made of gold. (Perhaps he is the model for the idol.)

As you know, God manifests His power by protecting Shadrach, Meshach, and Abed-Nego from the fiery furnace. Since the king doesn't learn humility, we are told in the following chapter that his boast as builder and master of Babylon led to the Lord humbling him. Slowly read Daniel 4:34–37 and observe the king's magnification of the true God and his self-abasement. James gives great advice on this relevant topic: "Humble yourselves in the sight of the Lord, and He will lift you up" (James 4:10).

Employment Point: *Humble yourself before the Lord, and let Him exalt you.*

DECEMBER 5

DANIEL 5–6, WITH
1 JOHN 4

I beseech you therefore, brethren, by the mercies of God, that you present your bodies a living sacrifice, holy, acceptable to God, which is your reasonable service (Romans 12:1).

HOW DO YOU BUILD THE COURAGE NOT TO COMPROMISE WHEN FACING DEATH?

The very thing that pleased God about Daniel—his faithfulness—is the same thing that landed him in the lion's den. Knowing that the petition is signed, he "prayed and gave thanks before his God, as was his custom since early days" (Daniel 6:10). Daniel's regular excursions into God's presence enable him to stand firm. The writer of Hebrews seems to be acknowledging him in Hebrews 11:33, which says about the hero of faith that he "stopped the mouths of lions."

Daniel exhibits a valuable lesson from the experience in the lion's den that John imparts to us: "There is no fear in love; but perfect love casts out fear, because fear involves torment. But he who fears has not been made perfect in love" (1 John 4:18). Basking daily in the light of God's presence develops one's character!

EMPLOYMENT POINT: *Draw upon God's power by daily entering His presence, to know His perfect person and develop unwavering convictions.*

DECEMBER 6

DANIEL 7–8, WITH
1 JOHN 5

———————

And this is eternal life, that they may know You, the only true God, and Jesus Christ whom You have sent (John 17:3).

DO YOU KNOW THE TRUE GOD?

Satan seeks to prevent everyone from knowing Jesus. As we have learned in 1 John, the spirit of the Antichrist has been prevalent for two thousand years. Daniel predicts the coming of the Antichrist (Daniel 7:8). The prefix "anti" can mean *against* or *in place of.* Satan will raise up the Antichrist who is opposed to Jesus Christ (2 Thessalonians 2:4) and seeks to replace Him.

Speaking of Jesus, John writes, "And we know that the Son of God has come and has given us an understanding, that we may know Him who is true; and we are in Him who is true, in His Son Jesus Christ. This is the true God and eternal life" (1 John 5:20). Both Father (John 17:3) and Son (1 John 5:20) are called the true God! It is our privilege to have a relationship with the Father through the substitutionary death of Jesus for us.

EMPLOYMENT POINT: *Know the Father and the Son personally through Jesus' finished work.*

———————

DECEMBER 7

DANIEL 9–10, WITH 2 JOHN

If you had known, even you, especially in this your day, the things that make for your peace! (Luke 19:42).

DO YOU HAVE THE RIGHT OPEN-DOOR POLICY?

Daniel gives us one of the greatest prophecies in the Bible: the seventy weeks (Daniel 9:24–27). This prophecy pegs the exact day that Jesus would declare Himself to Israel as the Messiah. It shows that from the commencement of the prophecy that Jesus would manifest Himself in 173,880 days. When Jesus says in Luke 19:42, "if you had known, even you, especially in this your day," Luke writes a second-class condition, showing that they didn't know. They should have welcomed Jesus. Sadly, John writes, "He came to His own, and His own did not receive Him" (John 1:11).

Second John and 3 John pertain to hospitality. John warns the church not to give hospitality to a false teacher. He commands, "do not receive him into your house" (2 John 10). A careful study of God's Word provides guidance for hospitality. Children of God need to heed the warning of not entertaining those opposed to the gospel of Jesus.

EMPLOYMENT POINT: *Carefully study God's Word, for the right open-door policy.*

DECEMBER 8

DANIEL 11–12, WITH 3 JOHN

———◆———

I have no greater joy than to hear that my children walk in truth (3 John 4).

WHAT IS YOUR HEART'S DESIRE FOR YOUR BIOLOGICAL AND SPIRITUAL CHILDREN?

Daniel cares deeply for the children of Israel. As he prays three times a day facing Jerusalem (Daniel 6:10), they are regularly in his prayers. He writes about the resurrection of the just and the unjust in Daniel 12. Concerning the saints' resurrection, he pens, "Those who are wise shall shine like the brightness of the firmament, and those who turn many to righteousness like the stars forever and ever" (Daniel 12:3).

The Lord desires to reward His followers at the resurrection; Daniel similarly desires his spiritual children to experience this eternal shine, reflecting God's glory. John also houses the heart of a shepherd and longs that his beloved children would "not imitate what is evil, but what is good" (3 John 11). They are to be like Demetrius (3 John 12) and not the self-centered Diotrephes "who loves to have the pre-eminence among them" (3 John 9).

EMPLOYMENT POINT: *Strive to keep your children on the path that produces an eternal shine.*

———◆———

DECEMBER 9

HOSEA 1–4, WITH JUDE

Fight the good fight of faith, lay hold on eternal life (1 Timothy 6:12).

HOW WELL DO YOU DEFEND THE FAITH?

The Lord shows the depth of His love for Israel through Hosea. His life becomes an object lesson to God's people. He marries a woman (Gomer) who is unfaithful to him (Hosea 3), and yet he seeks to restore the marriage. God loves the children of Israel and longs for them to be restored to Him; that is the message communicated from the book of Hosea.

Next, Jude desires to write about salvation and the Lord gives him a redirect to confront the church. He pens, "For certain men have crept in unnoticed . . . ungodly men, who turn the grace of our God into lewdness and deny the only Lord God and our Lord Jesus Christ" (Jude 4). How should we protect the borders of the church? Jude tells the saints "to contend earnestly for the faith" (Jude 3). In essence, fight for the body of truth handed down to you ("the faith") and keep the church pure.

EMPLOYMENT POINT: *Agonize to keep yourself, and the church, pure.*

DECEMBER 10

HOSEA 5–8, WITH REVELATION 1

Behold, the Judge is standing at the door! (James 5:9).

ARE YOU READY TO MEET THE JUDGE?

Jesus says about His designated role from the Father, "For the Father judges no one, but has committed all judgment to the Son" (John 5:22). The Revelation of Jesus Christ depicts Jesus in Revelation 1:13 as "in the midst of the seven lampstands" (the seven churches in Revelation 2–3), evaluating each one. Our Lord, who has eyes like a flame of fire, scrutinizes each church and renders a decision based upon His omniscient assessment of their works!

Furthermore, He is the One who unleashes judgment upon the world during the Tribulation, through opening each of the seven seals (Revelation 6–19). He then returns to the earth at the end of the Tribulation to "strike the nations" with the "sharp sword" that protrudes from His mouth (Revelation 19:15). Finally, He will sit upon the great white throne to judge the unsaved (Revelation 20:11–15). The book of Revelation shows Jesus, the Judge, fulfilling His assigned task.

EMPLOYMENT POINT: *Prepare to meet the Judge through purity of life, accompanied with righteous deeds.*

DECEMBER 11

HOSEA 9–11, WITH
REVELATION 2

Sow for yourselves righteousness; reap in mercy; break up your fallow ground, for it is time to seek the LORD, till He comes and rains righteousness on you (Hosea 10:12).

WHAT IS THE DISCERNING EYE OF THE LORD REVEALING ABOUT YOU?

Whether Old Testament Israel or the New Testament church, the Lord evaluates His people and reveals His prognosis. Observe the Lord's remedy for a hardhearted Israel: "Therefore circumcise the foreskin of your heart, and be stiff-necked no longer" (Deuteronomy 10:16). He desires a tenderhearted people.

Jesus describes Himself as He "who walks in the midst of the seven golden lampstands" (Revelation 2:1). The lampstands are churches (Revelation 1:20) and Jesus says to each one, "I know your works." Also, He says to each church, which means His message pertains to every church, "he who has an ear, let him hear what the Spirit says to the churches." Therefore act upon Jesus' words from Revelation 22:12: "And behold, I am coming quickly, and My reward is with Me, to give to every one according to his work." Present service will result in future recompense.

EMPLOYMENT POINT: *Dedicate yourself to serving Jesus, and await His rich rewards.*

DECEMBER 12

HOSEA 12–14, WITH
REVELATION 3

Behold, I am coming quickly! Hold fast what you have, that no one may take your crown (Revelation 3:11).

DO YOU HAVE A FIRM GRIP ON ETERNITY?

Jacob begins life by grasping his brother's heel; he clutches it while in his mother's womb. Decades later, after robbing his brother of his birthright and blessing (Genesis 25 and Genesis 27), he clings to the Angel of the Lord because he doesn't want Esau to kill him; it is at this moment that he authentically seeks the Almighty Father. Desperately, the supplanter grapples with God, seeking His blessing because he finally latches upon the need to have Him be his all in all (Genesis 32).

Hosea writes about the encounter, "Yes, he struggled with the Angel and prevailed; he wept, and sought favor from Him" (Hosea 12:4). Regretfully, Israel didn't cling to God. For this reason Hosea pens, "So you, by the help of your God, return; observe mercy and justice, and wait on your God continually" (Hosea 12:6). Moreover, Jesus is coming quickly and desires all churches to get a grip on eternity.

EMPLOYMENT POINT: *Hold fast to Jesus and labor for His eternal rewards.*

DECEMBER 13

JOEL, WITH REVELATION 4

So rend your heart, and not your garments; return to the LORD your God, for He is gracious and merciful, slow to anger, and of great kindness; and He relents from doing harm (Joel 2:13).

WHY DOES GOD HAVE THE RIGHT TO JUDGE AND TO CHOOSE THE JUDGMENT'S TIMING?

Revelation 4 and 5 take us to God's throne room just before His wrath is released. A storm of judgment brews, and we get a character sketch of the Father sitting on the throne (Revelation 4) and the Son who will have a personal hand in the impending judgment. Together, they will enact judgment upon the inhabitants of the earth, which testifies to their rulership over the earth.

The equality of the Father and Son are depicted by John's use of the word "worthy." First he uses it of the Father (Revelation 4:11), and then of the Son (Revelation 5:9). God has a right to judge according to His perfect timing because He is creation's Maker. John pens, "You are worthy, O Lord, to receive glory and honor and power; for You created all things, and by Your will they exist and were created" (Revelation 4:11).

EMPLOYMENT POINT: *Worship the Creator God, because He is worthy.*

DECEMBER 14

AMOS 1–3, WITH REVELATION 5

Surely the Lord God does nothing, unless He reveals His secret to His servants the prophets (Amos 3:7).

WHO IS WORTHY TO OPEN THE SCROLL AND TO LOOSE ITS SEALS? (REVELATION 5:2)

John is transported to heaven, because God has a message for His prophet. The Tribulation commences shortly, and the search is made to find a worthy candidate to open the scroll containing the seal, trumpet, and bowl judgments (Revelation 6–19). A strong angel makes a universal proclamation, only to discover that no one is worthy. The inquiry for a worthy candidate begins from the greater to the lesser as follows: "And no one in heaven or on the earth or under the earth was able to open the scroll, or to look at it" (Revelation 5:3).

John emotionally responds after the failure of the search, "So I wept much, because no one was found worthy to open and read the scroll" (Revelation 5:4). Suddenly the conquering Lamb emerges to fill this role. This is why the sevenfold praise occurs: "Worthy is the Lamb who was slain to receive power and riches and wisdom, and strength and honor and glory and blessing!" (Revelation 5:12).

EMPLOYMENT POINT: *Worship the Lamb who is worthy to enact God's judgment.*

DECEMBER 15

AMOS 4–6, WITH REVELATION 6

He rains ruin upon the strong, so that fury comes upon the fortress (Amos 5:9).

HOW SHALL WE LIVE, KNOWING THAT JUDGMENT IS COMING TO THE WORLD?

Revelation 6 officially begins the commencement of the Tribulation with the opening of the first seal. The catastrophes described in Revelation 6 are predicted by Jesus in Matthew 24:4–8. Referring to the wars, famines, and earthquakes, Jesus says, "All these are the beginning of sorrows" (Matthew 24:8). There will be clear signs that the Tribulation has begun. Those who dwell on the earth will experience these phenomena, which point to the wrath of the Lamb.

Are church-age saints to watch for the signs mentioned in Matthew 24? No! We will be delivered from the Tribulation because it is a period of God's wrath (Revelation 6:17). You and I are not to focus upon signs, but the One who will deliver us from this worldwide judgment. Paul writes, "and to wait for His Son from heaven, whom He raised from the dead, even Jesus who delivers us from the wrath to come" (1 Thessalonians 1:10).

EMPLOYMENT POINT: *Anticipate Jesus' coming, to deliver us from His pending wrath.*

DECEMBER 16

AMOS 7–9, WITH REVELATION 7

For the great day of His wrath has come, and who is able to stand? (Revelation 6:17).

WILL GOD SAVE SOULS DURING THE TRIBULATION?

The Tribulation will begin shortly after the church is raptured. Amos describes this period, "It will be as though a man fled from a lion, and a bear met Him! Or as though he went into the house, leaned his hand on the wall, and a serpent bit him!" (Amos 5:19). God's wrath on earth during the Tribulation will be unprecedented!

Jesus tells us that unless this period was limited (until seven years) there would be no survivors (Matthew 24:22). Massive numbers of people will die during the Tribulation. John writes about the pale horse personifying death, "And power was given to them over a fourth of the earth, to kill with sword, with hunger, with death, and by the beasts of the earth" (Revelation 6:8). Yet God "desires all men to be saved and to come to the knowledge of the truth" (1 Timothy 2:4). God will save 144,000 Jews during the Tribulation and dispatch them to evangelize (Revelation 7).

EMPLOYMENT POINT: *Evangelize the lost, even in troubled times.*

DECEMBER 17

OBADIAH, WITH REVELATION 8

Though you ascend as high as the eagle, and though you set your nest among the stars, from there I will bring you down (Obadiah 4).

WHY DO THE WICKED SEEM TO BE SHELTERED FROM GOD'S WRATH?

The small Book of Obadiah carries a large message: God will eventually capsize the arrogant. Esau's descendants, the Edomites, have nestled themselves on high in a seemingly impregnable terrain. Yet the Almighty reach them. As the wicked Edomites enacted violence toward the Israelites (Obadiah 10), God would display that "vengeance is Mine, I will repay" (Romans 12:19). Proverbs 16:18 captures the elevated Edomites' demise: "Pride goes before destruction, and a haughty spirit before a fall." The arrogant cannot indefinitely evade God's wrath.

Is it quiet before a storm? This is the case in Revelation 8:1. John writes, "there was silence in heaven for about half an hour." The seven seals will be followed by seven trumpet judgments and God will again display His wrath after the brief silence. Although the wicked might seem protected from God's wrath during a brief intermission, it will nevertheless come!

EMPLOYMENT POINT: *God's vengeance topples the arrogant in His perfect timing.*

DECEMBER 18

JONAH, WITH REVELATION 9

And they said to one another, "Come, let us cast lots, that we may know for whose cause this trouble has come upon us?" (Jonah 1:7).

DO YOU ASK IF YOU CAUSED THE TROUBLE IN A CRISIS?

The heathen sailors seek to know why they are experiencing a storm. Often Christians blame the unsaved for their problems; however, Jonah is the source of the storm, which impacts the sailors (Jonah 1:7–16). Jonah should be a problem-solver because he knows the Lord; pathetically, he brings trouble upon others, since he disobeys the Word of the Lord.

As the Lord hurled a storm at Jonah and the sailors, the Lord throws horrific catastrophes at the unsaved during the Tribulation (Revelation 9). "Like" and "as" appear more in this chapter than any other in the Bible to describe the indescribable. A contrast occurs because the sailors "feared the LORD exceedingly, and offered a sacrifice to the LORD and took vows" (Jonah 1:16), whereas the earth's inhabitants "did not repent of their murders or their sorceries or their sexual immorality or their thefts" (Revelation 9:21). Let's imitate the former!

EMPLOYMENT POINT: *Evaluate yourself first during a crisis, and seek to resolve it biblically.*

DECEMBER 19

MICAH 1–3, WITH REVELATION 10

The secret things belong to the LORD our God, but those things which are revealed belong to us and to our children forever, that we may do all the words of the law (Deuteronomy 29:29).

WHAT OBLIGATION DOES GOD GIVE TO EVERY BELIEVER?

A mighty angel reflecting God's glory descends from heaven carrying a little book (Revelation 10:1–2). His posture is that of putting "his right foot on the sea and his left foot on the land" (Revelation 10:2). Three times his positioning on land and sea is given (Revelation 10:2, 5, 8). Although John isn't permitted to write about the judgment coming in Revelation 10, we know that it will impact both land and sea because of the angel's stance.

Next, John takes the book out of the angel's hand as he is commanded and then eats it (Revelation 10:9–10). His mission is then given: "You must prophesy again about many peoples, nations, tongues, and kings" (Revelation 10:11). The Lord permitted John to be banished to the isle of Patmos in order to broadly proclaim the Word of God. He sets an example for all subsequent saints to follow!

EMPLOYMENT POINT: *Digest God's Word, and then proclaim it.*

December 20

Micah 4–5, with Revelation 11

—◦—

But you, Bethlehem Ephrathah, though you are little among the thousands of Judah, yet out of you shall come forth to Me the One to be Ruler in Israel, whose goings are from of old, from everlasting (Micah 5:2).

How can you effectively witness for the One who is born in Bethlehem and yet eternal?

Many Christians try to identify the two witnesses in Revelation 11 rather than try to understand how they powerfully witness for Jesus. John identifies the prophets as "two olive trees and two lampstands standing before the God of the earth" (Revelation 11:4). The terminology derives from Zechariah 3 and 4 and points to the supernatural enabling that God grants to Joshua the high priest (Zechariah 3) and to Zerubbabel the governor (Zechariah 4).

God calls this holy tandem to complete the work on the temple and energizes them for the stalled mission. The temple will be rebuilt "not by might nor by power, but by My Spirit" (Zechariah 4:6). As they tapped into God's power, so must we. Jesus says to His followers, "But you shall receive power when the Holy Spirit has come upon you; and you shall be witnesses to Me" (Acts 1:8).

Employment Point: *Tap into God's Spirit for witnessing power.*

—◦—

DECEMBER 21

MICAH 6–7, WITH REVELATION 12

He has shown you, O man, what is good; and what does the LORD require of you but to do justly, to love mercy, and to walk humbly with your God? (Micah 6:8).

DO YOU LIVE HUMBLY BEFORE GOD?

Satan originally walked with God in heaven. Ezekiel records, "You were the anointed cherub who covers; I established you; you were on the holy mountain of God; you walked back and forth in the midst of fiery stones" (Ezekiel 28:14). Pride led to his downfall; it can also lead to ours!

The wicked one exists because God created him (Ezekiel 28:13, 15), and has limitations as a result of not being eternal like the Holy One. He appears before God in heaven to give an account of his activities (Job 1:6; 2:1), until the midpoint of the Tribulation when he will be expelled from heaven (Revelation 12:7–9). God and pride don't mix like oil and water. For this reason James commands believers to bow before the Almighty. He writes, "Humble yourselves in the sight of the Lord, and He will lift you up" (James 4:10).

EMPLOYMENT POINT: *Wrap yourself with humility because God opposes pride, but gives favor to the humble.*

DECEMBER 22

NAHUM, WITH REVELATION 13

———◦◦◦———

Woe to the bloody city! (Nahum 3:1).

ARE YOU OBSERVING THE WARNINGS IN THE BIBLE?

Nineveh, the great Assyrian city, had repented under Jonah's preaching. A century later, she is judged for her violence. God crushes the arrogant empire. Nahum writes, "It shall come to pass that all who look upon you will flee from you, and say, 'Nineveh is laid waste!'" (Nahum 3:7).

We next learn about two scary beasts in Revelation 13: the sea beast and the land beast. The term "beast" conveys *a wild beast* or *beast of prey*. Beast number one from the sea is the Antichrist, and the second is the false prophet. The latter makes an idol (the abomination of desolation) that comes to life and advises the earth dwellers to murder the saints. John gives a warning in Revelation 13:9. He writes, "If anyone has an ear, let him hear." Then he points out that those who kill by the sword (the Antichrist and false prophet) will perish similarly (Revelation 13:10). The Bible repeatedly warns the unjust; their ways will not go unpunished.

EMPLOYMENT POINT: *Be encouraged that God's warnings are not mere lip service.*

———◦◦◦———

DECEMBER 23

HABAKKUK, WITH
REVELATION 14

———◦———

But the just shall live by his faith (Habakkuk 2:4).

WILL YOU FOLLOW JESUS BY FAITH UNTIL DEATH?

Habakkuk gives the standard for the saints; they must live by faith. The popular theme appears three times in the New Testament (Romans 1:17; Galatians 3:11; Hebrews 10:38). This is consistent with the following statement of the writer of Hebrews: "But without faith it is impossible to please Him" (Hebrews 11:6).

Early in the Tribulation 144,000 Jews begin their journey by believing on Jesus (Revelation 7); however, they will face severe opposition from Satan, the Antichrist, and the false prophet. Eventually they are martyred for their faith and are depicted with the Lamb who is standing (the posture of victory) on Mount Zion (Revelation 14:1). How committed are they to Jesus? "These are the ones who were not defiled with women, for they are virgins. These are the ones who follow the Lamb wherever He goes" (Revelation 14:4). Jesus made fishers of men from the 144,000 (Revelation 7:9). They follow the Lord until death. Will you?

EMPLOYMENT POINT: *Follow the Lamb by faith until death, and your reward follows.*

———◦———

DECEMBER 24

ZEPHANIAH, WITH REVELATION 15

The LORD your God in your midst, the Mighty One, will save; He will rejoice over you with gladness, He will quiet you with His love, He will rejoice over you with singing (Zephaniah 3:17).

DO YOU SING TO GOD AS HE SINGS OVER YOU?

Tribulation saints who are martyred for Jesus will rejoice. They are described as having "victory over the beast, over his image and over his mark" (Revelation 15:2). As a result they sing two songs: "The song of Moses, the servant of God, and the song of the Lamb" (Revelation 15:3). These saints focus on both the person and work of God. They acknowledge, "Great and marvelous are Your works, Lord God Almighty! Just and true are Your ways, O King of the saints!" (Revelation 15:3). Victory comes from one source, the Lord.

Moreover, He rejoices over us with singing and permits us to sing to Him. What a privilege! Psalm 100 exudes a spirit of thanksgiving. The writer seizes the essence of joyful living. He pens, "Serve the LORD with gladness; come before His presence with singing" (Psalm 100:2). Let's enjoy His presence as He does ours!

EMPLOYMENT POINT: *Sing to the victorious Lord, who sings over victorious saints.*

DECEMBER 25

HAGGAI, WITH REVELATION 16

———◈———

Thus says the LORD of Hosts: "Consider your ways!" (Haggai 1:5).

HOW CAN YOU EXPERIENCE THE LORD'S BLESSING?

Jesus informs the Tribulation saints how to be blessed: "Behold, I am coming as a thief. Blessed is he who watches, and keeps his garments, lest he walk naked and they see his shame" (Revelation 16:15). For the third of seven times, this Greek term "blessed" appears in the Book of Revelation. It means *to be favored* by God. The Lord lavishes the saints with His favor when they walk with Him, look for His return, and maintain moral purity.

The saints to whom Haggai writes neglect the rebuilding of the temple, but build themselves opulent homes. That's why he writes, "You have sown much, and bring in little; you eat, but do not have enough; you drink, but you are not filled with drink; you clothe yourselves, but no one is warm; and he who earns wages, earns wages to put into a bag with holes" (Haggai 1:6). Let's put the Lord first in all things.

EMPLOYMENT POINT: *Serve God while awaiting His return, to receive His favor.*

———◈———

December 26

Zechariah 1–3, with Revelation 17

Pray for the peace of Jerusalem: May they prosper who love you (Psalm 122:6).

Do you love what God loves?

The Lord chooses Abraham and Jewish people for Himself (Genesis 12:3; Deuteronomy 7:6–7). Although He humbled the nation through the Assyrians (722 BC) and the Babylonians (586 BC), He again puts His blessing upon Jerusalem. The Lord says, "I am returning to Jerusalem with mercy; My house shall be built in it" (Zechariah 1:16). Indeed, He restores the priesthood through Joshua the high priest (Zechariah 3), which shows His renewed favor to the children of Israel.

By way of contrast, He will permanently destroy Babylon (Revelation 17 and 18). He calls this wicked city, "BABYLON THE GREAT, THE MOTHER OF HARLOTS AND OF THE ABOMINATIONS OF THE EARTH" (Revelation 17:5). Why will He decimate this ancient city? She is opposed to God and His children and has martyred the saints (Revelation 17:6). The psalmist summarizes our lesson well: "You who love the LORD, hate evil!" (Psalm 97:10).

EMPLOYMENT POINT: *Embrace God, His holy city, and His people for His blessing.*

DECEMBER 27

ZECHARIAH 4–6, WITH REVELATION 18

But you shall receive power when the Holy Spirit has come upon you; and you shall be witnesses to Me in Jerusalem, and in all Judea and Samaria, and to the end of the earth (Acts 1:8).

ARE YOU ACCOMPLISHING GOD'S WORK BY THE SPIRIT'S POWER?

The Lord set apart two choice servants to accomplish the task of completing the building of the temple. Joshua the high priest and Zerubbabel the governor are His picks. Without the enabling power of the Holy Spirit the temple will not be rebuilt and God's witness to the nations stifled. Truly the Lord's work is "not by might nor by power, but by My Spirit" (Zechariah 4:6). When the task at hand seems impossible to complete, then God dispatches the Holy Spirit to finish the unfinished!

God's Spirit is a member of the Trinity and today baptizes us into Christ's body the church (1 Corinthians 12:13), permanently indwells us with His Spirit (1 Corinthians 6:19) and fills us for victorious living (Galatians 5:16–23; Ephesians 5:18–21). His person and work have been vital to God's children through the ages to accomplish the work of the Lord.

EMPLOYMENT POINT: *Depend upon God's Holy Spirit to equip you for service.*

December 28

Zechariah 7–9, with Revelation 19

Rejoice greatly, O daughter of Zion! Shout, O daughter of Jerusalem! Behold, your King is coming to you; He is just and having salvation, lowly and riding on a donkey, a colt, the foal of a donkey (Zechariah 9:9).

What is the difference between Jesus' two advents?

Approximately five hundred years after the prediction of Zechariah 9:9, Jesus rides into Jerusalem on Palm Sunday (Luke 19:37–42). The meek Lamb of God first appears to offer salvation; however, He is rejected. John records, "He came to His own, and His own did not receive Him" (John 1:11). Jesus' own brothers did not initially believe on Him (John 7:5), and the nation rejected their Savior!

Jesus' Second Coming is quite different. He rides upon a white horse with a two-edged sword in His mouth. Why does He come again? Our Lord returns to judge the nations and establish His kingdom. John pens, "Now out of His mouth goes a sharp sword, that with it He should strike the nations. And He Himself will rule them with a rod of iron" (Revelation 19:15). Our Lord vanquishes His enemies at Armageddon, and subsequently rules as rightful King. The Second Coming of Jesus differs greatly from the first.

EMPLOYMENT POINT: *Invite people to receive Jesus' gift of salvation before it's too late.*

December 29

Zechariah 10–12, with Revelation 20

Blessed and holy is he who has part in the first resurrection. Over such the second death has no power (Revelation 20:6).

Will you participate in the first or the second resurrection?

For the fifth of seven times the word "blessed" surfaces in Revelation. This term conveys *to be favored* by God. Resurrection number one has several parts; it includes various resurrections to raise the redeemed from the dead. For the believer at death his soul and spirit immediately go to heaven. Paul writes, "to be absent from the body [is] to be present with the Lord" (2 Corinthians 5:8). What a joy to know that Jesus' death emancipates us from the body of death.

The second death points us to Revelation 20:11–15, where all the unsaved are raised from the dead to be judged and eternally banished to the lake of fire. All unbelievers will spend their eternity forever tormented in this dreadful place. Therefore, the first death is physical and the second spiritual. The lake of fire exists for the devil and his angels (Matthew 25:41); don't go there by rejecting Jesus!

Employment Point: *Believe on Jesus who died for your sin and conquered death, and escape the second death.*

DECEMBER 30

ZECHARIAH 13–14, WITH REVELATION 21

———◈———

And in that day His feet will stand on the Mount of Olives (Zechariah 14:4).

DO YOU CONFIDENTLY LIVE KNOWING JESUS WILL RETURN?

Zechariah 14 describes Jesus' Second Coming and judgment upon His enemies at the end of the Tribulation. Jude also boldly predicts this event: "Behold, the Lord comes with ten thousands of His saints, to execute judgment on all" (Jude 14–15). The term "comes" occurs in the past tense in the Greek, which literally says, "the Lord came." Jude employs the word in the past tense, showing the certainty of this event; it is as good as done!

Our Lord's Second Coming will not only be to thwart His enemies but also to establish His kingdom. Subsequent to these events will be the creation of the New Jerusalem (Revelation 21–22). John captures God's words spoken from His throne about the new creation, "It is done!" (Revelation 21:6). Rest assured, child of the King, that the Lord is coming to judge the wicked, set up His kingdom, and subsequently to create a new heavens and earth; it is as good as done!

EMPLOYMENT POINT: *Live confidently, knowing that Jesus will return and fulfill all Scripture.*

———◈———

DECEMBER 31

MALACHI, WITH REVELATION 22

And there shall be no more curse, but the throne of God and of the Lamb shall be in it, and His servants shall serve Him (Revelation 22:3).

ARE YOU PRACTICING YOUR SERVE FOR THE NEW JERUSALEM?

I dreamed as a teenager of playing professional tennis. Often I would go to the local tennis courts and practice my serve alone; this prepared me for the countless matches I would play. Similarly, we are saved to serve God now, but this continues eternally. Experientially I came to know the benefits of serving thousands of tennis balls in an empty court because I was later rewarded when competing.

How well are you doing practicing your serve for Jesus? Our reward is also coming if we now faithfully practice our service for Jesus. He says, "And behold, I am coming quickly, and My reward is with Me, to give to every one according to his work" (Revelation 22:12). My aspiration to one day play at Wimbledon never came to fruition; however, all children of God will know the height of joy when we serve the Lord in the New Jerusalem!

EMPLOYMENT POINT: *Serve Jesus now to be richly rewarded when He returns, and to be prepared for service in the New Jerusalem.*
